The Fifteen Confederates

The Fifteen Confederates

Johann Eberlin von Günzburg

Edited and Translated by
Geoffrey Dipple

PICKWICK *Publications* • Eugene, Oregon

THE FIFTEEN CONFEDERATES
Johann Eberlin von Günzburg

Copyright © 2014 Geoffrey Dipple. All rights reserved. Except for brief quotations in critical publications or reviews, no part of this book may be reproduced in any manner without prior written permission from the publisher. Write: Permissions, Wipf and Stock Publishers, 199 W. 8th Ave., Suite 3, Eugene, OR 97401.

Pickwick Publications
An Imprint of Wipf and Stock Publishers
199 W. 8th Ave., Suite 3
Eugene, OR 97401

www.wipfandstock.com

ISBN 13: 978-1-4982-2671-4

Cataloguing-in-Publication data:

Dipple, Geoffrey.

The fifteen confederates : Johann Eberlin von Günzburg / Edited and translated by Geoffrey Dipple.

xiv + 194 pp. ; 23 cm. Includes bibliographical references and indexes.

ISBN 13: 978-1-62564-232-5

1. Reformation—Germany. 2. Reformers—Germany—Biography. 3. German literature—Early modern, 1500–1700. I. Eberlin, Johann von Günzburg, approximately 1470–1533. II. Title.

PT1101 D54 2014

Permission to reproduce the original woodcut title pages of each of the Confederates has been granted by the Bayerische Staatsbibliothek München.

Meiner Mutter
Mae Ellen Varano (née Steinbruecker)
1930–2009

Contents

List of Illustrations | ix

Acknowledgments | xi

Note on Translation | xiii

Abbreviations | xiv

Introduction | 1

1 The First Confederate | 21
A pitiful complaint to the Christian Emperor Charles concerning Doctor Martin Luther and Ulrich von Hutten. Also concerning the courtiers and mendicant friars. That His Majesty not allow himself to be led astray by such people.

2 The Second Confederate | 35
Concerning the forty day fast before Easter and others, and how wretchedly the Christian people are burdened by them.

3 The Third Confederate | 43
An admonition to all Christians that they take pity on cloistered women.

4 The Fourth Confederate | 53
On the long, wearisome braying which the spiritual monks, priests, and nuns call the canonical hours.

5 The Fifth Confederate | 61
An exhortation to all authorities of the German Nation that they reform the pulpit.

6 The Sixth Confederate | 69
Erasmus of Rotterdam, a prince among learned men in our age, writes about the preaching of the mendicant friars in the book entitled Encomion Morias.

7 The Seventh Confederate | 81
In praise of parish priests.

8 The Eighth Confederate | 91
Why Sir Erasmus of Rotterdam is translated into German. Why Martin Luther and Sir Ulrich von Hutten write in German.

9 The Ninth Confederate | 101
To all Christian authorities, both worldly and spiritual, of the German Nation, a wretched, fervent lamentation of all God-fearing monks, nuns and priests that one should come to their aid and save them from their unchristian neighbors.

10 The Tenth Confederate | 117
New statutes concerning reform of the spiritual estate which Psittacus brought from the land of Wellfaria.

11 The Eleventh Confederate | 131
A new ordinance concerning the secular estate written in Wellfaria, as described by Psittacus.

12 The Twelfth Confederate | 143
A friendly response of all God-fearing, decent, reasonable people in the German land to the pitiful complaint made to them by those in orders.

13 The Thirteenth Confederate | 153
A hopeful exhortation to the upright, honorable, strong, and Christian lords, officials, and subjects of the Common Confederacy (known as the Swiss) that they faithfully help to preserve evangelical teaching and devout Christians.

14 The Fourteenth Confederate | 161
Sir Erasmus of Rotterdam reveals in the book Encomion Morias the shameful service we render to the saints.

15 The Fifteenth Confederate | 171
To each and every believer in Christ, a wholesome warning to guard against new, dangerous teachings.

Select Bibliography | 179

Name and Subject Index | 185

Scripture Index | 193

Illustrations

Figure 1 *Der erst bundtsgnosz* | 20
Figure 2 *Der ander bundtsgnosz* | 34
Figure 3 *Der III. bundtgnosz* | 42
Figure 4 *Der IIII. bundtgnosz* | 52
Figure 5 *Der V. bundtsgnosz* | 60
Figure 6 *Der VI. bundtsgnosz* | 68
Figure 7 *Der VII.bundtgnosz* | 80
Figure 8 *Der VIII. bundtsgnosz* | 90
Figure 9 *Der IX. bundtgnosz* | 100
Figure 10 *Der X. bundtgnosz* | 116
Figure 11 *Der XI. bundtgnosz* | 130
Figure 12 *Der XII. bundtgnosz* | 142
Figure 13 *Der XIII. bundtsgnosz* | 152
Figure 14 *Der XIIII. bundtgnosz* | 160
Figure 15 *Der XV. bundtgnosz* | 170

Acknowledgments

In the course of translating this work I have relied on the support of a number of people. In particular, I owe an immense debt of gratitude to Dr. Stephan Lhotzky of the Department of Modern Foreign Languages at Augustana College. I began this project as a novice translator, and Stephan's help in the early stages was immeasurable. He read through the entire first draft of *The Eleventh Confederate* and made numerous suggestions for corrections. Since that time he has provided advice on several occasions about the translation of particularly difficult passages. Dr. Susan Hasseler, Academic Dean of Augustana College, found institutional funds to help defray the costs of reproducing the original woodcut title pages of each of the *Confederates*. Finally, I am very grateful to my wife, Sharon Judd, who has read more drafts of this translation than can be counted, and who, on each reading, patiently offered suggestions for stylistic improvement.

Note on Translation

THIS TRANSLATION OF *THE Fifteen Confederates* is based on the German critical edition by Ludwig Enders published in 1896. The following have also been consulted: Arnold Berger's editions of the first, eighth, tenth, and eleventh *Confederates* in *Die Sturmtruppen der Reformation: Ausgewählte Schriften der Jahre 1520–1525*, Karl Simon's editions of the tenth, eleventh, and fifteenth *Confederates* in *Deutsche Flugschriften zur Reformation (1520–1525)*, Adolph Laube's editions of the first, tenth, and eleventh *Confederates* in *Flugschriften der frühen Reformationsbewegung (1518–1524)*, and A. Enzo Baldini's Italian translation of the tenth and eleventh *Confederates* in *Gli "Statuti di Wolfaria" di Johann Eberlin (1521)*. The court of final appeal in cases of particularly difficult passages was the 1521 Basel edition of *The Fifteen Confederates*, which has been posted online by the Bavarian State Library.

Abbreviations

CE	Peter G. Bietenholz and Thomas B. Deutscher, eds. *Contemporaries of Erasmus: A Biographical Register of the Renaissance and Reformation*. Toronto: University of Toronto Press, 1985-1987.
ER	Paul Grendler et al., eds. *Encyclopedia of the Renaissance*. New York: Scribner, 1999.
JEvGS	Ludwig Enders, ed. *Johann Eberlin von Günzburg, Ausgewählte Schriften*, vol. 1. Flugschriften aus der Reformationszeit, vol. 11. Halle: Niemeyer, 1896; *Johann Eberlin von Günzburg, Sämtliche Schriften*, vol. 2. Flugschriften aus der Reformationszeit, vol. 15 (1900); *Johann Eberlin von Günzburg, Sämtliche Schriften*, vol. 3. Flugschriften aus der Reformationszeit, vol. 18 (1902).
FnhdG	Alfred Götze. *Frühneuhochdeutsches Glossar*. 7th ed. Berlin: de Gruyter, 1967.
NCE	Berard L. Marthaler, et al., eds. *New Catholic Encyclopedia*. 2nd ed. Washington DC: Catholic University of America, 2003.
OCD	N. G. L. Hammond and H. H. Scullard, eds. *The Oxford Classical Dictionary*. 2nd ed. Oxford: Clarendon, 1970.
ODCC	F. L. Cross and E. A. Livingston, eds. *The Oxford Dictionary of the Christian Church*. 3rd ed. Oxford: Oxford University Press, 1997.
OER	Hans J. Hillerbrand et al., eds. *The Oxford Encyclopedia of the Reformation*. Oxford: Oxford University Press, 1996.

Introduction

The Fifteen Confederates are a collection of pamphlets ostensibly written by a group of laymen, the confederates, who had sworn together to address the religious, social, economic, and political problems facing the German nation in the early years of the Protestant Reformation. They came off the presses sometime in the fall of 1521, in the unsettled atmosphere after Martin Luther's hearing at the Diet of Worms and subsequent disappearance, without indication of author, publisher, or date or place of publication. Evidence from other sources indicates that they were available at the Frankfurt book fair by 27 September and that very quickly they were known throughout the German-speaking lands. Not surprisingly, almost immediately they aroused the interest of ecclesiastical authorities. Still in September Johannes Cochlaeus, advisor to the papal legate at the Diet of Worms Girolamo Aleander, translated parts of the fourth and tenth *Confederates* and sent them to Aleander. By October, Johannes Eck, Martin Luther's opponent at the Leipzig Disputation, had taken a copy of the entire work to Rome.[1]

In a later pamphlet, Johann Eberlin von Günzburg, an apostate Franciscan preacher, admitted his authorship of *The Fifteen Confederates*.[2] Both Eberlin and *The Fifteen Confederates* were central to the pamphlet war that erupted during the early years of the Protestant Reformation, which Mark U. Edwards likens to a modern media campaign. Barely seventy years old at

1. The most complete discussions of the circumstances surrounding the appearance of *The Fifteeen Confederates* and the initial responses to them are provided by Peters, *Johann Eberlin von Günzburg*, 41–42 and Baldini, *Gli Statuti di Wolfaria*, 7. Cochlaeus' translation of parts of the fourth and tenth Confederates have been published in Baldini, *Gli Statuti di Wolfaria*, 71–77.

2. *Wider die falschen Geistlichen, genandt die Barfüsser und Franziskaner*, *JEvGS* 3: 85, 88.

the time, the moveable type printing press became an indispensable weapon in the religious controversies of the age. Scholars estimate that somewhere around 10,000 pamphlet editions were published in the German-speaking lands between 1500 and 1530. Almost 70 percent of these, over 6,000 editions, appeared during the crucial years between 1520 and 1526. Among publicists of the Reformation, Eberlin ranks sixth in terms of the number of pamphlets he wrote and the number of editions of his works produced.[3] Between 1520 and 1525, in addition to *The Fifteen Confederates*, he may have published as many as twenty-four pamphlets dealing with the reform of church and society (twenty of these can be reliably attributed to Eberlin, the other four are less sure). A number of these works ran into several editions.[4] Probably the most obvious sign of the notoriety of *The Fifteen Confederates* among contemporaries is the prominent place assigned to them in *The Great Lutheran Fool* by the noted Catholic pamphleteer Thomas Murner.[5]

Not surprisingly, Eberlin has been heralded at various times as "the Luther of southern Germany," "one of the most important and immediate links between Luther and the German people," "after Luther the most prolific Protestant pamphleteer," and "next to Luther, . . . the most trenchant of the pamphleteers of the early Reformation."[6] As a result, Eberlin and his writings have been favorite topics for German scholars in a variety of disciplines, including theology, history, literature, politics, and law. In addition, he has caught the attention of scholars working in English, French, and Italian, although here studies have stayed focused for the most part on

3. Edwards, *Printing, Propaganda, and Martin Luther*, 14–40.

4. The works safely attributed to Eberlin are contained in the three volumes of the critical edition of his writings edited by Ludwig Enders (*JEvGS*). Also included in volume three of that work (111–24) is *Der Glockenthurm*, one of the works whose authorship is less sure. At the beginning of the same volume (xxxiii–xxxv) Enders notes two further works some scholars have suggested as possible products of Eberlin's pen: *Das die Priester Eeweyber nemen mögen und sollen*, a translation of Phillip Melanchthon's *Apologia pro M. Barptolomeo Praeposito, qui uxorem in sacerdotio duxit*, and *Klag und antwort von Lutherischen und Beptischenn pfaffen uber die Reformacion so neulich zu Regenspurg der priester halben außgangen ist im Jar M D xxiiij*. Alfred Götze has suggested that another pamphlet, *Sendtbrieff an Pfarrer von Hohensynn. Doctor Martini Luthers Leer betreffennde*, is also the work of Eberlin, see "Ein Sendbrief Eberlins von Günzburg," 145–54. For a complete list of extant editions of works attributed to Eberlin, see Peters, *Johann Eberlin von Günzburg*, 339–74.

5. Murner, *Von dem grossen Lutherischen Narren*, 120–61.

6. Schmidt, "Die 15 Bundesgenossen," 5; Bell, "Wolfaria," 139; Ozment, "Social History," 189; Oberman, *Roots of Antisemitism*, 4.

Eberlin's social and political thought, especially alleged "utopian" aspects of *The Fifteen Confederates*.[7]

Despite Eberlin's prominence in his own day and his subsequent popularity among scholars, we know surprisingly little about his background and early life. In fact, much of the little we know has been reconstructed from biographical references in Eberlin's own writings, and these tend to concentrate on the period of his life after he had encountered the Reformation and to portray events in his former life from the perspective of his new allegiance. His birth date has been calculated as falling somewhere between 1460 and 1475 on the basis of four university matriculations for a Johann Eberlin: Ingolstadt (1473), Basel (1489 and 1490), and Freiburg im Breisgau (1493). However, there is no independent evidence that all of these records refer to the same person or that any of them refer to the author of *The Fifteen Confederates*.[8] On the basis of the Freiburg matriculation record, which mentions a "Mgr. Johannes Eberlein de Kleinkez Augusten. dioc.," Eberlin's birthplace has been identified as Kleinkötz, a small village six kilometers south of the town of Günzburg in the margraviate of Burgau in southern Germany.[9] In one of his later pamphlets, Eberlin indicates that he had been baptized in Günzburg, and elsewhere he identifies two of his relatives: Matthias Sigk, the municipal clerk in Lauingen on the Danube, and Johann Jakob Wehe, a parish priest in nearby Leipheim who was later executed for his role in the German Peasants' War of 1525.[10] Otherwise, we know virtually nothing about his social origins.[11]

7. For works focusing on *The Fifteen Confederates*, see the select bibliography at the end of this volume. More comprehensive bibliographies are available in Dipple, *Antifraternalism and Anticlericalism*, 216–38; Peters, *Johann Eberlin von Günburg*, 320–38; and Baldini, *L'Educazione di un Principe Luterano*, 155–88.

8. Peters, *Johann Eberlin von* Günzburg, 17–18 and Baldini, *L'Educazione di un Principe Luterano*, 15, have identified two other Johann Eberlin's to whom they might refer. Peters (16–32) provides the most comprehensive reconstruction of Eberlin's life prior to the publication of *The Fifteen Confederates.*

9. Mayer, *Die Matrikel der Universität Freiburg i. Br.*, 110; Deuerlein, "Nachtrag zu Johann Eberlin von Günzburg," 495.

10. *Mich wundert, dass kein Geld im Land ist, JEvGS* 3:169; *Vom Missbrauch christlicher Freiheit, JEvGS* 2:40; *Wie sich ein Diener Gottes Worts in seinem Thun halten soll, JEvGS* 3:184.

11. Hitchcock, *Knights' Revolt*, suggested that Eberlin was a scion of the lower nobility and that the reforming proposals in some of his pamphlets reflected the interests of that group. Hitchcock's conclusions were endorsed by Cole, "Eberlin von Günzburg and the German Reformation," 9, 42–43 and "Law and Order," 251–56, but challenged by Bell, "Wolfaria," 122n4.

About Eberlin's early life in the church we are not much better informed. He may have been ordained and served as a priest in the diocese of Augsburg, although, again, the evidence suggesting this activity could refer to another Johann Eberlin.[12] Eberlin himself indicates in two of his later works that he was encouraged to enter the Observant branch of the Franciscan Order by Johann Kröner von Scherdüng, at one time the preacher in Heilbronn, and that he had seen the triumphal entry of Cardinal Raymond Peraudi into that city. This suggests that he may have entered the order in Heilbronn sometime in 1500 or 1501—Peraudi visited the city toward the end of 1501. Kröner von Scherdüng may also have introduced Eberlin to the humanist movement in southwestern Germany.[13] Thereafter Eberlin likely spent some time in Alsace, perhaps as a member of the Observant priory in the town of Barr.[14]

The first clear indication we have of Eberlin's life as a Franciscan can be gleaned from statements in several of his later writings. In these he indicates that for a time he was a preacher in the Franciscan church in Tübingen. During this time he seems to have played an active role in serving Franciscan nuns, the Poor Clares, under the care of the Tübingen priory,[15] which may explain his concern for the plight of cloistered women in *The Fifteen Confederates* and in a number of his later works. Eberlin provides us with no indication of when he was in Tübingen or for how long, although Christian Peters, the author of the most recent and authoritative biography of Eberlin, calculates he must have been in the city as early as 1517 and

12. The first Basel matriculation identifies Johann Eberlin as "presbyter Augustensis dioceses" (Wackernagel, *Die Matrikel der Universität Basel*, 209). However, this could be another priest by the name of Johann Eberlin who remained loyal to the Catholic church, see Baldini, *L'Educazione di un Principe Luterano*, 15.

13. *Wider die falschen Geistlichen, genannt die Barfüsser und Franzikaner, JEvGS* 3:46; *Wie sich ein Diener Gottes Wort in seinem Thun halten soll, JEvGS* 3:205; Radlkofer, *Johann Eberlin*, 3n5 and 6. Peters, *Johann Eberlin von Günzburg* 19–21, makes the most complete case that Kröner von Scherdüng may have been Eberlin's introduction to the humanist movement.

14. Lucke, "Die Entstehung der '15 Bundesgenossen,'" 10–14. Throughout his writings, Eberlin makes frequent reference to people and places in Alsace, including a number of important Alsatian humanists: see *The First Confederate*; *The Third Confederate*; *The Eighth Confederate*; *The Fourteenth Confederate* all below; *Mich wundert dass kein Geld im Land ist, JEvGS* 3:160, 181; *Wider die falschen Geistlichen, genannt die Barfüsser und Franziskaner, JEvGS* 3: 70–71.

15. *Sieben fromme, aber trostlose Pfaffen klagen einer dem andern ihre Note, JEvGS* 2: 70; *Wider den Ausgang vieler Klosterleute, JEvGS* 2:136; *Wider die falschen Geistlichen, genannt die Barfüsser und Franziskaner, JEvGS* 3:67–69.

certainly by 1519.[16] Eberlin portrays himself as being at this time an ardent defender of the dignity and liberties of the clerical estate, and especially of those in religious orders. This has obvious rhetorical value when contrasted with his later conversion to the "cause of the gospel," but it may also provide us with some insight into his pre-Reformation activities. He indicates as well that he became involved in a theological controversy at the University of Tübingen, but provides no details about its nature. There has been some speculation that Eberlin may have entered into a dispute between scholastic and humanist faculty members on the side of the humanists.[17] It appears that shortly after this controversy, Eberlin was transferred out of the Tübingen priory. At one time scholars assumed that this might have been a form of punishment imposed on Eberlin as a result of the various controversies in which he was involved. However, subsequent positions of honor he held in the order suggest instead that it is best explained by the common practice of frequent transferals in the mendicant orders.[18]

Perhaps still in 1519, Eberlin was in Basel, where he became a member of a humanist sodality, which included the Franciscan prior Konrad Pellikan, the famed Alsatian humanist Beatus Rhenanus, and members of the prominent Basel publishing families of Froben and Amerbach. In this context he encountered some of Luther's most important writings of the early Reformation.[19] He may also have made his first foray into the realm of popular publishing. In 1520 or shortly thereafter the Basel printer Adam Petris produced a brief anonymous pamphlet entitled *An Epistle to the Parson of Highsense (Hohensynn), concerning Dr. Martin Luther's Teaching*. A

16. Peters, *Johann Eberlin von Günzburg*, 21.

17. *Sieben fromme, aber trostlose Pfaffen klagen einer dem andern ihre Not*, *JEvGS*, 2:70. Peters, *Johann Eberlin von Günzburg*, 21–28 provides a comprehensive overview of the possible participants in the dispute. Paul Scriptoris, an earlier resident of the Tübingen priory, had been a zealous defender of the new learning.

18. Lucke, "Die Entstehung der '15 Bundesgenossen,'" 12; Geiger, "Die reformatorischen Initia Eberlins," 180; Heger, *Eberlin und seine Vorstellungen*, 14. According to Neidiger, *Mendikanten zwischen Ordensideal und städtischer Realität*, 177, well-educated friars were regularly shuffled between friaries to fill various positions in the order which required their particular talents.

19. Riggenbach, *Eberlin und seine Reformprogramm*, 12–15; Radlkofer, *Johann Eberlin*, 8; and Heger, *Eberlin und seine Vorstellungen*, 14–15, assumed that Eberlin was transferred from Tübingen to Freiburg im Breisgau. Scholarly consensus now favors Basel, see Lucke, "Die Entstehung der '15 Bundesgenossen,'" 14–18; Wulkau, "Das kirchliche Ideal des Johann Eberlin von Günzburg," 11; Geiger, "Die reformatorischen Initia Eberlins," 180; Peters, *Johann Eberlin von Günzburg*, 28–29; Dipple, *Antifraternalism and Anticlericalism*, 42–43.

satiric comparison of the lives of contemporary clergy with the example provided by Christ, both its style and content suggest that it might be the work of Eberlin.[20]

In early 1521 Eberlin was transferred to Ulm.[21] In a later pamphlet addressed to the city council he indicates that when he arrived there he was not yet openly supporting the Wittenberg reform movement: "When I came to you, God placed a great desire in your hearts to learn his Word through me, but I failed, in part because I did not know it and in part because I was afraid to speak the truth. But through Dr. Luther's little book I became daily more learned and ready to preach the truth."[22] However, it appears that this state of affairs changed quickly. In a letter dated 15/16 March to the papal vice chancellor Guilio de Medici, the legate Aleander refers to "a friar of the Franciscan Observants in Ulm" who had been preaching in an orthodox fashion at the beginning of Lent, but who has since begun preaching material and defending propositions which the legate thought worthy of notice in Rome.[23]

If we can believe Eberlin's later account of events, his new activities raised the ire of his superiors in the order who then moved to silence him, apparently against the wishes of the city council: "Then God allowed the devil to prepare a game through my hypocritical brothers, by which I was driven from you despite the intervention on three occasions of the city council of Ulm, who earnestly—as they also found support among the common people—appealed to my superiors to keep me there."[24] If the council did intervene, Eberlin's opponents were eventually successful, and he preached his final sermon in the city on the feast of Sts. Peter and Paul (29 June 1521) and then departed the city.[25]

In this context Eberlin wrote the first works that would become elements of *The Fifteen Confederates*. Noting inconsistencies in the cycle—for

20. Götze, "Ein Sendbrief Eberlin von Günzburgs," 145, 150–53; Peters, *Johann Eberlin von Günzburg*, 29–30.

21. Peters, *Johann Eberlin von Günzburg*, 30–31.

22. *Die andere getreue Vermahnung an den Rath von Ulm, JEvGS* 3:2.

23. Radlkofer, *Johann Eberlin*, 8–9, first identified this friar as Eberlin. Aleander's letter has been reproduced in Brieger, *Aleander und Luther*, 106 and Radlkofer, *Johann Eberlin*, 9.

24. *Die andere getreue Vermahnung an den Rath von Ulm, JEvGS* 3:2. The *Ratsprotokolle* for this period make no mention of an intervention by the council on Eberlin's behalf, see Geiger, "Die reformatorischen Initia Eberlins," 182.

25. *Ein kurzer schriflicher Bericht des Glaubens, an die Ulmer, JEvGS* 2:173.

example, the *Third Confederate* reminds its readers of topics which are, in fact, not discussed until the *Seventh Confederate*—Johann Heinrich Schmidt concluded that Eberlin was not a logical thinker and suggested that the order of the individual *Confederates* could be changed without detriment to the impact of the collection as a whole. In response, Wilhelm Lucke argued convincingly that these works were written in an order different from that in which they appear in the collection. He suggested further that the idea of the collected work had not yet occurred to Eberlin when he wrote these first components. Lucke's revised chronology for the composition of the *Confederates*, with a few minor modifications by Gottfried Geiger, is now generally accepted by Eberlin scholars.[26]

According to the revised order of composition, the first *Confederates* to be written were numbers seven, two, three, and four. These deal with issues of concern to inhabitants of monasteries, touching either the nature of their vocation or their interactions with the laity: the sufficiency of the parish clergy and the spiritual services provided by them, the Lenten fast and its applicability to both those in monasteries and the laity, the plight of cloistered women, and the canonical hours. Taken together, they envision a reform of the monastic life and its place in society that would have fundamentally changed the nature of the institution. Under the circumstances, the response of Eberlin's confreres and superiors to his suggestions should come as no surprise. Furthermore, these works may not have been envisioned initially as published pamphlets. Aleander mentioned that Eberlin's questionable opinions were spread about in sermons and propositions. Peters suggests that the seventh and second *Confederates* could easily have been developed out of popular sermons and that the third and fourth retain elements of what could have been lists of theses.[27]

Wilhelm Lucke characterized this group of *Confederates* as focusing on individual abuses in the church, but as remaining within the bounds of orthodoxy and recognizing the authority of the church throughout. While they draw on elements of Luther's reform program, especially as outlined

26. Schmidt, "Die 15 Bundesgenossen," 13–15; Lucke, "Die Entstehung der '15 Bundesgenossen,'" 2–3, 32–39; Geiger, "Die reformatorischen Initia Eberlins," 182–84.

27. Peters, *Johann Eberlin von Günzburg*, 45–46. He identifies *JEvGS*, 1: page 30, line 24 to page 33, line 4 and page 38, line 9 to page 40, line 7 (below page 49, line 11 to page 51, line 22 and page 55, line 22 to page 57, line 15) as blocks of theses which can stand on their own independent of the surrounding material. Geiger, "Die reformatorischen Initia Eberlins," 184, initially suggested that the earliest *Confederates* may have first been sermons.

in the *Address to the Christian Nobility*, they avoid mentioning Luther by name.[28] Gottfried Geiger and Günther Heger argued further that while Eberlin derives specific complaints about abuses from Luther's work, the basic thought of these pamphlets reflects the Christian humanist reform program of Erasmus of Rotterdam.[29] Elsewhere I make the case that Eberlin's suggestions in these works are best characterized as a continuation of reform traditions within the Franciscan Observant movement, complemented with ideas drawn from the works of Luther and Erasmus.[30]

The next three *Confederates* to be written were numbers one, five, and eight in the cycle. The first, an appeal to Emperor Charles V that he take to heart the reform proposals suggested by Luther and the humanist poet laureate Ulrich von Hutten, was, unlike its predecessors, clearly intended as a literary work from the outset. Probably written during the first three weeks of April, it was part of a deluge of pamphlets aimed at influencing the authorities and public opinion at the time of the Diet of Worms and may have been modeled on several "manifestos" written in the preceding year by Hutten.[31] In *The Fifth Confederate* Eberlin continues to call for reform from those in power, but he changes the object of his appeal from the emperor to secular authorities at all levels in the German nation. It is tempting to see in this change disappointment with the outcome of the Diet of Worms. Eberlin admonishes all authorities to undertake a reform of the preaching office, arguing that secular authorities have not only the right, but also the duty, to oversee this task. Only with good, biblically based preaching can peace and social harmony be maintained. In *The Eighth Confederate* he changes his tack and defends writing and publishing in the vernacular as the only effective ways to fight the wiles of the church. Included in this work is a brief history of conflict between popes and emperors throughout the Middle Ages, suggesting a growing sense of nationalism likely derived from Hutten's writings, but also compatible with statements in Luther's *Address to the Christian Nobility*.

In this group of *Confederates* we see evidence not only of Eberlin's deteriorating relationship with his brethren and superiors in the Franciscan order, but also with church authorities more generally. In his letter first

28. Lucke "Die Entstehung der '15 Bundesgenossen,'" 42–48.

29. Geiger, "Die reformatorischen Initia Eberlins," 191–93; Heger, *Eberlin und seine Vorstellungen*, 20.

30. Dipple, *Antifraternalism and Anticlericalism*, 47–59.

31. Ahrens, "Gedanken Eberlins," 37; see also Peters, *Johann Eberlin von Günzburg*, 46.

calling attention to Eberlin's activities in Ulm, Aleander had suggested that the matter be brought to the attention of the emperor's Franciscan confessor, Johannes Glapion.[32] Likely in response to Glapion's involvement, *The First Confederate* calls on the emperor to refuse any counsel from his confessor relating to affairs of the realm, or better yet, to send him away and take as his confessor a true friend of the German people like Erasmus, Luther, or Luther's colleague in Wittenberg Andreas Bodenstein von Karlstadt. Eberlin's distrust of Glapion escalates into an outright attack on the Franciscan Observants in particular and the orders of the mendicant friars in general in this and the subsequent two *Confederates*. At the same time Eberlin is increasingly willing to defy the ecclesiastical hierarchy, suggesting a deeper immersion into Luther's writings and stronger commitment to his cause. However, Eberlin continues to portray reform at Wittenberg as an extension of that of the humanists, associated especially with Erasmus and increasingly with Hutten.[33]

After leaving Ulm, Eberlin probably first went to Switzerland. A character in one of his later pamphlets reports seeing him in Baden in the Swiss Aargau on St. Ulrich's day (4 July) 1521: "There he preached in a completely Lutheran sense against priests, monks, and nuns, much more earnestly than he had preached before."[34] Unfortunately, we have no direct information on Eberlin's other activities in Switzerland at this time. He may have been *en route* to visit Huldrych Zwingli in Zurich—there is evidence that he and Zwingli knew of each other when Eberlin was in Basel—but we have no confirmation that this was his intention or whether or not he reached his goal if it was. More likely he soon moved on to Lauingen on the Danube, where he spent the summer with his cousin Matthias Sigk.[35]

32. Brieger, *Aleander und Luther*, 106; see also Lucke, "Die Entstehung der '15 Bundesgenossen,'" 54.

33. For a summary of scholarship on Hutten's influence on these and subsequent Confederates, see Dipple, *Antifraternalism and Anticlericalism*, 67–73.

34. *Klage der sieben frommen Pfaffen*, *JEvGS* 2:71.

35. Lucke, "Die Entstehung der '15 Bundesgenossen,'" 20, first suggested that Eberlin's intended destination was Zurich. Strobel, "Nachricht von Johann Eberlin von Günzburgs Leben und Schriften," 369, speculated that Eberlin went from Baden to Basel and then Rheinfelden, although he likely confused Eberlin's activities in 1521 with those from a subsequent visit to the area in 1523. In his 1522 pamphlet dedicated to Sigk, *On the Abuse of Christian Liberty*, Eberlin recalls their conversations from the preceding summer when he stayed with Sigk in Lauingen. see *Vom Missbrauch christlicher Freiheit*, *JEvGS* 2:40.

During this time Eberlin penned four further *Confederates*, although the locations and precise order of their composition is unclear. *The Thirteenth Confederate* is an appeal to the Swiss for their help in defending the cause of the Gospel. This may be a printed version of the sermon delivered in Baden, although as Christian Peters argues, its content suggests that it could have been written at any point during the summer. Gottfried Geiger argued that this was the first pamphlet written after Eberlin had developed the idea of collecting his works together as *The Fifteen Confederates*. Peters counters, I believe more accurately, that this honor belongs to *The Ninth Confederate*, an appeal to the authorities of Germany to come to the aid of monks, nuns, and priests suffering under the unjust rules associated with their estate.[36] In both of these works Eberlin's denunciation of the evils perpetrated on Christendom by the monks and priests continues unabated. In *The Ninth Confederate* he focuses especially on the activities of the mendicant orders and here expands considerably a brief history of them contained in *The Eighth Confederate*.

Closely related to the themes of *The Ninth Confederate*, but also to the eighth's call for writing in the vernacular, are the contents of the sixth and fourteenth. Both consist of translations of parts of Erasmus' *Praise of Folly*, with comments on those passages by Eberlin. The sixth concentrates on Erasmus' pillorying of the preachers from the mendicant orders while the fourteenth reproduces his satire of abuses associated with the veneration of the saints. Eberlin takes the opportunity provided by the latter discussion to excoriate the mendicants' use of their patron saints to exploit the naivety of the laity.

Likely while he was staying with his cousin in Lauingen during July and August Eberlin wrote the next three *Confederates*, numbers ten, eleven, and twelve. Numbers ten and eleven are closely related, containing respectively the ecclesiastical and secular statutes of the imaginary land of Wellfaria brought to Germany by Psittacus (the parrot or "ear-blower"). In terms of both structure and content they invite comparison with Thomas More's *Utopia*, and are among the most popular and intensively studied of Eberlin's writings.[37] *The Twelfth Confederate*, an answer of the German

36. Geiger, "Die reformatorischen Initia Eberlins," 183; Peters, *Johann Eberlin von Günzburg*, 44–45. Lucke, "Die Entstehung der '15 Bundesgenossen,'" 95–97, argues that Eberlin may have derived the idea of collecting his reforming pamphlets together under the guise of a sworn confederacy from the writings of Hutten.

37. Studies on Eberlin's alleged utopianism are legion, see, for example: Hitchcock, *Knights' Revolt*, 57–77; Cole, "Pamphlet and Social Forces," 195–205; idem, "Law and

people to the complaints brought to them by monks and nuns dissatisfied with life in the cloister, offers a general dispensation to all who wish to leave their orders and suggests comprehensive reform of the monastic life. It is unclear whether Eberlin was still in Lauingen or whether he had returned to Switzerland when he wrote *The Fifteenth Confederate*, a warning against the new, harmful teachings threatening Christendom. This work sets out to prove that scholastic theology, not the ideas of the Reformers, represents the novelty in the history of Christian teaching. In the middle of this discussion Eberlin mentions for the first time some of the central themes of the theology coming out of Wittenberg. Gottfried Geiger characterizes these as foreign bodies in the context of the cycle as a whole, and Wilhelm Lucke suggests on the basis of Eberlin's reference to "a little book on confession," possibly Luther's *On Confession* at press in the middle of August, that Eberlin had established contact with the Reformers in Wittenberg.[38]

Extant editions of *The Fifteen Confederates* indicate they were a publishing success both individually and as a collected cycle. After its initial publication by the Basel printer Pamphilius Gengenbach, the collected work was reprinted three times: once by Jörg Nadler in Augsburg and twice by Johann Eckhart in Speyer. Gengenbach also published individual editions of each of the *Confederates* and even second editions of numbers twelve and thirteen. By far the most popular *Confederate* was the seventh which ran through six editions: two by Gengenbach in Basel and one each from presses in Zurich, Augsburg, Speyer, and Zwickau.[39]

In *The Fifteenth Confederate*, Eberlin first began to address some of the central themes of Reformation theology. The remainder of his publishing

Order," 251–56; Bell, "Wolfaria," 122–39; Seibt, *Utopica*, 71–81; Vogler et al., *Illustrierte Geschichte*, 159–62; Ozment, *Reformation in the Cities*, 91–108; Gorceix, "L'Utopie en Allemagne," 14–29; Geiger, "Die reformatorischen Initia Eberlins," 178–201; Plard, "L'Utopie Communiste," 387–403; Vogler, "Reformprogramm," 219–32; idem, "Von Eberlin zu Stiblinus," 143–50; Eliav-Feldon, *Realistic Utopias*; Heger *Eberlin und seine Vorstellungen*, 47–64, 111–16; Baldini, "Riforma luterana," 3–31; idem, "Nobili e contadini," 439–53; Bujňáková, "Eine Gesellschaftsutopie," 184–94; Opitz, "Social Vision of Eberlin"; Brinker-von der Heyde, "Neue Weltordnungen," 29–40; Baldini, "Istanze Utopiche," 43–58; Doku, "Lutheran Utopia,"; Rivoletti, "Strategie della finzione," 69–93; Lederer, "Welfare Land," 165–81.

38. Geiger, "Die reformatorischen Initia Eberlins," 198; Lucke, "Die Entstehung der '15 Bundesgenossen,'" 91.

39. Peters, *Johann Eberlin von Günzburg* 43–47 and 340–50, argues that Gengenbach published the editions of the individual *Confederates* as soon as Eberlin finished each of them, followed shortly by the cycle as a whole.

activity in many ways chronicles his increasing immersion in that theology, although the social, political, and economic concerns voiced in *The Fifteen Confederates* never entirely disappear from view in his subsequent writings.

Eberlin likely spent the winter in Switzerland, possibly with Konrad Pellikan, before he began making his way toward Wittenberg in early 1522. His later writings indicate more than passing knowledge of the reforming movement in Augsburg, suggesting that he stopped there on his way north. He may also have spent some time in Nuremberg, although the evidence for this is less firm.[40] In a pamphlet written in 1526, Eberlin reflected back on his arrival at the center of the Saxon Reformation, likely in early 1522: "Three and one-half years ago I came to Wittenberg and thought that I knew much in the Gospel, but, when I consulted with the Wittenbergers, I knew nothing."[41] Eberlin's presence in the city is confirmed by the inclusion of his name in the matriculation records of the university for the summer semester of 1522.[42] The only other information we have about Eberlin's activities at this time are two vague references from his later writings. In what was probably his first work published after his arrival in Wittenberg, he addressed the German bishops: "I have advised you in an innocent and friendly manner in a small book addressed to you which I wrote while bedridden in Leipzig four weeks ago."[43] And in a subsequent pamphlet he claimed that the bishop of Meersburg consulted with him during his stay in Leipzig.[44] Echoes of Eberlin's advice may be contained in *How Very Dangerous, that a Priest does not Have a Wife*, a thorough denunciation of compulsory clerical celibacy that draws on the writings of both Luther and Karlstadt on the subject. Christian Peters speculates, I believe correctly, that Eberlin intended this pamphlet as a means to recommend himself to the Wittenberg Reformers.[45]

It appears that after completing *How Very Dangerous*, Eberlin devoted himself to an intensive study of Reformation theology, which, as we have

40. Riggenbach, *Eberlin und seine Reformprogramm*, 80–81; *Eine freundliche Vermahnung an die Christen zu Augsburg*, *JEvGS* 2:137–52; *Klage der sieben frommen Pfaffen*, *JEvGS* 2:92.

41. *Warnung an die Christen der Burgauischen Mark*, *JEvGS* 3:275.

42. Förstmann, *Album Academia Vitebergensis*, 113.

43. *Wie gar gefährlich, so ein Priester kein Eheweib hat*, *JEvGS* 2:31.

44. *Trost der sieben frommen Pfaffen*, *JEvGS* 2:92.

45. *Wie gar gefährlich, so ein Priester kein Eheweib hat*, *JEvGS* 2:21–37; Peters, *Johann Eberlin von Günzburg*, 56–59. For an overview of arguments about the respective influences of the writings of Luther and Karlstadt on this pamphlet, see Dipple, *Antifraternalism and Anticlericalism*, 98–103.

seen, he claimed was a novelty to him at the time of his arrival in Wittenberg.[46] Not surprisingly, when he again began writing, he focused on some of the central elements of that theology. *On the Abuse of Christian Liberty* was published in the early autumn of 1522. It indicates that not only was Eberlin wrestling with the fundamentals of Luther's theology, but also that he may have had some reservations about positions he had taken in his earlier writings. For example, in contrast to his earlier insistence on fundamental and immediate changes to the cloistered life and religious orders, in this work he includes cowls and tonsures among the externals over which enthusiasts (*Schwärmer*) fight to no avail.[47] Closely related to *On the Abuse of Christian Liberty* was Eberlin's next work, *Against the Imprudent, Unreasonable Departure of Many Cloistered.* At the outset Eberlin refers back to his earlier discussion of Christian liberty and claims that the large numbers of runaway monks and nuns have occasioned the present work.[48] Similar themes also reappear in *A Friendly, Encouraging Exhortation to the Christians at Augsburg*, in which Eberlin sought to convey to friends in the south the fruits of his theological study in Wittenberg.[49] Also during this time Eberlin translated from Latin into German the autobiographical history of Jacob Probst, the prior of the Augustinian convent in Antwerp who had close ties to Wittenberg. In February 1522 Probst recanted his reforming teachings under pressure from the authorities, but he subsequently returned to them and his case was for a while a central feature in polemics both for and against the Reformation.[50]

46. Peters, *Johann Eberlin von Günzburg*, 59. Martin Brecht has pointed to a break in Eberlin's publishing activity after the completion of *How Very Dangerous*; all subsequent pamphlets cite Luther's translation of the New Testament, which came off the presses around September 21, 1522, see Brecht, "Johann Eberlin von Günzburg in Wittenberg," 48.

47. *Vom Missbrauch christlicher Freiheit*, *JEvGS* 2:39–55, especially 51.

48. *Wider den unvorsichtigen, unbescheidnen Ausgang vieler Klosterleute*, *JEvGS* 2:119–36, especially 122–23. Although the only extant version of this pamphlet bears the publication date of 1524, references by Eberlin to a work of this nature in pamphlets from 1522 and 1523 indicate that it was completed on October 28, 1522, see *Wider den unvorsichtigen Ausgang*, *JEvGS* 2:121; *Eine freundliche, tröstliche Vermahnung an die Christen zu Augsburg*, *JEvGS* 2:151; *Wider die falschen Geistlichen, genannt die Barfüsser und Franziskaner*, *JEvGS* 3:87. See also Riggenbach, *Eberlin und seine Reformprogramm*, 200; Radlkofer, *Johann Eberlin*, 82–83; *JEvGS* 3:xv; Brecht, "Johann Eberlin von Günzburg in Wittenberg," 50.

49. *Eine freundliche, tröstliche Vermahnung an die Christen zu Augsburg*, *JEvGS* 2:137–52.

50. *Eine schöne und klägliche Historie*, *JEvGS* 2:95–117.

Eberlin's subsequent works written during his first stay in Wittenberg can be divided into two distinct groups: anonymous pieces, often in fictional form, concentrating on pressing social concerns and signed works more explicitly theological in nature. In November and December 1522, Eberlin returned to the former format. In *Seven Devout but Disconsolate Priests Complain to One Another about Their Plight* seven new fictional characters discuss the predicaments facing godly clergy. The fifteen confederates then suggest solutions to the priests' problems in *The Consolation of the Seven Devout Priests*.[51] Closely related to these two pamphlets and written around the same time is *A New, and the Last, Statement of the Fifteen Confederates*.[52] In these works Eberlin cautions his readers to be judicious in their acceptance of some of the statements in *The Fifteen Confederates*. In the conclusion of *The Consolation of the Seven Devout Priests*, the fifteen confederates warn: "We ask that you read judiciously our first fifteen little books, which appeared among many in Basel in 1521, for not all things found there are articles of belief."[53] And *A New, and the Last, Statement of the Fifteen Confederates* points out the dangerous consequences of writing books on religious matters. It then concludes by announcing the retirement of the fifteen confederates and encouraging their readers to turn their attention to the Bible.[54]

After the retirement of the fifteen confederates and the seven devout priests, Eberlin returned to the format of the signed pamphlet in his own voice. One of the questions addressed in *A Little Book Which Answers Three Questions* is about the authority of a council to decide on matters of faith. This suggests that the book was written in early spring 1523 when plans for a general council in Germany were being proposed.[55] Shortly thereafter,

51. *Sieben fromme, aber trostlose Pfaffen klagen einer dem andern ihre Not*, *JEvGS* 2:57–77; *Trost der sieben frommen Pfaffen*, *JEvGS* 2:79–93. On dating these works, see Brecht, "Johann Eberlin von Günzburg in Wittenberg," 51–52; Peters, *Johann Eberlin von Günzburg*, 92, 107–8.

52. *Letzter Bundesgenosse*, *JEvGS* 1:171–205.

53. *Trost der sieben frommen Pfaffen*, *JEvGS* 2:93.

54. *Letzter Bundesgenosse*, *JEvGS* 1:202–5.

55. *Ein Büchlein, worin auf drei Frage geantwortet wird*, *JEvGS* 2:153–69. During the Nuremberg *Reichstag*, convened on 17 November 1522, a proposal was put forward for a church council which would include representation for secular authorities. On 8 February 1523 this proposal was presented to the papal nuncio and on 6 March was proclaimed by imperial edict. In the meantime it became widely known through informal channels. See Radlkofer, *Johann Eberlin*, 90–92; Heger, *Eberlin und seine Vorstellungen*, 26; and Brecht, "Johann Eberlin von Günzburg in Wittenberg," 52.

Eberlin wrote the first of two epistles to the citizens and council of the imperial city of Ulm, likely in preparation for a planned visit there in the summer of 1523. *A Short Written Report on Faith to the Citizens of Ulm* is dated 24 February 1523.[56]

Eberlin's' pamphlets written between the time of his arrival in Wittenberg and the spring of 1523 suggest that he had moved fully into the orbit of the Wittenberg Reformation. In the works in which he speaks with his own voice his goal is primarily to share with his readers the details of the Reformation theology he had encountered there. While he continues to address social issues associated with reform in the anonymous works cast in the voices of fictional characters, he tends to step back from some of the more radical and forceful statements of *The Fifteen Confederates*, and especially their criticism of members of the first estate. This trend seemed to reverse itself in the spring and summer of 1523.

In 1525 the Augsburg printer Heinrich Steiner published a pamphlet by Eberlin entitled *Against the Profaners of God's Creatures*. In it the anticlerical rhetoric developed in some of *The Fifteen Confederates* returns with full force, and Eberlin goes so far as to identify ordination with the mark of the apocalyptic beast.[57] Bernhard Riggenbach regarded this work as far too radical to have been written after Eberlin's arrival in Wittenberg. He suggested instead that it, too, had been written during Eberlin's convalescence in Leipzig, in support of Karlstadt, who had opted for an increasingly radical reforming trajectory in Wittenberg during Luther's stay at the Wartburg in late 1521 and early 1522, but first published by a member of the Karlstadtian party in 1525. Riggenbach's suggestion led to widespread speculation about the extent and duration of Eberlin's radical Karlstadtian phase.[58] More recently, however, Christian Peters has argued convincingly that this work was, in fact, written in mid-1523 in response to moves led by two Franciscans, Johann Fritzhans and Hans Seyler, to turn back the tide of reform in the city of Annaberg.[59]

Similar criticism of the first estate continues in *A Second True Admonition to the Council of Ulm*, written between 16 April and 23 May 1523.

56. *Ein kurzer schriftlicher Bericht des Glaubens, an die Ulmer*, *JEvGS* 2:171–92, especially 174.

57. *Wider die Schänder der Creaturen Gottes*, *JEvGS* 2:1–19.

58. Riggenbach, *Eberlin und seine Reforprogramm*, 81–83, 97–110; Radlkofer, *Johann Eberlin*, 52–62; Ahrens, "Gedanken Eberlins," 31n70; Geiger, "Die reformatorischen Initia Eberlins," 197–200; Heger, *Eberlin und seine Vorstellungen*, 23–24.

59. Peters, *Johann Eberlin von Günzburg*, 173–84.

Here Eberlin returns to his denunciation of the mendicant orders from *The Fifteen Confederates*, and he identifies the Dominicans and Franciscans as the main opponents of the Gospel in the city.[60] Eberlin's anti-mendicant polemics then reach a crescendo in *Against the False Religious known as the Bare-Footed Friars and Franciscans*, which was likely written between May and July. This work was part of a general campaign against the Franciscan order by its former members in the spring and summer of 1523, initiated, if not orchestrated, by Luther.[61]

While the pamphlet war against the Franciscans was still being waged, Eberlin left Wittenberg for a preaching tour of Switzerland and southern Germany.[62] Evidence of the message he preached survives in two works published during his travels: *A Splendid Mirror of the Christian Life* and a sermon on Luther's doctrine of the two kingdoms preached in Rottenburg am Neckar.[63] Eberlin's ultimate destination was Ulm. He must have arrived in the city by the middle of October and begun preaching immediately. By the end of the month open conflict between him and local Dominicans led to his ouster from the city. Eberlin may then have visited his cousin Johann Jakob Wehe, the reforming priest in nearby Leipheim. Wehe's sermons were enjoying some popularity locally, including among the citizens of Günzburg, whose priest responded by having the magistrates throw several of them in jail. *The Bell Tower*, an anonymous pamphlet denouncing the actions of the priest and magistrates of Günzburg has been attributed to Eberlin, although his authorship is by no means a sure thing.[64] Eberlin probably next traveled to Nuremberg, before returning to Wittenberg in late autumn 1523.[65]

60. *Die andere getreue Vermahnung an den Rath von Ulm*, *JEvGS* 3:1–40.

61. *Wider die falschen Geistlichen, genannt die Barfüsser und Franziskaner*, *JEvGS* 3:41–88. On the anti-mendicant campaign and Eberlin's role in it, see Dipple, *Antifraternalism and Anticlericalism*, 1–36, 131–62.

62. Peters, *Johann Eberlin von Günzburg* 185–222 provides the best summary of this period of Eberlin's life. A less thorough summary in English of Eberlin's activities is available in Dipple, *Antifraternalism and Anticlericalism*, 201–11.

63. *Ein schöner Spiegel des christlichen Lebens*, *JEvGS* 3:97–109; *Predigt von zweierlei Reich, gehalten zu Rottenburg*, *JEvGS* 3:89–95.

64. *Der Glockenthurm*, *JEvGS* 3:111–24. The debate about Eberlin's authorship of this pamphlet has continued for over a century, see Riggenbach, *Eberlin und seine Vorstellungen*, 194–96; Radlkofer, *Johann Eberlin*, 143–44; *JEvGS* 3:xxv; Leitzman, "Zu Eberlin von Günzburg," 277; Brecht, "Johann Eberlin von Günzburg in Wittenberg," 49n8; Laube, *Flugschriften* 2:937; Peters, *Johann Eberlin von Günzburg*, 242.

65. Statements in *Ein freundliche Zuschreiben an alle Stände deutscher Nation*, *JEvGS* 3:125–45, suggest that it was possibly written in anticipation of the Reichstag scheduled

In Wittenberg he continued to write, in part reflecting on the experiences of his travels. *How a Servant of God's Word Should Conduct Himself*, first published in 1525 but likely written in March 1524, is dedicated to Eberlin's cousin Wehe and consists of instructions for an aspiring evangelical preacher. It encourages proceeding cautiously in matters of reform and suggests that the enthusiasts pose a greater threat to the cause of the Gospel than do the papists.[66] He also began work on *I Wonder that there is no Money in the Land*, which revives the character of Psittacus and the social concerns of *The Fifteen Confederates*. Modeled closely on Ulrich von Hutten's *The Robbers*, this work claims to be the written transcript of a conversation between Psittacus and three south German commoners about the reason for widespread poverty in a land so richly endowed by God. Much of the blame for this state of affairs Eberlin still lays on the shoulders of the clergy, but he continues to caution against the activities of the enthusiasts and enters into a detailed critique of the writing and publishing of books. Among those denounced as having foolish titles which mislead readers is *The Fifteen Confederates*.[67]

Statements in *I Wonder* suggest that it was written piecemeal in 1523 and early 1524, and that it was finished after Eberlin had moved to Erfurt. When exactly he arrived there is not completely clear. His next pamphlet, *A Sermon in Erfurt on Prayer* is the printed version of a sermon he claims he delivered on 1 May 1524. This work continues to exhibit Eberlin's concern with the activities of the enthusiasts and his desire for measured, orderly reform.[68] Although he claims to have preached regularly in Erfurt, and possibly may have been recommended for a clerical position there by Luther, Eberlin was unable to find fixed employment in the city.[69]

Eberlin also claimed to have played a role in stilling unrest associated with the Peasants' War in and around Erfurt in the spring of 1525.[70] He eventually left Erfurt in search of settled employment, applying unsuccessfully for a position in Rothenburg ob der Tauber and ultimately successfully

to convene there on 13 November.

66. *Wie sich ein Diener Gottes Worts in seinem Thun halten soll*, *JEvGS* 3:183–232.

67. *Mich wundert, dass kein Geld im Land ist*, *JEvGS* 3:147–81.

68. *Predigt zu Erfurt vom Gebet*, *JEvGS* 3:233–52.

69. *Mich wundert, dass kein Geld im Land ist*, *JEvGS* 3:166.

70. *Warnung an die Christen der Burgauischen Mark*, *JEvGS* 3:282–87. Radlkofer, *Johann Eberlin*, 513–15 found some confirmation of Eberlin's clalims. For a good summary of this period of Eberlin's life, see Peters, *Johann Eberlin von Günzburg*, 279–91.

for one in the service of Duke George of Wertheim. In the support of his appeal for this position he wrote the last of his published works, *A Warning to the Christians of the Margraviate of Burgau.* Ostensibly a warning to Eberlin's friends and relatives not to heed those attempting to foment renewed rebellion, this pamphlet seeks to disassociate the Gospel from the events of the preceding year and to justify Eberlin's activities during the Peasants' War.[71]

Eberlin spent the next four years in the service of the Duke of Wertheim, first in the small parish of Remlingen and later in Wertheim itself. In the latter post he rose to prominence, being named superintendent and apparently becoming a close advisor of the Duke on religious matters. Unpublished writings from this period of his life indicate a strong interest in practical matters of reform and the establishment of a humanist educational program. However, Eberlin's position and influence came to an abrupt end with the death of Duke George on 17 April 1530. Further activity in Wertheim was impossible as a result of political pressures on the father of the deceased duke, Duke Michael, and Eberlin moved to a new position in the parish of Leutershausen. However, conflicts from his earlier activities followed him there and the last three years of his life were filled with strife. Throughout all this Eberlin's health continued to deteriorate, and he died in early autumn 1533.[72]

By any account, Eberlin's was an important voice in the early years of the Reformation. As such, it provides us with valuable information about the Reformation's message as it passed through the medium of popular pamphlets. One of the most striking features of Eberlin's writings is the fact that only gradually do many of the central themes of the new Wittenberg theology emerge in them. Only after he moved to Wittenberg and immersed himself in the theology of the movement there did he really begin to speak as we would expect a Protestant Reformer to speak. Luther and those associated with him do appear in Eberlin's earlier utterances, but there serve as beacons for the reform-minded in the German-speaking lands, associated more with addressing abuses in the church and society than with the finer

71. *Warnung an die Christen der Burgauischen Mark*, *JEvGS* 3:253–87.

72. A wealth of material has been published in German on Eberlin's last years, which is well summarized in Peters, *Johann Eberlin von Günzburg*, 292–314. Eberlin's unpublished writings from this period include the first German translation of Tacitus' *Germania*, supplemented with statements of other classical authors about the ancient Germans, and a treatise on the education of a prince. See Masser, *Ein zamengelesen bouchlin* and Baldini, *L'Educazione di un Principe Luterano*.

points of Reformation theology. Luther takes his place alongside Erasmus, Ulrich von Hutten and a host of other reformers, primarily from the ranks of the Renaissance humanists.

The subtitle of Christian Peters' biography identifies Eberlin as a Franciscan reformer, humanist, and conservative Reformer. *The Fifteen Confederates* occupy a crucial position in this evolution, chronicling his movement through the first two phases and his entry into the third. In the process, they give us a clear indication of how broadly reform could be conceived at the beginning of the sixteenth century. This is most obvious in the Wellfarian statutes of the tenth and eleventh *Confederates*, the first vernacular utopia of the age. Eberlin's later writings indicate that his growing connections to the Wittenberg Reformation led him to abandon or qualify some of his earlier enthusiasm and elements of his reforming agenda. However, they also indicate that his concern for social reform never disappeared entirely, even if *The Fifteen Confederates* were now to be read with caution.

Ein kläglichē klag an dē christlichē Römischen Kayser Carolum/ vō wegē Doctor Luthers vnd Vlrich von Hutten. Auch von wegen der Curtisanē vnd bättel münch. Das Kayserlich Maiestat sich nit laß söllich leüt verfüren.

Der erst bůdtsgnosz

Figure 1. *Der erst bundtsgnosz.* Bayerische Staatsbibliothek. München [Res/4 H.ref. 271 y]

1

The First Confederate

A pitiful complaint to the Christian Emperor Charles concerning Doctor Martin Luther and Ulrich von Hutten. Also concerning the courtiers and mendicant friars. That His Majesty not allow himself to be led astray by such people.

I, THE FIRST CONFEDERATE, was charged by my fourteen companions to bring honor to our confederacy, so I thought it useful to direct my words to the faithful, noble, Christian heart of our most gracious Emperor Charles, in the hope that if his majesty were well informed as our sovereign, all his other subjects would have prosperity and security. Do not be angry with me, Oh worthy Emperor, that I come so rashly into your benevolent presence, for I have been driven to this by our great need and by our great hope in you. There is such pressing need to report our common suffering that even the sun and moon and stars take pity on us, and we know of no one on earth we can appeal to aside from you, our sovereign, our long wished for and most welcome emperor. In you rest all our trust, our hope and refuge; let them be realized, Oh beloved Prince. Behold how mercifully our God has dealt with you. He wants you to be a blessed creation in body and soul, in honor and goods, whose equal has not been seen in a thousand years, and to whom so many lands and peoples, both here and beyond the seas, are subject without bloodshed or opposition. But in particular the German lands, at the very heart of Christendom, are willingly obedient to you, so that under you may be established through wise and prudent judgments a reign pleasing to God. Your predecessors among the German emperors have strived for this earnestly and often, but by God's special decree it has been reserved for you. Oh Christian Lord, would that you bear this in mind and take God's sword in your hand, protect and govern the noble and dearly ransomed Christian people, especially those of the German nation. This nation God has singled out so that from it more than any other you may establish a wholesome reign according to Christian principles. A Christian character consists in maintaining a devout heart to God and upright conduct with one's neighbors. Where such a Christian character is planted among the people, there the wise administration of your imperial majesty will be effective. And although this Christian character should fill the whole world, nonetheless it pleases God that it arise again first in the German lands, where, unfortunately, it has lain hidden for many years (as it has in all of Christendom). But now it pleases God that the entire world will again have a source of Christian character in the German nation, as previously occurred in Judea. And not without special provision from God has Germany always been obedient to a Roman emperor, so that with God's cooperation he would want to do great things on the basis of this obedience, as appears possible in these days. For many years now a seed of all good things has germinated unobserved in the German nation: a shrewd sense, clever inventions, consummate skill in all crafts, knowledge of all writings and useful languages, a new useful art of printing, a desire for Gospel teaching, and delight in all truth and honesty. All of these things had been concealed in our land by misfortune, but with heavenly help they are now emerging. Therefore, the German nation is wonderfully and suitably prepared, and as a passionate, robust, and obedient people, would be worthy of this task. And because you are the Christian emperor you are, this should move you to particular care and love for the German nation, and to promote, increase, and protect the above-mentioned divine seeds scattered by God in German hearts. Through this your empire, glory, and security will be increased and eternally secured. Know also, Oh mighty Emperor, that Johann Reuchlin,[1] famed throughout the world, is the source of all things useful in the German land. It was he who began to uncover the source of Christian character sown in human understanding and life, and therefore he is worthy of eternal glory. Thereafter, came Erasmus of Rotterdam, who, with angelic ingenuity and kindness, nurtured continually

1. Johann Reuchlin (1455–1522), humanist and noted Hebrew philologist. See *ER* 5:325–27; *CE* 3:145–50.

the godly gifts in us for our great benefit. And clearly the printing press has used these developments to good effect, as Your Esteemed Wisdom already knows. The above-mentioned two men have laid the first stones for everything beneficial, to which many others have also contributed, such as Jakob Wimpfeling,[2] Doctor Johann von Kaisersberg[3] in Alsace, Doctor Ulrich Kraft[4] from Ulm, Johann Oecolampadius[5] in Swabia and all of their supporters. Also very helpful in this matter has been the faithful and beneficial instruction of many excellent schoolmasters in many places, such as Crato[6] and Sapidus[7] in Schlettstadt, Michael Hilspach[8] in Hagenau, Simler[9] and Gerbelius[10] in Pforzheim, Brassicanus[11] and Heinrichmann[12] in Tübingen, Ägidius Krautwasser[13] in Stuttgart and Horb, Johann Schmidlin[14] in

2. Jakob Wimpfeling (1450–1528), Alsatian humanist, regarded as the father of German patriotic historical writing. See *ER* 6:311–12; *CE* 3:447–50.

3. Johann Geiler von Kaisersberg (1455–1510), renowned popular preacher and reforming theologian in Strasbourg.

4. Ulrich Kraft (ca. 1460–1516), humanist and member of an Ulm patrician family. He taught philosophy and law at the universities of Freiburg, Tübingen, and Basel. From 1500 to 1516, he was a priest in the Ulm cathedral.

5. Johann Oecolampadius (1482–1531), from 1522 Reformer of Basel. See *ER* 4:337–38; *OER* 3:169–71; *CE* 3:24–27.

6. Crato von Uttenheim (+ 1501), from 1490 until his death teacher in Schlettstadt in Alsace.

7. Johann Sapidus (1490–1561), rector of the Latin school in Schlettstadt. See *CE* 3:195–96.

8. Michael Hilspach (+ after 1546), rector of the Latin school in Hagenau and later in Pforzheim.

9. Apparently Georg Simler from Wimpfen (+1535/1536), rector of the Latin school in Pforzheim. See *CE* 3:253.

10. Nikolaus Gerbelius or Gerbel (c. 1485–1560), worked as the corrector of Reuchlin's works at a press in Pforzheim. In 1515 he moved to Strasbourg where he later became a committed partisan of Luther. See *CE* 2:90–91.

11. Johann Brassicanus (+ 1539), humanist and teacher at the Latin school in Urach (Switzerland) and later in Tübingen. In Tübingen his students included Phillip Melanchthon. See *CE* 1:191–92.

12. Jakob Heinrichmann or Henrichmann of Sindelfingen in Swabia (c. 1482–1561), humanist and student, then teacher, in Tübingen until 1506. From 1514 he was councilor to the bishop of Augsburg, canon at the cathedral in Augsburg (until 1521), and parish priest at Zusmarshausen west of Augsburg. See *CE* 2:177.

13. Ägidius Krautwasser, teacher of Latin in Stuttgart and later in Horb.

14. Johann Fabricius (Schmidlin), teacher in Esslingen and Ulm.

Memmingen, Cochlaeus[15] in Nuremberg, Nesen[16] in Frankfurt, etc. Now God the Lord, through the diligence and efforts of these men and others like them, and also through the earnest pleading to God of many devout people, has already prepared the minds and souls, and also the customs and hearts of Germans to desire a true Christian character. And since the time has arrived for your peaceful, God-pleasing reign to begin in Germany, God sent two specially chosen, daring, and enlightened messengers to prepare the way for your reign and to guide and direct you in your progress. Through their effort and exertion all that would lead you astray in your office will be brushed out of the way.

These two messengers are Martin Luther and Ulrich von Hutten; both are German born, learned, Christian men who have dedicated their days to promoting God's honor, as has been evident from the start. For, what does Martin Luther seek other than a pure,[17] unadulterated proclamation of gospel teaching in the schools and from the pulpits, where, for many hundreds of years by God's special decree, one has taught the world for God, Antichrist for Christ, Barrabas for Jesus, heresy for truth. All of Martin's efforts are directed toward bringing back to the light of day evangelical, Christian teaching. And God is with him, for many learned, brave men in all places, not only in Germany but in all of Europe, leap to his side and many pious Christians, women and men, priests and lay-people, monks and nuns, support him in their hearts, even if they are unable to voice their support openly.

Ulrich von Hutten wields the pen and the sword to awaken ancient German integrity through loyalty, faith and truth in the German nation, which has always been self-sufficient in all the necessities for physical life, in money, in the fruits of the earth, in useful customs and laws. Now, however, its integrity and resources have been wasted by useless people, as you will hear. We now know that unadulterated evangelical preaching, and also loyalty and faith along with the required physical necessities, are all needed for a wholesome reign in your German land. In this God will help you and your subjects through Martin Luther and Hutten. However, as much as God favors you, so much does the devil oppose you, and he will not rest

15. Johann Cochlaeus (1479–1552), humanist and rector of the St. Lawrence School in Nuremberg from 1510–1515. He later became a bitter opponent of Luther. See *OER* 1:369–71; *CE* 1:321–22.

16. Wilhelm Nesen (1493–1524), member of the Basel humanist circle and student of Erasmus. See *CE* 3:12–14.

17. "*luthere*" (*lauter*). Eberlin is likely making a pun on Luther's name with this term, as did many of his contemporaries.

until he is able to lead astray your upright heart. And would God that in your youth you never would have been ruled over by Dertusiensis,[18] from whom you were unable to learn much of Christian freedom or of other things that are necessary or may be useful for such a great prince. I fear that the evil enemy has prepared this, and God permitted it to happen to you, so that from it the whole world may know how noble your nature is, that even in your youth you could not be led into shameful humility. After that, through the devil's mischief, your upright conscience was entrusted to a barefooted friar from the ranks of the superstitious Observants[19] as your spiritual counselor. Many devout Christians lament this, and day and night they plead with God that He will stand by their upright emperor, and help him to take up his godly glory, and save him from the Grey Hypocrite.[20] For, where you are not cautious, God help you and us. And God will hear the devout prayer offered up for you, and give you help that you may escape the traps laid for you. Therefore, we (in our hope) have been moved by God to lay our complaints before you. Consider in your lofty understanding to whom it is that you entrust your secrets: he is a bare-footed friar from the arrogantly named Observants. Among them there has always been little knowledge and little wisdom, they appear better than they are, their great numbers are completely unknown, and if one in a thousand among them is intelligent or learned, he sits among the rest like Daniel among the lions. Furthermore, they have never considered your confessor Glapion[21]

18. Cardinal Dertusiensis, later Pope Adrian VI (1522–1523), was appointed Charles' tutor by the Emperor Maximilian. See *ER* 1:12–13; *OER* 1:8; *CE* 1:5–9.

19. The Franciscan Observants, members of the order intent on a more strict observance of the rule of St. Francis than were their opponents, the Conventuals. In 1415 at the Council of Constance the Observants of the French province were granted their own provincials and in 1443 Pope Eugenius IV gave the Observants their own provincial general. In 1517 they were formally separated from the Conventuals and declared the true Order of St. Francis. See *ODCC*, 634–36. In pamphlets of the Reformation era Franciscans were often referred to as "Barfusser," "barefooted" friars. This identification may derive from mid thirteenth-century polemics against the friars, in particular William of St. Amour's identification of the friars' practice of going barefoot with the Pharisees broad phylacteries and the enlarged borders on their garments mentioned in Matthew 23:5. See Dipple, *Antifraternalism and Anticlericalism*, 160; Szittya, "Middle English Literature," 298–99; idem, *Medieval Literature*, 39.

20. The Franciscans were also referred to as the Grey Friars on the basis of the color of their habits.

21. Johann Glapion (mid-fifteenth century to 1522), a Franciscan and father confessor of Charles V. See *CE* 2:103–5.

particularly learned or spiritual, and they themselves are surprised that you burden yourself with this person.

Oh devout Emperor, send the mendicant friars away from you, especially the bare-footed Observants, for your innocent conscience is too trusting of their deception. Inquire throughout the German nation, among all princes and lords, both spiritual and secular, all estates and cities which have anything to do with them; none are able to escape the bare-footed friars no matter how much they want to. Your predecessor, the blessed Maximilian,[22] also sometimes confessed to them, but he didn't decide anything to do with the affairs of the empire in consultation with his father confessor, neither before nor after confession. And during confession he did not want the monk to bring into the discussion anything dealing with his pleasure concerning the empire. He said to his father confessor: "Sir, concerning my affairs I have taken counsel with wise people, do not question me about them. What I confess, absolve in God's name." As soon as he was finished confessing he sent the monk away. When he wanted to confess, the monks did not send him a learned man, both because they do not permit such honors to the learned among them and because they were well aware that Emperor Maximilian would not ask for special counsel. In such matters follow his example, devout, beloved Prince, and you will have good fortune, security, and great favor from the German land. We often think that it was through the devil's cunning that you came to be taught by Dertusiensis and Glapion, so that your empire would never be purged of false teaching and dishonest activities. The courtiers and mendicant friars have hindered the common good, and the devil's cunning has almost succeeded in deceiving you into believing that Luther and Hutten are worthy of disdain, but God's grace did not allow you to be blinded. Know, Oh Christian Emperor, that courtiers and mendicant friars are a particular poison for true Christianity in the German land. They oppose the blessed Luther and the Christian, noble lord von Hutten, and also all those who counsel beneficial things for your Christian people. Christian, evangelical teaching is a beginning of all things helpful. Luther strives the hardest for its advancement; the mendicant friars, especially the bare-footed Observants, who rely on their false renown and claim often to counsel the simple people, oppose it the most. Ulrich von Hutten has taken it upon himself to advance the cause of German honor, freedom, and self-reliance as much as possible, but the courtiers stand in his way. Therefore, everything evil directed against

22. Emperor Maximillian I (1459–1519). See *CE* 2:410–14.

you or your empire comes from the papist folks, because the mendicant friars and the courtiers are the sworn servants of the Roman pope.

Take note, devout Lord, the two breeds mentioned above want to deceive you so that you would regard even your best friends as sworn enemies. Who is a greater friend to you and your empire than Luther or Hutten, who seek only the well-being, honor, fortune and happiness of you and all your subjects? They are willing to place at your service themselves and all their supporters, their bodies and honor, their goods and lives; for this reason they have often placed themselves in mortal danger, and still they do not give up, even in the face of your apparent displeasure. For they love you and the truth so much that even if you never thanked them, they would wish, nonetheless, to do you good. But the mendicant friars and courtiers seek to harm and corrupt you and your empire and to promote their own interests. If any of them were to suffer one-thousandth for your sake what Hutten and Luther have endured, they would leave you to fend for yourself and give you the finger.[23] Indeed, they advise you to spurn your own friends so that there will be no one to warn you against their evil ruses. Not without reason do the mendicant friars fight against Hutten. The bare-footed Observants alone take out of your Upper and Lower Germany in one year 200,000 florins in cash and valuables. Although they refuse to touch money when anyone is looking, they have managers who handle their transactions more precisely than any prince does. In fact, it has been calculated that annually the four mendicant orders collect more than 1,000,000 florins in the German nation. This they suck out of the poor and rich, the lords and servants. Then, what should I say about the papal see which annually relieves the German nation of 300,000 florins? And what is drawn from the German nation to Rome as a result of the mischievous legal trade is impossible to calculate. Still less can one reckon what is stolen and pillaged by the courtiers from the cloisters, hospitals, parishes, and benefices of the German nation. In addition, the people must pay legitimate annual taxes to you and other lords, they must feed themselves, and also support so many monks and priests, not only those in the monasteries, but also those with benefices outside them, not to mention the mendicant friars. How, then, can the German nation flourish when so many harmful animals in it devour all the good pasture? All that would be tolerable if they jeopardized only our goods. But they have also tried to do harm to our bodies and freedoms, and

23. *"zaygen dir die fygten,"* an obscene gesture involving sticking the thumb between the first two fingers, indicating contempt and scorn. See *JEvGS* 1:209.

so they are happy to see that we are unable to endure our secular lords on account of the taxes they levy. And they insist that what we give to them is a gift to God and may not be reduced, but the taxes of the princes might be held back. Now, if we are unable to support both the pope and the princes, they say that we should first forsake the princes. That we don't want to do, so they are accustomed to making themselves arbitrators and intermediaries so that they can gorge themselves on our strife. For this reason so often the Roman pope sends emissaries into all lands to sow discord among the princes and lords. And what is more serious, the courtiers and mendicant friars bring from foreign lands, especially from Rome and Italy, all falsehood, fraud, unfaithfulness, and deception, through which trust and faith are destroyed, and hardly one brother dares to trust another. Contrary to the ancient integrity of the German nation and by such mischief the monks absolve everyone on the basis of the freedoms of their orders and the courtiers on the basis of their indulgence letters and the grace of Rome. And to promote injustice, and also so that God's anger will come upon us and remain on us, they falsify the Gospel teaching from the pulpit. They encourage us in our envy and hatred, and they say that one may certainly hate the sin, but not the sinner. One may certainly avoid and shun someone and still not be his enemy. One may certainly take interest on a loan to a friend. One may certainly employ cunning if it's not harmful cunning. One may certainly have the pope dispense him from a written oath. One may certainly wage deadly warfare in defense of his own interests when he appears to have credible justification. Masses said by even evil priests redeem souls. We may, through our own abilities and without grace, guard against sin, and we can acquire grace for ourselves. It is better to give money for Roman indulgences than give it to other poor people in obvious need. Everyone may and should seek his own interest. Within limits one may avenge wrongs done to him. A government is no more required to do everything it can for its Christian subjects than the Turk is for his subjects. This and similar Aristotelian, heathen teaching they instill in us from our youth onward so that we never recognize the gospel truth. To ensure that God is our enemy they produce all such antichristian teachings. And since Dr. Luther wishes to root out all such things for the good of us all, the courtiers, the mendicant friars, and even the whole Roman curia oppose him and wish to besmirch your good reputation. To pervert your Christian judgment, to turn from you devout German goodwill, they try to draw you, Oh blameless Emperor, into their antichristian sect. But, Oh Emperor, we trust in your righteousness, and we hope that you are so devout that on the basis of good intelligence you would never have judged Luther and Hutten as erroneous and dangerous. Therefore, we do not abide by any decrees dealing with such matters promulgated under the name of Your Imperial Majesty. We assume that either you do not know of them or else that you are not correctly informed about the matter. Therefore, we appeal to you to allow us to advise and inform you about the evil reports and the deceptions of Romanists around you. In the meantime, we will read what Hutten and Luther have written or will write in the hope that the Romanists' deceit will soon come to light, so that you would outlaw and ban the mendicant friars and courtiers. We do not doubt that God will soon bring this about, for God so loves you that he will not long leave you in error. Now that the true light has been made clear to you by Luther and Hutten, would that you soon throw off the errors of the Romanists and those who preach them. However, as I said at the beginning, Oh devout Prince, it is evident our distress is so great that we can no longer hold ourselves back from pitiful complaints. As you can see, our minds have been opened by God's grace so that we recognize from the old histories how fortunate our land once was and how terrible our situation is now. We are vexed by the great deception and superstition among us, which we cannot escape because they are sustained by Roman statute and canon law. As a result, no one can be secure in his affairs; there are always little loopholes through which one can find a way to squeeze the poor. For this reason the barristers and lawyers go to school so they can support themselves from this activity. Our ancestors had few laws but great faith, and it was not fitting for anyone to take his legal affairs out of our land. But now, if I have dealings with the mendicant friars, my opponent drags me from one conservator[24] to the next in both Upper and Lower Germany, and finally to Rome where he wins praise and glory. With the priests it is the same. And from this we lay people learn about pretext and objection, and to answer deceit with deceit. Everything is expensive among us, the money is debased, and no gold can be found anymore. Rome swallows up everything gold and silver, and the lazy mendicant friars and courtiers make even the water expensive. It is said that our learning leads us to the pulpit with a fool's bridle. If God took from us the error of our darkness, and we wanted to learn and hear the Christian truth which nourishes our

24. A bishop named by papal privilege for each province of the mendicant orders to act as judge in cases in which the legal rights of the friars were infringed upon in secular matters.

souls, there would be no one who could tell it to us. For the mendicant friars do not want to be the ones to show us where we have gone astray; they would much rather let us remain longer in our error. To this end they have directed all their abilities and wish to frighten us with papal bans promulgated against the truth, with imperial mandates commanded without your well-informed judgment, with ancient customs of our mistaken ancestors, with the illustrious appearance of their orders, with the numbers of their followers. And the more they strive to keep the Christian law from appearing purely among us, the less can we be at peace because of the godly compulsion within us. So we have been cheated out of goods, lives, honor, and even our souls. And we have given up on expecting any help from the pope, or from many of the bishops, who are worm-eaten by their greed and wish to have three or four bishoprics with papal dispensation, that is, by leave of the antichristian law. They want to take on the offices of abbot, prior, or provost of a monastery *in commendam*[25] despite the fact that they are not monks and have no desire to become monks. And so they don't want to attend to their bishoprics, but instead attach themselves to the king or great princes, which they are unable to do without papal dispensation. Although there are also many bishops who would gladly give aid to the gospel truth, they are overwhelmed by fear of the pope. To whom, then, should we pour out our troubles, besides you, our devout emperor and lord, from whom we expect all good. Although, we are alarmed by your father confessor, who boasts far and wide that you regard him not only as your confessor, but as your mentor in all matters. But we hope that you would be of sounder judgment than to allow an insolent cheese hunter[26] to rule you and your empire. Nonetheless, there is now a great number of simple folk who are frightened and saddened by this and therefore have said: "Woe unto us, woe unto us, must we longer be subjected to the degrading tyranny of the monks? We hoped that the noble blood of Charles would have saved us from this. God have pity that an unlearned, ambitious, miserable monk should rule the entire Roman Empire, how will we ever be saved?" We fifteen confederates have heard such restless complaints among princes, nobles, burghers, and peasants and have undertaken with all our abilities to wipe out such an evil misperception of you among the people so that the German nation does

25. "*Commend*," the administration of a vacant ecclesiastical office until the position is refilled. In the sixteenth century this system was abused to allow one ecclesiastic to enjoy the benefices from several offices. See *ODCC*, 383.

26. "*käßiäger*," a common term of abuse for members of the mendicant orders at this time, likely because they would beg for cheese. See *JEvGS* 1:209.

not become displeased with you. We have said to them that you will turn to neither papal legates nor mendicant friars. And if you have already released decrees against Luther and his followers, as has been alleged, that is because you were not completely informed of matters or you will soon change these; that you would rather turn to Christ, who speaks through Luther and Hutten, than to the entire world; that you would send away the Grey Monk and take Erasmus of Rotterdam, or Luther or Karlstadt[27] or someone similar as your confessor and spiritual counselor. You would take as your closest advisors especially the secular Electors and your upright cousins, the Bavarian lords,[28] and the noble Franz von Sickingen, Ulrich von Hutten, Duke Frederick Count Palatine,[29] and others like them. You would outlaw and banish all courtiers and mendicant friars. You would allow no bishop to be an Elector. You would allow absolutely no cardinals in Germany. You would command that the wholesome teaching of the three languages[30] and other honest arts be advanced in schools, that only the gospel truth be preached from the pulpit, and that whoever wishes to oppose these things should be punished. You would decree that from now on no more palliums[31] be purchased from Rome, that no more annates[32] be paid, that no more indulgences be allowed to come into our land, that no mendicant friar be allowed to collect alms—instead they should support themselves by suitable and worthy work. That from now on no one be allowed to enter a mendicant order; instead the orders should be allowed to die out. That from now on no one should be excommunicated on account of debt. That no priest may hold more than one benefice. That each priest must inhabit his own living. That all parish priests and bishops fulfill the duties of their own offices themselves through preaching and other services. That from now on no

27. Andreas Bodenstein von Karlstadt (1480–1541), at this time Luther's reforming colleague in Wittenberg. See *OER* 1:178–80; *CE* 2:253–56.

28. Dukes Ludwig and Wilhelm of Bavaria had not yet declared themselves openly against the Reformation at this time. See *JEvGS* 1:209.

29. Count Palatine Frederick, later Elector Frederick II. See *JEvGS* 1:209.

30. The three "biblical" languages: Latin, Greek, and Hebrew.

31. A circular band of woolen material worn as part of the vestments of the pope and metropolitans. In the ninth century John VIII commanded all metropolitans to petition the pope for the pallium within three months of their election or confirmation. Thereafter it became a symbol of the jurisdiction conferred on the metropolitans by the pope. See *NCE* 10:807–8.

32. The first year's revenue from an ecclesiastical benefice paid to Rome. See *ODCC*, 71.

monk or nun be allowed to take the three vows before the age of thirty. That all monks and nuns be allowed to leave the monastery if they discover that the monastic life poses a danger to their souls. That from now on no courtier may seize a benefice. That under no circumstances may one seek justice or a dispensation from Rome, but instead all spiritual matters should be brought before the local bishop. That a set amount be established for the goods one may take into a monastery, and no more be permitted. How many priests there should be in each city, and no more. That from now on no anniversary masses or benefices be endowed without specific permission of the emperor. That all monks and nuns in all orders be subject to their local bishops. That all priests be allowed to have wives so that so much shame and sin will be avoided. That no legal proceedings, including those involving secular law, should be drawn out for more than a year, because this causes so much hardship for the poor. That from now on Your Imperial Majesty will employ nobles in imperial offices and in your councils and not allow so many Johns and Conrads and Henrys and similar vagabonds and clerks and usurers to manage the great affairs of the Roman Empire any longer. For this reason the nobility now have their children study and be instructed in knowledge and morals. That from now on soulless, callous soldiers who take money and contract with the devil will be abolished. Instead, each land will help its lords, and the nobles, whose role it is, to wage war. That Fuggerei[33] will be destroyed. That drunkenness, a source of all vices, will be seriously punished. That scandalous clothing for both men and women will be abolished. That public blasphemy, notorious adultery, and drunkenness be regarded as sufficiently serious crimes that on account of them all one's honor will be lost. That from now on rent charges will not be sold on landed property, and that one may pay off all interest on goods in a reasonable amount of time.[34] That no war shall be waged without the permission of Your Imperial Majesty and the Imperial Electors.

33. "*Fuggerei*," usury. Eberlin here adopts the common early sixteenth-century identification of the prominent Augsburg banking family, the Fuggers, as the embodiment of usury. See Laube, *Flugschriften* 2:716.

34. The rent charge was an archaic financial instrument which permitted property holders, either owners of the property or holders of a heritable tenancy, to raise sums of money and provided purchasers with steady incomes. A property holder would sell a rent charge to a person or institution for a sum of money, thereby encumbering the property with the obligation to pay rents for a set time period or in perpetuity. Rent charges were regarded as real property and could be taxed, sold, or bequeathed by the holder. They appear to have been popular among ecclesiastical institutions because they provided regular income without the bother of maintaining and managing real property.

These and similar matters we have brought before the German nation with our mouths and pens, both openly and privately, so that you will direct all your efforts to address them before all other matters. Afterward God will give you victory and security before all your foes. Then the stout Germans will arise, pledging themselves and their possessions to march with you against Rome and make all of Italy subject to you. You no longer need to enlist the support of either pope or cardinal. From now on they will have to be confirmed by you and your successors, but all of your authority will come to you through the strength of your election by the Imperial Electors. In this way you will become a mighty king on the earth; if from now on you do God's work, then God will do your work. Therefore, we fifteen confederates beseech Your Imperial Majesty in the name of the German nation that you arouse your virile, noble heart and support our proposals before the common people; thus will you keep the love of the people. Prefer your willing German nation to the bare-footed Observants who will not remain faithful to you in the long run, as almost all princes and lords, both spiritual and secular, and lands and cities in the German nation can attest. If someone bestows great benefits on them and, as is sometimes necessary, requests a prayer from them, they forget about everything else and drop from their prayers other important matters, with great vexation for both rulers and ruled. This happens often with them and, as a result, the hearts of nearly all princes and cities have turned against them. Also, sometimes they plot against bishops and parish priests, cities and lords with their arrogant bulls and their intemperate preaching before the simple people. With this I conclude my and my comrades' heart-felt complaint to you. Act as a faithful father, as a merciful lord, as a courageous emperor, and give thanks to God and the German nation and come to our aid. God keep you and us prosperous for a long time. Amen.

See Buck, "Perpetual Rents," 23–33.

Der ander bundtsgnosz.

Vom fasten der .xl. tag
vor Osteren vnd andern/ wie do mit so
jämerlich wirt beschwärt das
Christenlich volck.

Figure 2. *Der ander bundtsgnosz*. Bayerische Staatsbibliothek München [Res/4 H.ref. 271 y#Beibd.1]

2

The Second Confederate

Concerning the forty-day fast before Easter and others, and how wretchedly the Christian people are burdened by them.

We fifteen have sworn together that we would reveal to common Christians what shameful, unbearable burdens have been laid on them, and that each of us should bring to the light of day his own advice and concerns, along with suggested solutions and their consequences. And so each, before he began his deliberations, in the presence of the holy crucifix asked God, as it pleased Him, for inspiration and help in this undertaking. And having done this, I, the second confederate, resolved to write about the forty-day fast, about which many people complain. And may God help me that I write the truth. Everyone knows that all Christians who wish to live in obedience to the Roman bishop are compelled from the pulpit and the confessional to fast each year from Ash Wednesday to Easter. And this every day without exemption or exception, unless one has permission from his father confessor, whom he invited to his house for Shrovetide, whose gullet he filled, and to whom he promised a good, fat chicken. Now I ask, dear friends, that you consider my advice carefully and thoughtfully and then draw the conclusions that seem fitting to you.

Is it not a blind people which believes the full, bulging preachers who say to you that the Christian church has commanded on pain of mortal sin that one must fast so many days without interruption? What is even more disgraceful, they record with mathematical calculation who is, and who isn't excused from it. And they always leave a prick of scruples in the conscience, as perhaps when one believes too much in one's own weakness, so that Christian hearts are always troubled. And through this the father carousers and fairy-tale preachers[1] are always able to ply their trade with the people, judging their consciences with rabbinic[2] authority and terrifying them. Albeit they can't prove that this fast has been commanded for the whole of Christendom, and even if such a commandment were found, there is no solid proof that it should apply to all on the pain of mortal sin. And so it should not be regarded as such. In the harsh law of Moses there is much written about fasting, but in no place will you find that someone who breaks the fast has committed a mortal sin. How is it, then, that some mountebank can be so bold and claim, without justification, that in the new law it is commanded in this way? For under the new law we are released from such heavy burdens, as the teachings of Paul prove. See what heavy work there is for all people in the German land. It is said that a cardinal once saw this and showed the pope how hard-working the German nation is and suggested that a strict fast not be laid upon them. Nonetheless, this fast has not been taken from them; rather, it remains still as a reward for excessive labor. In the whole year there is no busier time for field work than during the fast. In addition, in many places in Germany there is little food, and in only a few places wine. In many places, even with hard work, one has to be satisfied with a few peas, beans, and hard pears known as *Hutzlen*.[3] In no place do olive trees grow to provide oil. Who could say that the mild, merciful mother of Christendom would lay such a heavy yoke on hard-working lay people, whose consciences are set in an uproar when sometimes they need to break this tyrannical command to meet their basic needs? The full monks, who every day at a set time have a well prepared meal on the basis of their leisurely work, performed in the shade without sweat or serious effort, claim that they do something special with their fast and want to impose the same command on the lay people. Such a command they would not keep even if they were given twice as much to eat with half the work as they burden the lay people in their hardship. Furthermore, if

1. *Buchvätter und marlin prediger*. *Buchvätter* (*Bauchvätter*), literally "stomach father," is a parody of *Beichtvater*, "father confessor."

2. *Parnosisch*. On the possible meanings and origins of this term, see *JEvGS* 3:376–77.

3. Dried pears. See *FnhDG*, 127.

someone wants to eat moderately during the fast, it is clear that this will involve greater expense, and as much if not more desire will be aroused by it, than in three months outside the time of the fast. Who says that the Christian church prescribed that for so many days each year the costs and charges laid on food and drink should double as a form of penance, or else that one should eat so poorly. And it would come as no surprise that if one held this command up to a heathen land, even if otherwise inclined to the faith, it would renounce all Christian practices before submitting to this yoke. The majority of people are not bound to observe this fast; they may eat and drink as often during the day as necessity demands. And necessity shouldn't be defined in terms of extremes, but rather as enough to satisfy one's hunger and thirst while at work without danger to one's health. However, my wish to bind the rich loafers strictly to this commandment to fast is in vain since they pay no attention to what I say. Among a hundred of them barely three can be found who would want to be bound by such a strict commandment. How can one make a general rule on account of the smallest minority?

I don't believe that such a commandment was given by the church, and even if it were, it is neither valid nor binding. Similarly, it is not the custom among lawmakers that onerous, dangerous commands or prohibitions be imposed on the people for the sake of the smallest minority without special provision for exceptions. For this reason, my companions and I do not commend preaching that all persons without explicit dispensation are bound by mortal sin to fast during this time. One should excuse them on a reasonable basis. But then it would become apparent that hardly one or two would be bound by it. And so they have to preach that whoever has none of their numerous dispensations is bound by mortal sin to fast, but how foolishly this pronouncement is observed is readily apparent. And soon some mad fellow rushes forward and wants to provide evidence for the forty-day fast from the ancient teachings, as if we hadn't read them. I don't deny that in former times in rich lands people were admonished, both individually and together, each year to shun common, overly festive fellowship, since there were still many remnants from heathen ceremonies. But I do contest that we are commanded to fast forty days before Easter in honor of Christ's fast and in anticipation of future feasts, just as we are to make new Christians through baptism and to give the sacrament of the altar to those already Christian. One also need not abstain from wine, meat, milk, butter, eggs and other things so necessary for daily nourishment, but rather from long drinking parties or sprees, from drunken lazing about, from excessive feasting, which consume much time and money.

But now in our lands (through God's grace) such heathen excess is unknown. If one fears he has sinned, he can do enough through natural means; it is not necessary to make such a fuss with this commandment. A senseless commandment like this only vexes consciences, scandalizes the simple, and encourages backbiting among the spiteful. And so a respectable man hardly dares to eat publicly with his neighbors during the fasting time, even if he is compelled to this not by his desire to eat, but by social ties or inner affliction and a burdened soul, which he hopes to ease through good company. If one places uneducated, inexperienced, foolish people in the pulpit and confessional, they don't know how to recognize the intent of human law, but rather (being themselves inexperienced) they measure all things by the simple literal meaning. Thus do they make others and themselves into fools or bring the scorn of sensible people on the laws and on themselves. It is no argument that Christ fasted this long and therefore we should do the same each year, for one does not read that Christ observed such a fast every year. Furthermore, he did not command that we should fast this long. Had you only read Chrysostum on Matthew 6,[4] maybe you wouldn't have spat out such nonsense so defiantly. I recognize that fasting is a commandment of Christ and the apostles, but not like the fast we observe, giving up completely so many common foods for so many days and only eating once during the day, etc. Rather, a Christian fast is nothing other than a willing, deliberate renunciation of so much and for so long as is necessary for you to castigate your flesh and to subject it to the well-intentioned spirit, as your own circumstances dictate. Such a thing cannot be commanded for all in the same way since there are great differences in natural, physical constitutions and in the extent to which the heart is armed with divine inspiration, without which this would be in vain. This great, onerous commandment has been forced upon us by the Romanists and the pope's courtiers. From this a compelling argument can be drawn: since the fast is broken in the courts of the pope and cardinals, at the tables of the bishops and abbots, with the knowledge of the prelates and without any opposition from them; in fact, since during the entire period of the fast butcher shops in Rome remain

4. John Chrysostum (c. 347–407), *ODCC*, 342–43. Presumably Eberlin is referring to Chrysostum's comments on Matthew 6:16 in "Homily XX." See Pelikan, *Preaching of Chrysostum*, 153–56.

open and meat is bought and sold just as it is during the rest of the year, it is clear that such a commandment should be imposed even less on our rugged German land. For the breach of a human law with the knowledge and tacit consent of authority voids the contract. And if some foolish little priests and monks each year exaggerate the importance of the commandment to fast, they do this more from their own misunderstanding than at the command of the prelates of the church. And as these practices grow up without sound judgment, they want to teach others according to their own schemes and ideas, and each makes a fool of another.

See how the holy popes give dispensations for money to consume milk, butter, cheese and eggs during the fast. Bishops allow marriages during the 70 days.[5] Monks, priests and nuns enjoy Shrovetide as much as possible. What isn't observed, can't be decreed, but you, Dolt, wish to lay such a strict commandment without limits on average Christians. Such a commandment is the cause of a hundred thousand mortal sins each year, as everyone devises some mischievous plan with which to lighten the anticipated limitless fasts. This they wouldn't do if the fast weren't coming. For during the entire year no such foolishness is displayed as before Shrovetide, although during the rest of the year it would be more fitting. One might claim that in February the heathens, too, practiced such tomfoolery. And perhaps, to put an end to such foolishness in a suitable, but also hypocritical,[6] Christian way, an order was established to ensure that indecent pleasures were shunned, which at the same time prohibited decent pleasures such as wedding celebrations. Nonetheless, it would appear that such commandments are no longer valid, for they are ignored and weddings openly permitted in exchange for money. Also such a commandment should be legitimately done away with as one sees from the experience of many hundreds of years that no improvement has come from it, but rather more guilt from its non-observance.

My fourteen companions and I advise that no layperson, be he young or old, rich or poor, healthy or sick, should be bound by mortal sin to observe the fast before Easter. However, we do not wish to stand in the way of anyone who observes it voluntarily, although we will not much praise this activity either. Our honest advice would be that one should boldly eat

5. In preparation for Lent the medieval church forbade marriages from *Septuagisma* (the seventieth [day]) Sunday until Easter. See *JEvGS* 1:210 and *ODCC*, 1483.

6. *Angenummer*. Eberlin is playing on the terms *angenem* (useful or suitable) and *angenumen* (hypocritical). See *FnhDG*, 9.

meat, eggs, cheese, butter, and milk—in short, all the usual foods—because at that time, since almost everyone is burdened then with greater work than at other times, small transgressions may occur. But such a breach should occur with the advice and help of the spiritual and secular prelates. And one should not be concerned if a few people abuse this, for wine and bread, even the Holy Sacrament, are abused and nonetheless they are not abolished as a result.

Human folly is so great that to put an end to particular abuses, general restrictions or prohibitions are placed even on decent, necessary things.

The preachers and father confessors should admonish the Christian people to moderate use of the necessities of life, to sincere hatred of vice out of love for virtue, and to zealous and earnest prayer to God. In this sometimes a moderate abstention from food and drink is very helpful in keeping one more alert while praying to God. I commend greatly observing the four Lords' Fasts[7] in a year, and fasting on the eves of Christmas, Easter and Pentecost, while taking part in public processions and ceremonies, and joining in common prayer to God about matters of immediate concern. But the people should not be taught that such fasting is a command of God, but rather that it rests only on the external decrees of the church. Common Christians should be taught how to fulfill God's commandment of diligent prayer with temperance and moderation of physical necessities. For God has commanded each person to turn to Him in sincere prayer to request everything necessary and to give thanks for all things good. Such prayer requires tempering the reason, and such prayer is called fasting by Christ and St. Paul. But the Jewish fast that the gluttonous monks with their bulging bellies now observe and teach others, calculated right down to the day and the number of days, of abstaining from necessary common foods, and having a full meal at midday and more than a little for the *collation*,[8] has no basis in scripture and is a mockery of the consequences of faith. Don't concern yourself that certain teachers such as Thomas[9] and others like him,

7. The Ember Days, groups of three days (Wednesday, Friday, and Saturday) of fasting and abstinence observed after the feast of St. Lucy (13 December), Ash Wednesday, Pentecost, and the Exaltation of the Cross or Holy Cross Day (14 September). They were commonly referred to as the Lords' Fasts because these days were often chosen as the deadlines for the payments of rents and taxes. See *JEvGS* 1:210 and *ODCC*, 543. Cf Eberlin's discussion of fasting in *The Tenth Confederate* below.

8. "*uff den mittag vol und zü Collatz ler.*" The *Collatio* was the light meal allowed on days of fasting in addition to the one full meal at midday. See *ODCC*, 375.

9. Thomas Aquinas (c. 1225–74). *ODCC*, 1614–17.

have held to this or other Roman or human ordinances. For they lived in the obvious darkness that God allowed to engulf Christendom for two hundred years. I believe that these same teachers, who perhaps are with God in heaven, have compassion on us that we have been led astray by their error, and they diligently plead with God that we would be enlightened. And God has heard their pleas, for in the last hundred years and more disdain for such ceremonies has continued to grow, as you read in Scotus, Ockham, Gerson, and recently in the Epicureanism of the doctors who subscribed to the advice of Gabriel Biel on fasting.[10] But God has obviously taken pity on the world in our day when the freedom of the gospel shines and human laws become less severe. But I will no longer detain you, Oh reader, that you become irritated or weary, and I, too, will hold to the prescriptions of my confederates, from some of whom you may yet hear much pleasing advice.

Conduct yourself well, the time approaches.

10. John Duns Scotus (c. 1265–1308), *ODCC*, 513–14; William of Ockham (c. 1285–1347), ibid., 1745–46; Jean le Charlier de Gerson (1363–1429), ibid., 669–70; Gabriel Biel (c. 1420––1495), ibid., 207–8. What Eberlin means by the "Epicureanism" (*epikierung*) of those who subscribe to Biel's advice on fasting is unclear. See *JEvGS* 1:211.

Ein verma
nung aller christē
das sie sich erbar-
mē vber die klosterfrawē.

Thů kein Tochter in ein
kloster / du lässest dañ
diß bůchlein vor.

F W

Der. III.
bůdtgnosz

Figure 3. *Der III. Bundtgnosz.* Bayerische Staatsbibliothek München [Res/4 H.ref. 271 y#Beibd.2]

3

The Third Confederate

An admonition to all Christians that
they take pity on cloistered women.
Don't put your daughter in a convent until you've read this book.

J W

Now it is my task, as the third confederate, to try diligently to reveal to the world a great grievance. Since my colleagues have already spoken about vigils and masses, as well as fasting,[1] I thought it would be good to write about cloistered women. And no one should turn up his nose until he reads and reflects on my proposals.

Whenever I consider the general state of persons known as cloistered women, my heart is moved entirely to pity, for who could think on their torment without great sorrow. They are taken during their high-spirited, innocent youth into a captivity, from which they will never be saved, where they are neither able nor allowed to complain of their predicament, and if they complain, no one may help them. Believe me, for the most part they are deceived into believing God has called them, either by the "good advice" of their friends or by the pleasing appearance of the convents; thus are they snared by the devil.[2]

1. I.e., in *The Seventh Confederate* and *The Second Confederate*, see Lucke, "Die Entstehung der '15 Bundesgenossen,'" 38.

2. "*so sy der butz hat beschissen*," literally, "so the masked one has shot them." See *JEvGS* 1:211.

Often parents are responsible for this because they place their child in this condition, either on account of poverty, from which they desire to save her with years of constant begging, or from devotion.

I will tell you a true story about what a cloistered woman once said to me. She said: "If I knew my parents were in hell and I could release them by praying an *Ave Maria*, I would pray instead that they remain there because they brought me into these miserable circumstances. If they were unable to find a nobleman to marry me, they could have found a peasant."

Oh foolish parents, how can you lead your child astray on account of your silly delusions? How can you cast away your own flesh and blood by surrendering your child to the roasting spit of a cloistered life? I would not take this amiss if things were as before when a poor child was put in a convent until someone came and requested a well-bred maiden for his wife (as is still the case among free women).[3] And I would not object if one placed a child in a convent and the time came that it was clear to her she wanted to pass her life in purity and peace. Rather this I would commend in all seriousness. But binding young children with such perpetual chains I challenge before all people.

You put your child in a convent to preserve her dignity, but you would bring her greater honor if you found her an honest boon companion to marry, even if he is a laborer. That your noble daughter becomes a peasant would not be regarded as such a base thing. And you don't realize that putting your daughter in a convent gives everyone reason to judge your poverty.

Oh mother with a heart of stone, how faithless you are to your child. Do you think she is made of wood or iron, that she will not necessarily feel the burning desires of the flesh, just as you felt them, and they will be so much more difficult for her the more the passions of inexperienced desire tempt her womanly soul.

You don't want to place your child in a poor marriage in which she might weather with decency and peace of mind the desires and aversions, the peace and agitation, of the flesh. And you must expect the day when her passions burst forth, and in disgrace and sin she succumbs to a lowly stable-hand or cow-hand; indeed, when she stays with him and there follows, no less shocking, the sin unnamed even among evil spirits, as unfortunately is now obvious in many places. And if she retains her normal appearance, one fears that conception has been prevented or its consequences destroyed, or

3. Presumably Eberlin is referring here to the inhabitants of the convent in Andlau mentioned below, see 49n11.

the new-born child murdered, or that the child is intentionally given to the wrong father, which leads to endless gnawing at the conscience.

Ah, how often and how long do these ideas torment a maiden's heart when for so many years, so many hours and days, so many moments she is drawn to the joys of the world, to dancing, singing, idle talk or even greater things that catch her fancy. For even if your child is hidden away in hardened stone, nature is not idle. And the more foolish she is by nature, the more she will follow her own will, as one also sees among cattle.

You should also be aware that the more bow-legged and deformed she is, the more she wants to be loved.

She will be imprisoned, unheeded, without comfort, not for a day or year, but without any hope for her entire life. Oh, hard mother, how can you have this on your conscience? It would be easier for your child to be martyred like St. Agatha than to suffer such a long ordeal. You say: "Aha, God gives grace to those who call on Him." But, I answer: "Purity and martyrdom are not given to all who desire them, but only to those it pleases God to give them—this the Gospel teaches us." You say: "One comforts the other." But I answer that usually one plays the devil to the other so that they make the convent and order too crowded, and sometimes a kind hearted person complains more of mistreatment by her fellows than of all other tribulations. Oh, the great torment of a neglected, cloistered young person who ponders how she might escape to free air, whether she would enter a common house, whether she would flee to a foreign land and not return, whether she would give herself as a spouse to the devil; thus she plays with images and thoughts, thus she becomes weak in the flesh, while asleep or awake, and as a result the conscience does not rest. Think how, as a result, through all this misfortune and suffering she becomes a devil's martyr. If she has a vindictive abbess or prioress or if she angers a sister especially beloved by her superiors, she will never have rest or peace. She sits and laments her fate, then along comes the devil and tries his luck to see if he can more easily lead her heart astray in the midst of her sorrow. And frequently he succeeds: many have such a feeble mind that the cloistered life becomes a prison for them; many have such restless minds that the seclusion[4] becomes a purgatory; many have such a tender, simple, humane heart that cloistered churlishness is hell for them. You say that if the mother superior

4. *Ainigkeit*. Enders suggests the term should be interpreted as *Einsamkeit*, although he also allows that it could be understood as *Vereinigung*—association, union, or assembly—as a reference to the common life of the religious, see *JEvGS* 1:211–12.

of the convent says many good things about your child, then she must be especially dear to her, as she is to you. But you don't understand that the envy and feminine jealousy of many others will not stand for it if she wants to give comfort to your child in particular. And so often a mother superior may not do the smallest thing for her sisters in the convent in front of the others because envy in the cloister knows no bounds. Think, Oh pitiless mother, from now on your child may not eat when she is hungry, she may not drink when she is thirsty, rest when she is tired, but rather she must do these things at set times when it suits others. Indeed, she must make herself just like the others despite great differences in temperament. Think what a great cross you lay on your child, under the weight of which she may sink forever. God does not give to all people the grace to come to the Christian faith, and He reveals His unfathomable election and damnation in unbaptized children, who, without personal, actual sin, are cast away from His presence forever. Nor does He make the way easy for all Christians who take it upon themselves to ascend to the high counsels of chastity and the complete renunciation of temporal goods. These are granted only to those whom God has chosen in eternity. Before entering the cloister too few think too little about what is pleasing to God.

You say: "I want to give my child peace so that she doesn't have a miserable marriage like I do." But look, your basic assumption is wrong, and you encourage the same mistake in your child. Who can say whether God will give your child a happy or unhappy marriage? Who can say whether God will grant your child less trouble in a convent than in a marriage? All of this comes from doubting God, and it can never be pleasing to God. You hitch your child to a cart, which she must pull until judgment day. Perhaps you think that in the convent she can serve God without hindrance. If I had the time, I could show you that there may be more dangerous and difficult obstacles to true Christian worship in the convent than there are in the world. Unless God cooperates in particular with His grace, no one can render true Christian service, neither in the cloister nor in the world. And there may be more people given this grace (by God's hidden decree) in the world than in the convent.

Oh, woe, the great blindness of those in the monasteries, how deeply they have sunk in their ignorance of true salvation. Oh, abyss of God's judgment, how you blind with the veil the so-called "spiritual" people.[5]

5. ". . . *wie verhengst du ein wiß uber die genanten gaistlichen*." Eberlin's meaning is not completely clear here. This translation is suggested by Ender's interpretation of the

To require the same food, drink and clothing, waking, resting, fasting, working, etc. of different temperaments is an unbearable burden, and fine to propose, but almost impossible to endure. And that's only speaking of the physical burdens, now consider seriously the burdens placed on her soul and conscience.

Even if your child is not weighed down by all these burdens and still wishes to dedicate herself to service to God, the convents are now in such a state that one should flee them.

There is an old saying of the saints that if a wicked person is tormented by one devil, then an upright person is tormented by ten or twenty. But who doesn't know the different tricks and temptations of the evil spirit which your child must expect in the convent; all suffering in the world, all faithlessness, is nothing compared to them. Then your child should rely on the salutary teaching of Holy Scripture, for God's word is a sword of the spirit. Your child also needs the trustworthy advice of learned people. In the convent this is denied her, because the nuns don't understand Latin, and yet every day, at meals and in the choir for ten hours, they have to occupy themselves with Latin, whether for singing, reading, or praying. Therefore, this time is both useless and difficult for them. And don't say to me: "They don't understand it, but God and the angels do." I say to you: "Your comments are nothing but water and air, for it hardly pleases God that people spend their entire lives without understanding." Perhaps you have a point when one reads or has read, out of devotion and honor for God's word, an obscure text of Scripture, containing higher truths than are evident in the literal sense of the words. But God finds little—I would even say no—pleasure in a complete lack of understanding of the language. And even if she already understands the Latin that has been in use for many years, still there is not enough wisdom written in such "kitchen-Latin" for your child to find proper instruction about the perfect service to God for which she entered the convent. Such great ruin has come upon the convents because we neglect Christian teaching; how you eat your fare determines how you get your meat, and as your teaching is, so are matters close to your heart and your customs.

Note here that true understanding and devotion come from frequent reading of the Holy Bible, along with ancient commentators, such as Origen, Chrysostum, Jerome, Augustine, and others.[6] But how will you

passage, see *JEvGS* 1:212 and Baur, "Rezension Eberlins Schriften," 5.

6. Origen (c. 185–c.254), *ODCC*, 1193–95; John Chrysostum (c. 347–407), ibid., 342–43; Jerome (c. 345–420), ibid., 867–68; Augustine of Hippo (354–430), ibid., 128–30.

understand this teaching if your father confessor and lector[7] don't know it? Further, even if you were already well versed in Latin before you entered the convent, you will not be allowed to read good books once you are there. For coarse, unlearned, foolish monks are assigned to the convents; for them it would be painful if the nuns know more than they do, and so they don't tolerate those who are more knowledgeable than they are. This they justify under the cover of claiming that studying is not appropriate for nuns, that it places obstacles in the way of humility, piety, etc. Thus has folly given rise to all these burdens. Originally convents were nothing other than schools of God's law, as the wise Philo demonstrates in his book on contemplation[8] and the ancient histories inform us. Now nuns don't know anything except silly stories and foolish tricks, and how to read from German books. As a result, sometimes a nun reaches the age of forty without having read for herself the four Gospels or the Epistles of Paul. Now tell me, to whom should your child turn with her troubles if, perhaps, (with good reason) she dare not trust her father confessor, or if he shows her no favor or mercy, or perhaps if they have an unseemly relationship, so that the confessional is then nothing more than a tryst? Another will not take her on for counsel and absolution in fear of causing suspicion. And only grudgingly do they allow other religious than those appointed to attend to and teach the nuns. And their monks preach fables and foolish things, just as they learned them. Thus is the devil victorious by promoting misunderstanding of wholesome teaching. For the devil opposes nothing so much as the proper understanding of the Holy Scriptures. For this reason he leads Christians, body and soul, to false peace,[9] so that in complete blindness the above-mentioned cloistered people insist they are enlightened and on the right path. Father and mother, to this you bring your child, and to this you entrust her.

Therefore, if you have a daughter who wishes to remain chaste, keep her in your house while you are alive; nowhere is she better protected (if she agrees) than in her father's house. Have her do reasonable work around the house, so she has something to do. At the appropriate times, let her hear God's word and have her say her prayers to God. If she doesn't want to do

7. "*läßmeister*": teacher of theology and philosophy in the monastery, see *JEvGS* 1:212.

8. *De vita contempliva* of Philo of Alexandria (c. 20 BC—c. AD 40). See *JEvGS* 1:212 and *ODCC*, 1279–80.

9. ". . . *zeücht er mit fryde umb als ein fäder spyl, die lyb und selen der christen menschen*, . . ." literally, ". . . he surrounds with peace as a decoy the bodies and souls of Christians . . ." See *JEvGS* 1:212.

that, then she doesn't have a true calling. In this way, you can better care for her needs and she for yours. If you don't want to bear the expenses of your child,[10] how do you expect strangers to do it in a convent where one can hardly stand to smell the breath or see the shadow of another? You commit a serious sin if you are unwilling to care for the child God has given you. If you are poor, be patient and trust in God, He will watch over your child if she is God-fearing, even without the convent.

Teach your child that every day she should pray to God for mercy, so that she finds herself in a blessed condition, and commend her to God; He will watch over her like a father.

My advice is that from now on the three vows not be permitted in any women's convent.

That all convents be reorganized along the lines followed by the honest, free women at Andlau in Alsace.[11]

That all women's convents should be made into schools for the teaching of Christian character; also that one trains children there for household management and work, so that if they someday marry, they will know how to keep house.

All windows through which one currently speaks to the nuns[12] should be torn out so they can be seen and heard if relatives or respectable, good friends come, or if one wishes to win a respectable wife there.

I am in no way suggesting, though, that men be allowed to enter the convent, because this is unnecessary and it provides no secure refuge.

Every man should regard it as a favor from God if such a well-reared, chaste, modest maiden from a convent should fall to his share. They should also be treated respectfully by men; and where this does not occur, the authorities should punish the guilty parties according to the details of the case. On this matter it may be better to forbid useless things and worldly pleasures for these children, so they are encouraged to shun such things until they enter the married state when they will have both the opportunity and the right to them. They should be allowed to go to the baths and to visit close friends, if this is deemed necessary or useful and undertaken in

10. Presumably Eberlin is here referring to the cost of assembling a dowry.

11. A convent in Andlau near Barr in Alsace established in 880 by the wife of Charles the Fat. In the 1470s the convent caused a stir because of the strictness of the reform measures introduced to it, see *JEvGS* 1:212 and Peters, *Johann Eberlin von Günzburg*, 19n23.

12. "*redfenster*." A small opening in the cloister wall, covered by a grille or grating, through which one could speak with the inhabitants, see *JEvGS*, 3:395. Cf. Kerr, *Life in the Medieval Cloister*, 69.

good company. However, if one of them, out of a special sense of devotion, wishes to remain chaste in perpetuity and free of the company of people, and if she has good opportunity to do this, she may remain behind in the convent and dedicate herself to God.

The convents are sufficiently well endowed to support their inhabitants that they may give to a sister who chooses to leave as much as she brought when she entered the convent. However, in cases of impoverished convents, it is better just to let her depart and use the resources to support another.

None should wear the veil, even if she wishes out of special devotion to remain behind in the convent, nor may she begrudge the others their progress.

Singing and the canonical hours in the churches should be short and reasonable, and their statutes bearable.

The vows, which until now the cloistered women have taken, do little to restrain them. If they discover that they are unable in this way to maintain their health or purity, my confederates advise them to renounce the common, cloistered life and take a husband or in some other way serve God and the world in a Christian manner, as they are able. For God will not recognize such superstitious, thoughtless, foolish—yes, I would even say dangerous—vows. If you can realistically hope that your bishop will give you permission for such a departure, then petition him for it. But if you cannot expect this from him, then we fifteen confederates will give you dispensation on the basis of God's mercy. Join together with an upright companion in marriage and devote yourself to God, or support yourself in another godly and respectable way. The time will soon come when you will not need to fear opposition from the authorities if you have left the convent. Above all, seek God and His commandments and you will find Him, whether in the convent or outside of it. But, if you do not seek God, no collar will help you at the gallows.[13]

No man should fear or be ashamed to marry a nun who has left the convent under the circumstances I have described above, because he does a good and praiseworthy work and God will reward him.

It is certainly right to take pity on the women's convents, which are burdened with so many unreasonable statutes made by superstitious,

13. The remainder of the text was likely added to the original pamphlet when it was reworked for inclusion in *The Fifteen Confederates*, see Lucke, "Die Entstehung der '15 Bundesgenossen,'" 40.

unlearned, inexperienced monks. With singing, fasting, reading, keeping vigil and other such things they compel the poor children to as great, if not greater, tasks than are laid on the monks. This certainly ought to move one to pity.

Often the nuns have to fast when the monks are eating boiled or roasted meat. In fact, the nuns must cook this, but they are not allowed to enjoy it themselves.

The nuns are forbidden to see their father and mother, while the monks seek far and wide for any new, curious thing.

The poor children are forbidden to enjoy fresh air, to travel to a spa, even in the case of an emergency to visit their dying father or mother, while the monks run hither and thither throughout the land without any cause, to the annoyance and burden of the people.

Pointless running around or outings are also not allowed to upright women in the world, but necessary outings should also not be forbidden to the nuns; but whoever makes these puts herself in God's hands.

If one objects to my advice for those already in the convent, then let him at least prevent anyone from entering it in the old way.

Whoever causes the nuns to sing excessively in the church has already been cursed by St. Jerome.[14]

Whoever interferes with their diligent study of the godly law sins against God and their souls.

If it were generally known on what foolish foundations the monastic rules are built, they would not be held in such high regard. But maybe one of us who knows more about these things will have something to say on this matter.[15] I will leave things at that since my time is up. But I urge all nuns to confidently call on God for help and to desire to lead a Christian life with God's help, either inside or outside of the convent; God will hear them.

With God is help.

14. The reference here is not completely clear. It may be to Jerome's comments in Epistle 108 when he admonishes St. Paula in response to her excessive prayers both day and night: "Constantly did I warn her to spare her eyes and to keep them for the reading of the gospel . . ." Later in the same letter he describes the daily routine in the monasteries founded by St. Paula as a judicious mixture of Psalm singing and work (Schaff and Wace, *St Jerome*, 203, 206).

15 Eberlin is likely referring to the further discussions of the monastic life in *The Ninth Confederate* and *The Twelfth Confederate*.

Von dem langē ver
drüssigen geschrey/das die geistlichē
Münch/Pfaffen vnd Nunnen die
syben tag zeit heissen.

Hör zů münch/pfaff vnd nunn/
Groß gåben din vorfaren drumb/
Das sie mich håtten vorgelåsen/
Eb sie kamen in solichs wåsen.

Der.IIII.bůdtgnosz

Figure 4. *Der IIII. bundtgnosz.* Bayerische Staatsbibliothek München [Res/4 H.ref. 271 y#Beibd.3]

4

The Fourth Confederate

On the long wearisome braying which the spiritual monks,
priests, and nuns call the canonical hours.
Monk, priest, and nun prick up your ears,
Well would it have paid those in former years,
Had they read my humble advice,
'ere they entered such a life.

Come Lord Jesus to my aid, so that I, the fourth confederate, might fulfill my promise for the good and comfort of the world, so that superstition might be reduced and your holy praise encouraged. I have long contemplated writing about the ecclesiastical prayers known as the canonical hours[1] and the more I think about them, the more I am amazed by human folly. Look, dear friends, our monks, priests, and nuns have led us to believe that nothing is more pleasing to God than their birdsongs which they call the canonical hours. As a result we don't consider ourselves true Christians unless we become accomplices to them from time to time with all our belongings and goods, from which they become fat and lazy, and through which, besides, true service to God—which consists in love, faith and hope, and help for the poor—is neglected.

1. Eberlin uses the terms *hore canonice* and *die syben tag zeit* to refer to the canonical hours established by the church for communal prayer by the religious at set times throughout the day: Matins, Prime, Terce, Sext, Nones, Vespers, Compline. He appears also to connect the canonical hours to the seven petitions of the Lord's Prayer, see *JEvGS* 1:212 and *ODCC*, 795.

But what is more shameful to hear, they themselves are so foolish that they regard their obligations as so great that any neglect in observing the canonical hours amounts to a mortal sin.

In no rule will you find that outside the community one is individually responsible to say the canonical hours as now occurs in the choir. That subsequent statutes require this is no concern of mine. I would love to hear from the temple servants a clear explanation of the reason for their claims.

It is important to remember that the institutions we call chapters and monasteries began as schools where one learned skills and wisdom. There, school masters were paid a well-deserved wage, and also poor students who wanted to study were maintained, who afterward could be of use in filling public offices for the entire land, especially in educating people. A similar system is still in place at the universities in the form of scholarships established to support poor students.

Also, if one wished to spend his days in such a place, serving God in peace and quiet, with reading, teaching, and contemplation, etc., whether he was a nobleman or a peasant, he had the time, place and means.

For this reason, certain times in the day were set aside so that together in common prayer they could appeal to God on behalf of the living and the dead; thus did this institution have its beginnings. Afterwards, through crafty schemes, a prison was made of the monasteries and a collection box of the chapters. On judgment day I wouldn't want to be in the shoes of those responsible for this state of affairs. I also want to point out that many places now in the hands of the cloistered people and the canons were originally founded as respectable accommodations for the aged, the poor, the ill, or for those unfit for civic life because of mental defect.

Now see what obvious evidence you have that what were once distinct monasteries are now incorporated into other monasteries, what were once women's convents have been allowed to die out and their goods transferred to monasteries for the monks. Many monasteries were attached to hospitals, then the clergy also sought to take control of the hospitals and were called hospitalers,[2] such as the Brothers of Saint Anthony, the Knights of the Holy Cross or Holy Spirit, the Teutonic Knights, the Knights of St. John,

2. "*Spittel herren*." The term hospitalers is usually applied to the Knights of the Order of the Hospital of St. John of Jerusalem, known after 1310 also as the Knights of Rhodes and after 1530 as the Knights of Malta, see *ODCC*, 794–95. Clearly, Eberlin is using the term more generally to describe orders associated with hospices and infirmaries, especially those caring for pilgrims during the crusades. See *JEvGS* 1:212–13 and *ODCC*, 1594–95 for further details on some of these orders.

etc. And many free parishes were incorporated into the chapters, abbeys, and the like, and the terrible consequence was the prostitution of the clergy, that is, leave was given to the monks to gamble, to ride, and to wage war.

You foolish Germans, how long do you want to remain blind and use your goods and labor for such evil ends? If someone just recites the canonical hours somewhere, you have no qualms about giving any amount, no matter how else he might live. And where the most goods are, there you donate the most, just as the parable about the power that perhaps compels you to do this states: "The devil shits on the biggest pile."[3] The canonical hours are of dubious origins; they have never had a commonly accepted, reasonable justification. But the current situation came about gradually, step by step, for human excess knows no bounds. This began first among the monks, and then the foolishness and generous gifts of lay people tempted the selfish monks to set this profitable activity at the pinnacle of service to God. When the priests saw what was happening, they thought that this could profit them and they, too, instituted the canonical hours. And so all the priests on the land and in the cities babble the canonical hours more than they pray devoutly. But who can say a pious prayer when he has to recite the canonical hours? As a doctor[4] has attested, this is impossible in the normal course of things.

Therefore, hear what I and my fourteen confederates think about the canonical hours.

Singing or reading the canonical hours is work like any other physical work. And all who feel themselves bound to this task sin before God when they shirk their duties from faithlessness or laziness, just as they would sin in any other work which they undertake for pay and livelihood.

It is a dangerous thing to support oneself with the canonical hours. Whoever is unable to do anything more useful or better than cry and mumble in the church, either because he lacks commonsense or because he is unsuited in some other way, may support himself with the canonical hours. For all others, relying on this is a precarious occupation.

In the chapters and monasteries time can be better spent in studying or teaching, and no one who is capable of these activities is bound to observe so many and such long canonical hours.

Those who preach to the people in the chapters or monasteries, if they perform their offices diligently by studying pressing matters, are not bound to observe the canonical hours.

3. For the background on this earthy proverb, see *JEvGS* 1:213.

4. It is unclear to whom Eberlin is referring here.

Stewards in the chapters and monasteries, if they perform their duties faithfully, are not bound to observe the canonical hours, even outside of the choir.

All those in the chapters or monasteries who diligently study useful things, or who teach them to others, are not bound to observe the canonical hours.

Father confessors who fulfill their office in a knowledgeable, faithful, and Christian manner, are not bound to observe the canonical hours. For hearing confessions in a truly Christian manner is a great work.

Parish priests who themselves preach and perform other parish duties are exempt from observance of the canonical hours.

Hired curates or helpers of the parish priest are not bound to observe the canonical hours.

Whoever, on account of illness, is unable to serve in the choir, even if his illness is not deadly, is not bound to observe the canonical hours at that time, nor is he bound to make them up later.

Those who are so feeble-minded that they are unable to earn their daily bread in any other way, or who are so poorly educated that they are unsuited for any public service, may commit themselves to such divine service as the canonical hours to support themselves, and they should perform these tasks decently and faithfully just as one expects of any other faithful worker. If foundations are established for the children of poor nobles and others like them, and no provisions are made that the canonical hours must be observed in them, the residents should not be required to observe them, and they should praise God that they are free.

All of the above-mentioned preachers, father confessors, office-holders, sick persons, etc., should diligently come before God each day in devout prayer in whatever way is suitable to them and to their immediate needs. But as to when, and for how long and how much to pray, these things are not stipulated. If you are unable to go to the choir, or if you must leave the choir on account of physical necessity or to earn your daily bread or to help your neighbor or because of civic responsibilities, you are not bound on the pain of mortal sin to repeat the canonical hours or to meet this obligation. But instead, beseech God diligently on behalf of those who commissioned you to say the canonical hours.

Monks in the monasteries and priests at the chapters who are fit to lecture in the schools, or to preach, or to fill the office of parish priest or his helper may leave the monasteries where they are only bound to observe the canonical hours and depart the chapters, and support themselves by such useful work. If the chapters and monasteries were returned to their original forms, one could begin to accomplish or undertake these things in the monasteries. But since things are such in our time that only with great difficulty can they be done, the above-mentioned persons should be free to leave the monastery and chapter and to go forth from them.

Those in the monasteries who are able to support themselves by the strength of their bodies or work of the mind other than through canonical hours, should try to do this in the monastery by helping those in need. If they are unable to do this in the monastery, or if their help is not needed, and instead they are forced to continue with the indolence of the canonical hours, they should leave the monasteries. God's command to feed ourselves by the work of our hands is greater than any human ordinance. The canons, monks, and casual chaplains or altar servants[5] of the temple lie when they claim they would be happy to stand before God and explain how they fulfill this commandment.

Now you see how foolish these people are. When they casually skip over the opening lines; or on account of pressing business, they do not hear or miss a verse, a Psalm, a response or a Bible reading; or, because of the call of nature, they must leave the choir, afterwards they are so concerned to fulfill their duty and recite the words left out. And they are even more anxious to confess this lapse, even though they are not bound to this observance. Yet they have little or no concern about helping their neighbor and rendering the assistance that God has commanded.

Item. If one has to undertake a journey because of pressing needs, he is not obliged to carry the breviary with him. If he conducts himself in an honorable and Christian manner in other things, that suffices. What you find in episcopal or papal laws, or in the legends and histories of the saints, or in chapter or monastic statutes that disagrees with this advice, understand in light of my counsel, or else ignore such prattle which reflects more superstition than God's command.

Don't think that you do a better work in observing the canonical hours than if you sowed your field or mowed your meadow. What the Holy Spirit prescribes as true service to God does not bring in great heaps of worldly goods to support sumptuous, luxurious, useless, slothful temple servants. But the spectacle of divine service, devised by human schemes and desires, is directed entirely at earthly gain, and God allows that such gain often comes to them, and thus do they come under even greater judgment. So you see how monasteries and chapters have come upon such great riches,

5. "*Altaristen*," holders of minor benefices endowed at specific altars, see *FnhdG*, 8.

and how their inhabitants have so much to do that they scorn God and forget all about good deeds, or only superficially observe them. At least once every day each Christian should turn to God in prayer for God's help and support and in thanks for everything good; this prayer can take place in a house or in a church. It is a praiseworthy thing to go to church once a day with other people and to pray together as a group. Whoever can sing and read should help the priests in the choir, especially on feast days. On Sundays such communal gatherings should not be neglected. When in the church, God's word should be preached and the priest and people should say a common prayer for the living and the dead. But my confederates and I regard as useless that one occupies the people with lengthy singing of the canonical hours or with singing many offices that are incomprehensible to them. One hour of preaching and half an hour of praying is long enough. Whoever wants to do more makes a long day for himself; it's not necessary that the whole parish follow such a person in his schemes. Believe me, if such singing in the monasteries and chapters weren't so profitable, there wouldn't be so many people in them. Even if one barely fulfills his duty in one place, still he wants to be a canon in three or four chapters, not for the office, but rather the profit. And if the lay people knew how fed up the monks and priests are with this temple service, and how unwillingly they perform it, they would let these fattened pigs look after themselves and would neither give nor lend anything to support such hypocritical bawling to God. It's incredibly arrogant of these monks and priests to claim that their service to God is more worthy of reward than other prayers of pious lay people, as if keeping the house and the daily work of the laity were not also service to God; and because these are commanded by God, they are even more worthy than the bawling and buzzing of the temple servants that God never commanded. I believe that if a prelate prays diligently for his people, that is highly valued in the sight of God, and if he calls together his people in the church and they pray together, that is entirely useful and beneficial. But so much singing of masses, vigils, canonical hours is a human invention; God well knows how useful this is. It's on your conscience. Believe me, if you turn to God in personal prayer at a time that is suitable for you, then the canonical hours are an unnecessary prayer. For few monks and priests understand what they sing and read, and those who understand are unable to grasp the meaning and reflect on it as a result of this deception; for where there is no time for reflection, how could such singing be of use? The nuns and lay people who listen to them understand absolutely nothing of what is going on. One could rather place thrushes, nightingales, and finches in the church;[6] they would earn nothing by their singing, they wouldn't be under any obligation, and then they wouldn't sin. In this way are the chapter and cloister fools subject to so many burdens, and they clearly violate God's command to support themselves through hard work.

I'm amazed the simpletons don't realize that the canonical hours, as observed in the choir, resemble in no way how they speak to someone else; and if one spoke to another person the way they speak to God, he would be mocked. One answers his own queries both before the Bible reading and again after, before the collects[7] and then after, thus does one say prayers, read responses, etc. And they insist that the prayers must be said precisely according to human formulas and nothing changed, even though the holy *pater noster* is taught, prayed, and written out differently in Matthew and Luke; where one includes a word, the other leaves it out.

If God does not regard it as a mortal sin to innocently change one's prayer, then how can you say that the prayers required by your rule are so strictly commanded. I know well that the unlearned, lazy, bulging monks and priests say, "What would we do the whole day long if we were not in the choir?" But whoever diligently studies the Holy Scriptures discovers that he has too little time and too few hours in the day; he has enough to do and finds that the canonical hours stand in the way of better activities.

I certainly believe that in the past monks and priests came together in the churches daily or frequently and there heard readings from the Holy Scriptures and debated useful matters, as is now supposed to happen in the universities. Perhaps such activity also encouraged apish imitation in the canonical hours instead of useful study. But I will bring my writing to an end here in hopes that my colleagues will do their part, so that this and other abuses will be challenged and redressed.

From the prayer to us by Christ taught,[8]
Have the canonical hours been wrought,
Greed alone inspires their observance;
Love of neighbor is completely neglected.
This age certainly will witness God's vengeance.

6. Eberlin introduces this list of song birds with the terms "*mär stell*," the meaning of which is unclear. See *JEvGS* 1:213. Here my translation follows the suggestions of its possible meaning by Baur, "Rezension Eberlins Schriften," 5

7. "*Collecten*." Eberlin may be referring here to the first and last prayers of the mass, a prayer said at the altar for the congregation, or the offering. See *FnhdG*, 138 and *ODCC*, 375–76.

8. See above, 53n1.

Der.V.bundtsgnosz.

Ein vermanung zu
aller oberkeit Teütscher Na
tion/das sy den Predig
stül oder Cantzel
reformieren.

BIBLIOTHECA
REGIA
MONACENSIS

Figure 5. *Der V. bundtsgnosz.* Bayerische Staatsbibliothek München [Res/4 H.ref. 271 y#Beibd.4]

5

The Fifth Confederate

An exhortation to all authorities of the German Nation
that they reform the pulpit

WITH GOD'S HELP AND inspiration alone do I, the fifth confederate, undertake to write an exhortation in simple words on the reformation of pulpits in the German nation. Since all efforts and proposals, both spoken and written, put forward by God-fearing and sensible people have so far made little progress, for the pulpit is still unreformed, I want to direct this address to the secular authorities who alone can carry out this reform.

Consider seriously, Oh you regents of the German Nation, both on the land and in the cities, to what God has called you. You should use the authority entrusted to you to establish, to encourage, and to uphold true Christian living. For that you bear God's sword. To that you should dedicate your honor, body, goods and soul. This is demanded by your oath, which you swore to God at baptism and from which no pope can absolve you, and by the loyalty and vow, through which your office binds you to your subjects. Now I wish to show you a handy, useful way to fulfill the duties of your office so that the subjects entrusted to you may live in peace and safety, and with them you may have God's blessings here and eternal blessedness hereafter. The best and most effective means to encourage Christian living among Christian people lies not in many statutes and territorial laws, in harsh penalties, in unbecoming severity, but more in the diligent proclaiming of God's word by those appointed to this task. For the word of God alone is effective in punishing evildoers, in correcting sinners, in helping the good. What God's word cannot accomplish, no human fear or effort will bring to pass, for God's word is like a sword that cuts through not only the body, but also the soul and spirit. By the sword of God's word we are driven from heathen ways to Christian living, from sin to decency. And should we again fall from this, it alone can bring us back to the right path, for all are turned from evil by fear or love of God. God's word alone calls forth this love or fear in us. Where the word of God is steadfastly proclaimed, purely and faithfully, much misfortune will bypass your land and cities. God judges by His word, and whomever God does not call, remains unmoved. But above all, think seriously about who should preach to you. It would be most useful if the parish priest himself does this. And so the parish priests should be learned or teachable people, good-hearted and prudent, who can pursue ways and means that will serve the people according to their own character. Also, no one else should frustrate his good plans, because the pulpit is in his power. On this matter, it would be good if one could test a candidate's abilities as a preacher and counselor before he is appointed to the designated post, and then the choice should lie with the common people and the authorities whom he will serve. Where it is not possible to bring in a parish priest, or to have such a parish priest, another possibility is to install a second preacher who will faithfully teach the people. But in this one must be careful and together diligently pray to God for a priest learned in, or willing to study, the Holy Scriptures; who has a sensible moral judgment and some experience of public life; and who is a compassionate, unassuming man with the gift to present the scriptures in a useful and organized fashion. Moreover, one should examine five or six candidates more than once before choosing one of them, and then establish a good living for the preacher, so that he may live according to his rank. If you find such a one in a cowl, you may take him on with the permission of the prelates, should they agree. Should they not, do it anyway, for a suitable monk is more obliged to teach the people, if called to this task by a community in the city or on the land, than to attend to the arbitrary demands of his abbot in the monastery. Thereafter, apply yourselves diligently to establishing such a relationship with the preacher that you will not dismiss him, nor will he leave you, without just cause. It takes more than a week for a preacher to learn the customs of a people and for people to accommodate themselves to a preacher. Otherwise, little of use can be accomplished; in this St. Paul is a great witness for us. Many cooks and a variety of foods do not make for a healthy body, and frequent and regular changes of the preacher bring uncertain convictions and morals. From uncertain morals the land and people become restless. If a preacher knows that he may not change positions without good reason, he must be more careful to conduct himself in a decent and courteous manner with his listeners. And if one cannot dismiss him without good cause, then he is more bold to speak the truth dictated by his conscience. From this it follows that yearly servants, curates, or priests' helpers[1] are not entirely suited to instructing the people, for they are generally young and inexperienced apprentices, and they can be dismissed or take their leave for matters of no significance. It also follows that the mendicant friars are not suited to this task since they are under the authority of their order. Either their preaching serves no purpose on account of their inexperience—they show up and babble nonsense, they wish to overturn this or set up that, neither of which are of use to the local community—or they offend with their odd schemes or bickering with some of the people. And they think to themselves: "If you are here today, tomorrow you will be somewhere else." As a result, the people become restless and the word of God is obstructed. But if the preacher must remain, he will think about things much differently from the beginning.

Item, often when a preacher is agreeable to the people, the monks become envious of him and he must leave. Often no one can prevent his departure, with great harm to the people.

Item, if someone preaches the truth of the Gospel, and this causes grumbling among some people who find the truth strange and shocking, immediately the monks dispatch a preacher to forestall disfavor and disagreement. For the mendicant friars fear terribly the hostility of the people, unless they can respond with mischief. Or if someone preaches the apostolic teachings, by which the unfounded doctrines and scandalous lives of the monks are recognized, from that moment on they seek, both inside and outside the cloister, reasons to transfer such a useful preacher to another position, with harm to God's word. Because where the word of God bears any fruit, no one can tolerate it less than the monks and clerics.

The mendicant orders were initially well received in the belief that their voluntary poverty would make them more daring in preaching the gospel since they have nothing to lose. But things have gotten turned

1. "*Järlich knecht, mütherren oder pfarr helfer*," helpers for the local priest on annual contracts or otherwise temporarily engaged, see *JEvGS* 3:389, 393.

around so that their hypocritical, compulsory poverty discourages them from speaking the truth. Even if one or another of them should come to his senses, the crowd stands against him and he has to bow to their will; otherwise he remains among them in constant fear. And so, we have now reached the point that you dare not expect clear evangelical and apostolic teaching from the mendicant orders. See, who opposes the clear truth more than the mendicant orders? Note clearly here, you innocent Christians, your ancestors received the mendicant friars out of charity and allowed them to build small dwellings among you so that sometimes they could preach to the people. And at first they were very simple and humble toward the parish priests and other priests, toward secular authorities and toward everyone. With such an appearance they became so firmly rooted that they were able to defy magistrates and judges, parish priests and other priests, and everyone else. For they cultivate support among the common people, whom they beguile in the confessional and elsewhere, so that if one wishes to resist them, he must fear a popular uprising. To this end, they threaten with empty, hollow papal bulls, and so they frighten the faint-hearted. And thus it has come about that they build extravagant houses and churches, have many people, have valuable trinkets and furnishings, and suffer no true want, even if appearances are otherwise. Sometimes they purchase rents and interest. Indeed, an entire city hangs in the balance when one stirs them up. But there is no better way to stand up to them than to have a suitable preacher (whether from the secular or the regular clergy), who is agreeable to the people and who generally presents useful things to the people so that the people themselves note what the monks have been up to until now. Furthermore, everywhere order is pitted against order, monk against priest, and often their sermons disagree; from this arise different opinions among their listeners. If you go to hear a sermon in one monastery, the preacher says red. If your wife goes to a different one, the preacher says blue. If your relatives go to the priests, the preacher says white. As a result, even in one house there is rarely a single understanding of basic Christian teachings. How, then, can one give consistent advice in the council or courtroom? How can there be a people well-grounded in true Christian peace? Furthermore, from this comes discord in the conscience and many questions and complaints arise. All of this brings honor and profit to the monks, as you can see by how busy they are and how discord in hearts and consciences is their larder.[2] Should a preacher now wish to bring to

2. "*Schmaltzgrub*," literally, lard pit, means of living. See *JEvGS* 3:396.

the people the true, solid foundation, so that honor and profit of the monks and priests are diminished, then he must be silent or suffer great torment, for until the firmly grounded teaching is brought to the people, he will experience nothing but misfortune. The secular authorities are certainly equal to this task and they can bring it to pass if they hold true to course. If they find a good preacher outside the cloister, then they don't need the monks, and they should command the monks not to mock him so that the people don't fall away from his teaching. If they find a good preacher among the mendicant orders, still they should appoint him. If the mendicant friars don't want to allow this, then the authorities have the power to expel them completely from the city or to reduce their provisions. And so the monks will not deny to a city the bread of God's word which can be provided by a suitable preacher. Don't let yourselves be hampered by the claim that their orders hold the rights to appoint preachers. It's not true. Frequently and often they want to arrange a good cover-up before the people because of their quarrels and suspect ideas. You should also not fear rebellion among the people on account of the monks, for, if the people note your seriousness in this, they will come over to your side. Furthermore, do not fear the bulls and bans of the monks, for they have such little worth that often the monks laugh at you for placing such stock in them; fire and water will dispense with such bans and bulls. Don't expect any help from the bishops and pope, for the mendicant friars are mixed up with them and they with the friars, so that they all follow suit. As a result, true Christianity wanes and superstition and heathen ways wax. Since you have accepted the mendicant friars on account of their wholesome preaching and you experience the opposite from them, it is fitting that you drive them back out on account of their opposition; in that you would do a service to God. Without them you already have enough priests and monks who mock you and fleece you of your goods and then devour them in their laziness. When you have found a man, either inside or outside one of the religious orders, who, by common consent, serves you well, you should commission him to begin preaching to you evangelical and apostolic teaching with the commentaries of the ancient teachers—Origen, Chrysostum, Augustine, Jerome, Bede, etc.[3]—and to omit the quarrels of more recent scholastic teachers. Furthermore, don't burden yourself with lawyers and Aristotelian teaching, which cause

3. Origen (c. 185–254), *ODCC*, 1193–1195; John Chrysostum (c. 347–407), ibid., 342–43; Augustine of Hippo (354–430), ibid., 128–30; Jerome (c. 345–420), ibid., 867–68; Bede (c. 673–735), ibid., 177–78.

great difficulties for the people and diminish enthusiasm for God's word. From now on sermons should be taken from the pure fountains of the Bible and ancient holy teachers, not from the pits, cisterns and caves of the new preaching books, as has occurred in the last 300 years, when the monks unveiled their indulgences, good works, praise for the saints of their orders, with all their self-seeking and ambition. The time has come that such things should be done away with. Oh, how praiseworthy, honorable, useful and wholesome it would be if you had such a preacher; in a few years you would have a well-cultivated Christian people. Then you would discover how usefully I have counseled you. Therefore, boldly seize the initiative. Is there a spark of godly seriousness in you? Is there a drop of Christian blood in you? Are there virile human sinews in you? Then show it in your actions. Oh you regents of God in the worldly estate, don't push this responsibility off yourselves and on to the bishops and so-called spiritual folk. All Christians are spiritual people: they have all received the Holy Spirit in baptism, they are all part of the suffering of Christ and they all have the holy sacraments, one faith, one calling, on the basis of which one is truly called spiritual. Preaching is for the whole community, and as rulers over Christian people, it is fitting that in your official capacity you take charge of matters that serve Christian teaching. Do you want to please God, cast off your sins, obtain remission from them,[4] do great good for an entire land or city? Would you like sometimes to be God's friend? Then take the matter in hand, don't delay. Today someone may die. If there were wholesome teachings, things would go better for him, because without wholesome teaching, no one can be saved. But such teaching has been hidden for many years, and it is obvious and evident that we hear useless fairy tales from the pulpit. Why do you want to delay so long, then, on matters concerning your soul? To hold a sermon on one day or in many places, one preacher suffices for 10,000 people. Each man should be on his guard against many different kinds of preaching because this encourages doubt-filled hearts and brings other great mischief. Well then, you dearly ransomed Christians, do you want to repay God for his great love for you, then provide help and counsel so that the Christian law will be preached purely and truly. If you have already experienced opposition to your efforts, endure it, don't give up, God will be with you. Believe me, this is more meritorious than if the Turk struck you down on account of your faith. No one does greater harm to true essence of Christianity than such unlearned, lazy, foolish, self-serving dream

4. "*Ablaß erlangen*," literally "procure an indulgence."

preachers, who, under good appearances, turn the people away from Christ. Therefore, one does not immediately recognize their deceit. But no one challenges the unbelievers. Why is there war, hail, crop failure, and other plagues? Because the word of God is abused in the churches and no one does anything about it; God cannot let this go unpunished. I want my soul saved. I have warned you truly, God will punish your laziness with disgrace and poverty, or in other ways, so that you recognize your fault.

Therefore, beloved, devout Christians, especially officials in secular office, do you want to be protected against injury and disgrace? Do you want to rule effectively in peace? Do you want your children to carry on happily long after you are gone? Do you want to die in a state of grace? Then take on this service to God. Forcibly reform your pulpits. Forbid those who preach contrary to what I have said from preaching any more. Oppose them with force. Pay no regard to any old customs, to the freedoms of orders, to papal bulls. Fear God more than men. Have a stout heart. Carry out God's will by promoting His law. Whoever opposes this, whether of secular or spiritual estate, against him use your authority, to correct or to punish, as is fitting. If you are already burdened by some offences, God will punish you less severely if you promote His law to others. I hope that you also will be delivered from your sins through grace. Such acts are better than all alms; they help the souls in purgatory greatly and are a beginning of eternal life. May God help us in this. Amen.

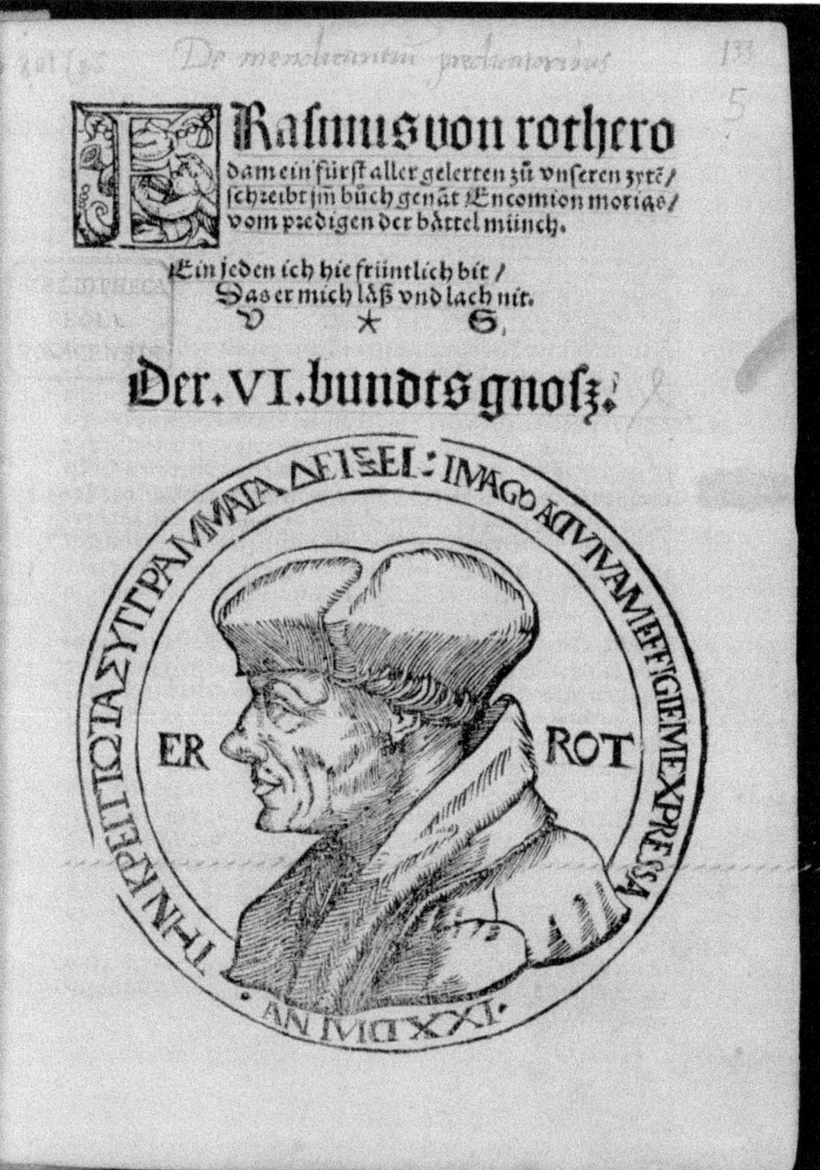

ERasmus von rothero
dam ein fürst aller gelerten zů vnseren zytē /
schreibt jm bůch genāt Encomion morias /
vom predigen der bättel münch.

Ein jeden ich hie früntlich bit /
Das er mich läß vnd lach nit.
V ★ G.

Der. VI. bundts gnosz.

IMAGO AD VIVAM EFFIGIEM EXPRESSA
ER ROT
AN MDXXI

Figure 6. *Der VI. bundtsgnosz.* Bayerische Staatsbibliothek München [Res/4 H.ref. 271 y#Beibd.5]

6

The Sixth Confederate

Erasmus of Rotterdam, a prince among learned men in our age, writes about the preaching of the mendicant friars in the book entitled *Encomion Morias.*

To each and every one I appeal,
That he not laugh when he reads what I reveal.

B G

I, TOO, AM ONE of the fifteen confederates, and as the sixth, I am now called on to do my part. So I thought it good to present what Sir Erasmus has written about the errors which the mendicant friars ply in their sermons and to which they themselves foolishly fall victim.[1] Whoever stirs up the supposedly humble mendicant friars, on him they take their revenge in public preaching, and they point out their adversary with such veiled words that everyone knows whom they mean. Furthermore, they don't stop railing against him until someone fills their mouths with porridge. Indeed, what minstrel or peddler of theriac[2] is more ridiculous to see than the mendicant friars? In their sermons they try to present themselves

1. The material contained in the next eight paragraphs is a loose translation/paraphrase of Erasmus' satire of mendicant preaching in *Praise of Folly*, see Erasmus, *Collected Works of Erasmus*, 27:132–35. On the preaching of the friars and the humanists' criticism of it, see Edwards, *History of Preaching*, 210–82.

2. Theriac was an antidote to bites of poisonous animals, especially snakes. See *JEvGS* 1:56 and *FnhdG*, 55. Today we would likely refer to such a person as a snake oil salesman.

as experts in the art of public speaking. And although their method is disgraceful and does not agree with the teachings of proven rhetoricians, nonetheless, they insist that it pleases well their listeners. From this arises, then, much laughter among wise people, for self-satisfaction among fools is comical. Oh God, how they distinguish themselves with their gestures, how they alter their voices, how they sing in the pulpit, how they praise themselves, how they contort their faces, how they fill the entire church with the braying of oxen. And they guard their preaching strategies as great secrets; they refuse to teach them to any strangers, but only pass them on from one monk to another. But now we've gotten hold of and learned from them their methods, so that the foolishness they carry on in the pulpit can be revealed to the people.

They begin with a prayer, something they have learned from the poets who initially call on their muse. But neither Augustine nor Jerome nor others have encouraged such a prayer because they assume that the people have already done that. Then, as an introduction to the sermon, they produce something that has nothing to do with its subject. For example, if they want to say something about love, they take for their introduction something about the Nile River in Egypt. Or, if they want to say something about the Holy Cross, they make an introduction about the dragon called Bel in Babylon. Or, if they want to say something about fasting, they begin to talk about the twelve signs of the Zodiac, as if fasting were justifiably prescribed for the springtide or March because of the favorable influence of the heavens at that time, which is, of course, utter folly. Or, if the sermon is meant to be on matters of faith, their introduction is on squaring a circle. I have heard one of them preaching—a very foolish, I should say, very learned, man—who wanted to reflect on the Holy Trinity. He wanted to demonstrate his foolishness, or ability, and he began speaking about the ABCs, and about syllables, and about an entire oration, also about how verbs and nouns should work together according to the rules of grammar, also about the ordering of adjectives and nouns. At this some of his fellows were astonished, as if this were a lofty matter, and they whispered the words of Horace: "Where can all this talk go next?"[3] Finally, he brought the sermon to the point where he would also explain the mystery of the Holy Trinity through basic grammar, as clearly as any mathematician could draw a triangle in the dust. And he would have had to spend eight whole months studying for such a thoroughly theological sermon, with such diligence and

3. Horace, *Satires* II.VII.21 in Horace, *Satires, Epistles, and Ars Poetica*, 227.

seriousness that he now doesn't see as well as a mole, because he focused his eyes inwardly to sharpen his understanding. But he doesn't grieve over his lost sight; his only concern is that he captured honor (as he foolishly imagined) from his precious sermon.

Furthermore, I know an eighty year old who was such a good Scotist, it was almost as if he were a second Scotus.[4] He wanted to preach a sermon in praise of the name Jesus. And he showed most foolishly, I meant to say subtly, that everything one would ever want to say on the subject is hidden in the name Jesus. He said that grammatically the name Jesus has only three cases, which signifies the Holy Trinity. Then he continued, the first case ends in an s, the second in an m, and the third in a u (for one declines it Jesus, Jesum, Jesu). The three letters s m u show that he was the sum, the middle, and the ultimate.[5]

Further, he revealed a great secret hidden in the name Jesus: it is of great significance that there is an s in the middle of the name. He explained that the Jews call the letter s syn, and in Scotland syn means sin, which clearly means that Jesus takes away the sin of the world. When his fellow theologians heard this, they were so astounded that they very nearly turned to stone like Niobe;[6] and this is not surprising, for when did Demosthenes and Cicero use similar introductions in their speeches?[7] The famed rhetoricians of old teach that it does not stand well when the preamble does not accord with the intended subject matter, just as if swineherds, uncharacteristically, did not draw their speech from the experience of nature.

But the mendicant friars claim that their preambles are artfully constructed. If they have little to do with the intended subject, then the listeners are left to wonder where the preamble is leading. And so, having begun by saying a special prayer with the people, followed by their inappropriate preamble, in the third place, instead of giving the intended address, they

4. John Duns Scotus (c. 1265–1308), a medieval philosopher and theologian, and member of the Franciscan order. He was known as Doctor Subtibilis. See *ODCC*, 513–14.

5. In Latin, *summus, medius, ultimus*.

6. In Greek mythology Niobe's children were killed and she was turned to stone after she boasted that she was at least equal to the Titaness Leto because she bore more children. See *OCD*, 735–36.

7. Here Eberlin omitted an important further comment by Erasmus: "As for me, I nearly split my sides like the fig-wood Priapus who had the misfortune to witness the nocturnal rites of Canidia and Sagana, and with good reason; for when did Demosthenes in Greek or Cicero in Latin think up an exordium like that?" See Erasmus, *Collected Works of Erasmus*, 27:133–34. In the process Eberlin clearly changes Erasmus' meaning.

read aloud a passage from the Gospel, but quickly and superficially, as if one needs say nothing other than the words of the Gospel. In the fourth place, they distinguish themselves highly and ponder what they regard as a profound question from the great teachers. This is, in fact, much less useful to the people than is usually thought. It deals with neither heaven nor earth, although they claim it comprehends both. Then they display true theological seriousness and bring forward their lofty teacher, subtle teacher, most subtle teacher, seraphic teacher, and they call forth similar splendid titles.[8] Also, in the pulpit they make use of syllogisms, conclusions, *corrolaria*,[9] points, articles; indeed, they lay before the simple people all sorts of scholastic rubbish. In the fifth and last place, they attempt to complete their great masterwork, and take a superstitious fable from a book of *exempla*,[10] which they then interpret spiritually. In this way they conclude their rude sermon, which is so clumsy that one can hardly describe it. But it insults them to take note of this. They at some time heard that a speech or sermon should not begin with a great clamor, but in a more quiet voice. This they misunderstood such that the beginning of their sermons are whispered so softly that they themselves can hardly hear them, and the beginning is nothing more than a mumble, just as one speaks so that no one can hear.

They have read somewhere that it is useful in appealing to the affections to employ the device of raising one's voice. This they do in such a way that after mumbling quietly for a while, they very cunningly begin to shout as if they were crazy. Such shouting has never been heard, not even at sites of martyrdom. You would think that they were in need of some hellebore.[11] It's as if it doesn't matter where in the sermon one shouts. They have also heard that as a sermon progresses, it should become more impassioned, so they become so animated that by the end they have become completely faint.

Finally, they have read that the great teachers of rhetoric have described how a funny story complements well the material, if one uses the joke at a suitable or appropriate time. Therefore, the mendicant friars also

8. Here Eberlin is following Erasmus' parody of the titles given to the great scholastic teachers, for examples, see 71n4 above and 74n17 below.

9. Corollaries, addenda, additions, see *JEvGS* 1:214.

10. Illustrations. For an identification and classification of medieval sermon *exempla*, see Edwards, *History of Preaching*, 228–31. Edwards (230) defines an *exemplum* as "a short narration given as truthful and intended to be inserted into a speech (usually a sermon) to convince an audience by means of a salutary lesson."

11. A plant believed by the ancients to cure madness.

wish to put jokes in their sermons, but their jokes are no more suited to the material than an ass is to playing a lyre.

Sometimes they pretend that they are serious about punishing great offenses, but their seriousness incites more than it restrains, and, in truth, they are never greater flatterers than when they want to appear the most serious. In short, all their preaching is arranged so that you would swear that they learned the art of preaching from the peddlers of theriac. No matter how much more elevated they are than these, the speech of both groups is arranged such that you can certainly recognize that one group has learned from the other. And no matter how superstitious the things they preach are, nonetheless, they are able to find people who are so pleased by this that one would think they heard Demosthenes or Julius preach.[12] But their teaching is especially appealing to merchants and women, and the mendicant friars seek to please women and merchants in particular. For, merchants, if they are pleased by the preaching, will share with them some of their plunder, and women are favorably inclined to the mendicant friars because they can pour out to the monks in the confessional all their vexation with their husbands. Furthermore, with such superstition and preaching they hope to master all men.[13]

All lay people should keep fixed in their memory this gem from the writings of Erasmus. And when they hear a preacher playing such a tune,[14] they would do God a great service if they left the church and in this way mock the preacher. It's a sad thing that such great, asinine ignorance reigns in the monasteries, also that they are unable to write half a page of letters half decently according to the rules of correct spelling. And what small children now know, old men in the monasteries are ignorant of. There was once great learning in the cowl. But now, beloved reader, if you know a little Latin and look into the *Kartünfflin*[15] which a cheese-hunter[16] carries with him, and from which he reads the foolishness he lays before the people, you will find in the writing neither correct spelling nor style. On the basis of what little understanding is left in reading or in speaking they don't even

12. Julius Caesar, who was also a renowned orator. Eberlin substitutes Julius for Cicero in Erasmus' text.

13. Eberlin's paraphrase of Erasmus' work ends here.

14. "*Uff solicher lyren machen*," literally "playing on such a lyre."

15. Enders (*JEvGS* 1:215) could find no definition for this term. Presumably it refers to the manuals used by mendicant preachers.

16. A derogatory term for the mendicant friars, likely referring to their begging for their sustenance.

know the correct accents or common vocabulary. So that your child, if he has been to school for two years, will notice immediately their folly and laugh at them. And if your child wrote and read before other students at school as they do, he would be beaten with rods. But when such a fool commits such folly in the mass and sermon, he is rewarded with cheese and fat.

You lay people know that you are responsible for the folly of the mendicant friars (I won't speak of the others for now) since you give them alms indiscriminately. If some fool comes to you, you give him as much as if he were Erasmus or Luther. Through this you encourage their excessive, lazy begging, and instead of teaching they rely on their unashamed begging and roaming about. Their superiors have noted this, and so they do not esteem learned people. There is no place for a clever man among them. If one of them becomes learned, he dare not stand out from the other fools and he must atone for the knowledge, which he should enjoy. And since their superiors are unlearned, they oppress the learned people who are different from them. If one of the superiors is learned, he wants to be seen as unique and will tolerate no one as his equal. In the process he notices that the unlearned can roam about the land just as well as the learned, and they do this happily, and they are not ashamed to fleece the poor of the rewards of their sweat by lying and cheating. Thus can the superior provision his monastery and alone be a fitting lord. In this way, many clever minds go to waste, which is something to be lamented. And everyone should counsel and help clever people in the monastery to escape the suffering they experience through their superiors and others. Close your wallet and cash box to the fools in the monastery, and very soon they will have to sing your song and let learned people take the lead among them.

But you say: "I am a simple layman, I don't know if someone is learned or not." Well then, I'll explain it to you.

You have just heard from Erasmus how you can recognize a prattler, or a fairy-tale preacher: when they use violent gestures in the pulpit; relate many fables or examples that are not written in the Bible; when they quote canon or secular law; when they frequently mention Aristotle, Scotus, Thomas, Bonaventure, Lyra, Hugo, etc.[17] When they employ

17. For Scotus, see 71n4 above. Thomas is the famed Dominican theologian and philosopher Thomas Aquinas (1225–74). Bonaventure (c. 1217–74) was a Franciscan theologian often referred to as "Doctor Seraphicus." Nicholas of Lyre (c. 1270–1349) was a renowned Franciscan biblical exegete. Hugo is either the theologian Hugh of St. Victor (d. 1142) or, more likely, the Dominican Professor at Paris, Hugh of St. Caro (d. 1263). See *ODCC*, 222–23, 800–801, 1151, 1614 and *JEvGS* 1:215.

much buffoonery and sarcasm which one is meant to laugh at. Be on your guard especially when they sneer at the authorities and priesthood, which certainly pleases the common man but is poison. When they chastise silly things, such as yellow veils, low-cut shoes, or clothing of this or that color. When they have a lot to say about indulgences, about the saints of their orders, about the good that occurs in their orders. When they have much to say on general fasting, on special little prayers, such as the rosary, Our Lady's Psalter, and the Crown Prayers.[18] When, with many words, they proclaim that one should give them alms, which they then collect.

When you notice this about someone, then you know he is a useless preacher. He knows nothing. He seeks honor, or profit, or compensation for himself. Give him nothing, leave the church, you will be doing God a service.

But when a preacher has much to say from the gospels; when he refers frequently to Saint Luke, Saint Mark, Saint Matthew, Saint John, Saint Paul, Saint Peter, Saint James, Isaiah, Jeremiah, David's Psalms, etc., then he is on the right path, for this is God's word. When he has much to say about love of God and neighbor, about contempt for the perishable world and eagerness for eternal salvation.

When he champions the home and people and the sick.

When he speaks of faith and hope in God.

When he speaks of contempt for the self.

When he preaches against slander and backbiting.

When he preaches against false judgments and hopes and seemingly good works, and grounds all his teachings in the Holy Gospel and in the epistles of St. Paul, and in the Holy Bible, he is on the right path.

Item, if a preacher sits among the lay people and has much to say about his own and his brothers' holiness, scorns other orders, scorns the priesthood in front of the laity, and nobles in front of the peasants, if he always lies to say what is pleasing to the people, he is a hypocrite, he is false, a seducer. See, I have pointed him out to you, don't let him lead you astray.

Item, if they speak about the great usefulness of masses, such as the thirtieth and golden mass,[19] about the endowment of anniversary masses, about confraternities and joining them, etc., then close your wallet.

18. Our Lady's Psalter was also known as the complete or Dominican rosary because it consisted of 150 "Hail Marys." The Crown Prayers were a devotional exercise associated with the rosary consisting of 33 "Our Fathers" and 5 "Hail Marys." See *JEvGS* 1:215–16. See also, Eberlin's comments in *The Tenth Confederate*.

19. The "thirtieth" was a mass celebrated in honor of the departed on the thirtieth

Item, if they speak in praise of the monastery, so that they regard the secular life as nothing, be on your guard around them.

This applies above all else to your alms; give first to the paupers in your parish, and afterwards give to foreign beggars, whether they be lay people or monks. Whoever teaches otherwise errs.

When the monks tell you about the great privileges of their orders, be on your guard.

In short, when a preacher points you to the Holy Gospel, to brotherly love, to well-founded humility, and demands more or as much for other paupers as for himself and his brethren, stay with him. Otherwise, beware.

You simple lay person, beware the mendicant friars, for they often come in sheep's clothing, but they are secretly ravenous wolves. And often it is the case that the more spiritual the appearance, the more fleshly the substance.

It would be even better to keep foreign monks and clerics out of the pulpit unless they have been first carefully examined by the local bishop and licensed to preach. Sometimes one is fortunate with his own parish priest, then I would silence the others.

But the layman is so foolish that he regards what is foreign and unfamiliar as much more clever and better than what is familiar.

You simple layman, you should be more diligent about how the good, wholesome teaching is proclaimed to you than you are about your bread and wine; for without this wholesome teaching, all your work is for naught. Therefore, pray to God faithfully every day for a wholesome preacher and message, and don't believe immediately what someone says, even if he has a holy appearance. Judge his teaching according to the instructions I have just given you so that you are not led astray. When the monks come alone and preach, if they want to take up a collection or they insist they should live well, give them nothing, for they are duty-bound to preach to you often, and that for God's sake. It is certainly true that years ago the preaching of the mendicant friars was held in high esteem. However, they were different people years ago. But now their preaching is dangerous and untrustworthy, and one should question them and examine them even more diligently than others before letting them preach.

---

day after the death or funeral, see *FnhdG*, 54 and Koslofsky, *Reformation of the Dead*, 24, 167n31. Cf. Eberlin's comments in *The Seventh Confederate*, below. What exactly Eberlin is referring to as a "golden mass" is not completely clear, although it may refer to an elaborate celebration lasting up to three or four hours. See *JEvGS* 1:216 and Eberlin's comments in *The Fourteenth Confederate*, 167 below.

It is wrong when the mendicant friars quarrel and wrangle from the pulpit, when they want to contest their privileges and their orders, to the amusement of the people.[20]

The bare-footed friars[21] want to make their Francis so great and raise him so high that any reasonable person can't listen. They do this not to honor the saint, but to be regarded highly by the people on account of the saint. Were they as meek as their name indicates, they would know that preaching about humble Francis in a more restrained manner would do him a greater service.

One can't lavish too much praise in honoring Christ and Mary, but it is clearly possible to overdo it with the other saints. Do you want to venerate the saints, then honor Paul, honor Peter, honor Augustine, Jerome, honor John the Evangelist, the Baptist, Chrysostum, etc.,[22] from whose lives and teaching you truly come to know Christ in the holy gospels. Let your Francis be who he is. But you bare-footed friars, although you regard many things as fables which others describe as great marvels, nonetheless, your desire for honor is so great that you spread these things among the people. Your order is not better than other orders; it is not especially praiseworthy. Be on your guard against others who would do something special. Furthermore, you should no longer spread such things among the people, or someone will throw them back in your face. The Preachers[23] want to be alone regarded as learned and defenders of the faith, to have their teachers alone recognized. This has brought them to such foolishness that everyone ridicules them and their teachers. Their teachers are not particularly elevated; they have written many good things, but also many bad things. What sort of thread their cloth is made of, everybody knows. The Carmelites lie and deceive so much with their St. Anne fraternity when recounting their origins, that soon Christ will bring their lies to the light of day since they have no basis in the Gospel. Where have you read that St. Anne had three daughters, that John and James were the sons of her daughters, and many similar things?[24] But

20. "*mit anlachen des volcks*." Eberlin's meaning is not completely clear here, but Enders (*JEvGS* 3:375) suggests this interpretation.

21. The Franciscans, see *The First Confederate*, 25n19.

22. In addition to the bibilical saints, Eberlin here refers to the church fathers Augustine of Hippo (354–430), *ODCC*, 128–30; Jerome (c. 345–420), ibid., 867–68; and John Chrysostum (c. 347–407), ibid., 342–43. At this point he appears to shift his address away from the laity to members of the mendicant orders.

23. The Dominicans, the "Order of Preachers."

24. This likely a reference to claims made by the Dominican James of Voragine in *The*

if you have money from the people, then you leave the others well enough alone. You want something special to set you above the other orders so you call yourselves Our Lady's Brothers.[25] Oh, you insolent rogues, as if our lady had such greedy, unchaste, insolent brothers. To my mind, all pious Christians are her brothers and sisters, also her sons, indeed, her children; and my opinion has a basis in the Gospel, while your fable is nothing but water and air. Also pay attention to the other circumstances in which the monks go around and in which they exploit the pulpit, keeping people from the pure Gospel and taking from them the fruits of their bloody sweat and hard labor, to the detriment of other paupers. God will not tolerate this much longer. But be warned you simple lay person, you must also beware because they often preach and write more on the basis of what they hear in people's confessions than what they read in the Bible. But I will not write further on this, my time is up. Let my faithful exposé be of service to you.

The peasant is getting wise.

Golden Legend (completed c. 1265). See Jacobus de Voragine, *The Golden Legend*, 520.

25. The Carmelites, the "Hermits of the Blessed Virgin of Mount Carmel" were particularly dedicated to the veneration of the Virgin Mary, see Andrews, *The Other Friars*, 52–59.

Dz lob der pfarrer
Vnd dē vnnützē
kosten der gelegt wirt vō dē
gemeinē vnuerstēdigē volck
vff mäß läsen/volgungen/begreb-
nüß/sybend/dryßigst/jartag ꝛc. Vñ
vom lob der Pfarrer vnd irer nöti-
gen Caplon.

Der. VII. bundt
gnosz.

Figure 7. *Der VII. bundtgnosz.* Bayerische Staatsbibliothek München [Res/4 H.ref. 271 y#Beibd.6]

7

The Seventh Confederate

In praise of parish priests
Concerning the useless sums paid out by the common, unsuspecting people for mass readings, funerals, internments, sevenths and thirtieths,[1] etc. And in praise of parish priests and their necessary chaplains.

HERE BEGINS THE PRAISE of the parish priests and their necessary chaplains, and a report on the abuses of funerals, mass readings, etc. Also how, from now on, each Christian should deal with these things

Often and frequently I consider the common complaint of the world that everything is increasingly topsy-turvy, and furthermore that the chief and greatest cause of this is the misunderstanding, laziness or malevolence of the authorities. And such a complaint very often is discovered to be true. But I can also well imagine that in many cases the common people do more to encourage these abuses by adhering to and supporting them than the authorities could ever do to remove them. This I want to report in as few words as possible, so that I can give reasonable people (of which there are now many in the community) cause to think further on these things, and with God's help to limit these abuses.

1. "*sybend, drysigst*," masses held for the departed soul on the seventh and thirtieth days respectively after the burial. Anniversaries, also known as obits, were masses celebrated once a year, usually on the anniversary of the death. See *FnhdG*, 54, 201; Koslofsky, *Reformation of the Dead*, 28, 167n31. Cf Eberlin's comments in *The Sixth Confederate*, above 75–76n19.

It is obvious that four things are highly regarded in the German nation. The first of these are the ceremonies known as burials or funerary processions, through which we believe one can give assistance or succor to the dead who now stand before God's terrible justice without resources of their own. The intent of these I do not condemn, because both natural and Christian love demand it. But the means, pursued without limit or justification, no reasonable person can defend. And, nonetheless, the common people in our land are so devoted to these practices, as a result of long-established custom (as they imagine) and because of the self-serving teachings of the kitchen preachers both within and outside of the religious orders, that such madness will not quickly be driven from them without special divine illumination. So burdened by all sorts of superstition is human folly. And I could not put an end to such vain imaginings of the people in hopes of bringing about improvement, had I not now noted the sunshine with which God wishes to enlighten the human soul, either by speaking directly to it or through heavenly influence, so that it recognizes, is disgusted by, and therefore puts an end to so many idolatrous activities in which, unfortunately, we and others have been mired for so many years. I wish, Oh reader, that you will calmly read this advice or recommendation and consider how it contributes to our preservation or improvement. If, however, you would judge this writing harshly, then do so on account of the abuses discussed and not my poor treatment of them.

That German Christians want to aid the dead pleases me so, that I wish that in all sermons they be earnestly admonished to cultivate such pious love of their neighbor. But since under this honorable cover is concealed such a dangerous Shrovetide prank, offensive to God, rooted in self-interest and human blindness, and a hindrance to real help for the dead, I can no longer keep silent about exposing this evil nor hold back from a useful admonition to all well-intentioned (but little-understanding) Christians.

Who can but be astonished if he takes this seriously and notes the commerce and trade carried on in masses. Look, if your father and mother, siblings, relatives, friend or another is called from this life, the light of nature teaches you, and the intent of Christian rite makes you willing, to give them aid in escaping their torments (assuming they are suffering torments) and in obtaining the wished-for salvation. Now you need to know of more suitable means to these ends, so that you do not put great trust in things that do them little or no good and that are harmful to both your possessions and your judgment. Therefore, follow this advice until things get better for you.

Stand before God with great trust and ask for His help and comfort for the dead person. Also, consider the innumerable wrongs by which we daily and hourly anger almighty God in this life, for which we deserve God's strictest judgment, and in which even our righteousness is displeasing to God. And the more seriously you take these two things to heart, the more earnestly you will pray. And so that you place great hope in God's mercy, which is so much more inclined to the departed souls the more they need it, and so that your intercessions become stronger and more pleasing to God, entire groups of friends and neighbors should direct their prayers in this way. Thus has it become the custom that all neighbors accompany the corpse to the grave and that along the way bells are rung so that all Christians who hear them are admonished to at least ask God to help this dead person. And all preachers who proclaim God's Word should encourage this and declare it to the Christian people in all sermons.

Thereafter, when the people come together in the temple on feast days, one should list off to them, either individually or as a group, all those who departed in the preceding days, and encourage them to pray for the departed. This should happen not only in the common prayer said by the preacher and the people immediately after the sermon, but they also should beseech God's help for the dead in all prayers the Christian people say to God during the entire mass on that feast day and during the following week. It is also especially helpful to teach the people that one will be shown as much mercy by God after one's death as one now tries to help the dead (even the undeserving) through one's prayers.

That one holds a burial or anniversary mass and in this way brings the people together and admonishes them to pray for the dead, too, is helpful and comforting for the dead in my opinion. For even St. Monica[2] requested that after her death she be remembered at Christ's altar. Another way to help is to do something for the poor, which pleases God greatly, and by fulfilling this commandment to love one's neighbor moves Him to have pity on the departed soul. And also, the poor should be obligated to pray earnestly. That a very useful (but little recognized) aid to the dead is the improvement of the lives of their relatives still among the living is clear from the words of the rich man, who also anticipated that his punishments would be lightened if his brothers were saved from a hellish prison by improving their ways. There is no activity more pleasing to God the Lord than when a Christian remembers in his prayers the suffering souls, and

2. St. Monica (c. 331–87), the mother of St. Augustine. See *ODCC*, 1104.

especially those to whom he or she has a special connection. This, too, is very helpful to the dead. These means have been proclaimed to us to aid the dead. If you take on others beyond those discussed here, you will certainly expend much effort, but do little to comfort the dead.

Unfortunately, human superstition has reached the point that much money and effort is expended on things such as vigils, candles, numerous masses, the endowment of anniversary and perpetual masses, which accomplish at best only part of the intended goal of helping the dead. Similarly, if a person dies, all efforts are turned toward preparing the pall; toward the bier; and toward useless and very expensive preparations, like wax and candles; toward hiring a great number of priests; toward arranging wearisome, excessive and unobserved vigils. I don't deny that all this serves worldly purposes: it brings frivolous esteem to the living. But that it serves the dead as a direct and powerful means of consolation cannot be established except through self-serving, unsubstantiated teachings, which are convincing only to those of mediocre understanding. I wish to show that such outward practices actually serve as a great obstacle to helping the dead. The fairy tale and kitchen preachers have established that the beginning and end of all help for the dead comes especially from such outward, showy things, through which hidden and unnoticed neglect grows in the human heart, so that the people come to believe that the dead receive sufficient help through masses, vigils and anniversary masses. And as a result of this their relatives leave off offering daily personal prayers for them and (so they intend) hand them over to the temple servants and others. But the temple servants (I mean the monks, priests and nuns) are as careless and weary in performing these as they are nimble and determined in receiving payment for them.

One complains daily about the great, unbearable crowd of ignorant priests and cloistered folk, whose only purpose is to take up space, cast shadows and eat up the food that should go to the poor, and yet, no one will consider seriously the proper means to reduce their numbers. But one sees how, without skills, without cares, without work and undeservedly so many thousand are able to maintain themselves through private mass reading, in which hardly a word is even spoken correctly, much less understood; and how with petitions and money they are forcefully drawn, urged, and pulled to these activities. Don't you think that it is human laziness that leads so many people to make use of this, to reconcile themselves to it, and that makes so many monks and nuns take the temporal goods of other Christians, empty their wallets, and in this way lead a full, lazy life? Through this the common people are daily blinded and God is dishonored.

However, while superstition and abuses are so revered by the simple, obliging people, the temple servants are clever and shrewd, and they prattle such superstitious ideas in the confessional and from the pulpit, and also fabricate various signs and appearances of departed souls. In this way they move the simple and naive people to endow perpetual masses, anniversary masses, and to multiply vespers for the souls, vigils and masses on the seventh and thirtieth [days after the burial], through which the monks and priests are maintained and fed until almost the whole world is beholden and indebted to them. And appeasing them only weakens useful governance and hinders the spread of Christian teaching, as is apparent to all who read about the nature of the priests and Pharisees in the gospel, and about the resistance of the servants of idols in the saints' legends, and about monks and priests in our time, among whom the reforming of Christendom will make less progress than among the Turks and heathens. And so it comes about that they are maintained by the endowments and benefactions of the simple folk, as if offering them many temporal goods (amply given) would move them to conscientious and regular intercession and help for the dead, for whom, in fact, no one does less than those who receive the most for their efforts. And so is fulfilled the maxim: what seems a service to God has given birth to riches, and the daughter has devoured the mother. Now look on in amazement at how the mass priests run willy-nilly to the churches where they have their prebends, laughing and chattering both before and after the mass, and how they rush through their canonical hours. One eggs on another to finish his mass quickly so that he can begin his own sooner. One spits out the mass and rushes off without even saying an Ave Maria either before or after. Oh, what frivolous conversations take place in the choir and sacristy during masses for the dead, what jeers when women go to the sacrament, as the temple servants stand around and play their parts, one after another. What consolation such a mass brings to the poor souls every Christian can imagine. Similarly, hardly every tenth word in the vigils is spoken, as anyone who can read has noted. Over the grave one mumbles broken words shortly afterward; this is deemed a fair exchange.

But what should I say about villagers who are so misled by their people's priest that not only do they give the priests valuable *presentia*,[3] but

3. Payment for being in attendance at, and taking part in, spiritual services such as masses and masses for the dead. See *FnhdG*, 40.

they also provide meals and banquets not only for the priests of their village, but they also invite monks and priests from far away, so that each priest will have his plunder. In his village one holds the priest in such high esteem that the peasant is skinned and scraped and so many charges are laid on him to bring his dead friend to the thirtieth day that he and his relatives could live for a whole month on the cost. And little, if any, attention is paid to the poor and homeless. What's happened to the words of Christ in Matthew chapter 9: "I desire mercy, and not a sacrifice?" Some wish to avoid this and they bring gold and silver to the monks in the cloister, hoping that they will do more for the dead. And they don't know that even less, or just as little, will be done, for seldom is more than one mass said specifically for an intended anniversary mass. And although they all stand around the altar in black vestments, such masses they leave to others they designate, so much so that hardly a memorial is held for a particular dead person. Nonetheless, if you wish to accomplish much and therefore fill the capes or purses of an entire convent, know that God and the souls would have had more help and been more pleased had you given a homeless neighbor enough to pay his taxes or to feed his small children. Some want to have a thirtieth read and do not know that there are so many obligatory masses among the priests and monks that often three thirtieths are rolled into one, and yet full payment is taken from each of them.

What should I say, then, about endowed anniversary masses that are seldom observed for more than 20 or 30 years. And if they are held, then so poorly that often four or five are said together and, nonetheless, each yields the prescribed *presentia*. Go ahead, foolish layperson, and give away your money to fill up the temple servants, neglect the dead while emptying your wallet. From this nothing comes except that you are counted among those who hold the usual customs; for there is nothing to recommend these practices other than the fact that they are regarded as customary. As if one has to incur such costs for the benefit of the dead. How long will you be so foolish; if you weren't, the stud-horses and temple servants wouldn't make such a fool out of you on account of your diligence.[4] But you should refuse the superfluous costs and be attentive to the homeless, whose need you see. I don't dispute the purchased rents[5] that are already in the hands of the temple servants, but the daily, useless offerings given to them I can't see. If you feel that the masses of

4. "*blütigen schweiß*," literally "bloody sweat."

5. See the discussion of rent charges in *The First Confederate*, above 32–33n34.

your parish priest and the common prayers of your fellow parishioners are insufficient, then turn to the priests who hold benefices in your parish and be satisfied with them. And don't say "Ah, but it's the custom." For if one were a bit more determined, in a short time these and other abuses would be reduced. To give an honest and fair gift to the poor of the parish in front of the church is praiseworthy in the eyes of God and the world.

Dear Christians in the German land, hold back such gifts to the temple servants so that their lazy, useless and vexing lifestyles are stopped. It does not upset me that established benefices are left as they are, but no new benefices should be endowed. The parish priest deserves his income and God wishes that each parish have a properly established parish priest with full authority, not just a temporary or even permanent vicar, and beside him two or three priests, also well supported, to help with the responsibilities when necessary. A mass in the parish church along with the prayers of the parishioners, are good help for the dead; I advise you not to arrange additional masses. Is it not a pity that so many people are maintained in the monasteries, especially in those of the mendicant orders, alone on the basis of the organized clamor they sing in the choir, which, nonetheless, they do not understand on account of their stupidity, which they can't follow on account of the speed with which they proceed, and which they don't want to take note of because of their vexation. How God regards all of this any Christian heart can imagine. And where enlightened Christians withdraw their support from this sort of activity, such hopeless cages would be done away with and the basis for many sins, about which I do not wish to write, would be withdrawn. What great troubles there would be among us if it were no sin to enjoy unearned food. Oh, how great is God's anger over the unknowing, lazy, superfluous people in monasteries who hope to earn their keep by gnawing away in the cage of the monastery and reciting the canonical hours in choir like a magpie, with no understanding of their meaning.[6] My companion will write more on this topic.[7] For we fifteen have sworn together to expose all such things to the world.

6. Eberlin here uses the term *taflen*, the meaning of which is not completely clear, although it likely refers to the act of mouthing words without an awareness of their meaning. See *JEvGS* 3:379.

7. Probably a reference to the discussion in *The Fourth Confederate*. These and subsequent references to the other Confederates were likely added after Eberlin conceived of the plan to publish the collection of pamphlets as *The Fifteen Confederates*, see Lucke, "Die Entstehung der '15 Bundesgenossen,'" 39.

Therefore, beloved Germans, beware new endowments, but keep the old ones; if a good friend dies, help him by using the means outlined above. Be content with the masses said by your parish priest, or at very most, with the masses said by priests with benefices in each diocese. Give alms to the poor, help the needy, support your priests with ample provisions, for which they may have both the great and the small tithe. During the time of mourning one may invite good friends to a meal, among whom may be included the parish priest and two or three other priests—that I don't forbid. But feasting the entire day I do not condone. If you want to endow an anniversary mass, don't establish it for more than thirty years, for it will not be held or will be poorly observed. And even so it will cause great harm to the consciences of the temple servants. Don't fall for the usual abuses, as if it were established that such customary ceremonies were commanded for the dead in the churches. Rather daily in one's prayers one should think on the status of the departed, tormented souls and plead for them as one would want to be pleaded for after one's own death. This not only helps the dead, but also warns the living about their own fate.

Oh, you dearly ransomed Christians, when will you think things through and boldly take the lead in doing away with such superstitions? Do you not see that God is reaching out His hand to you and wants to help you? This you can see in the fact that God has awakened so many brave heroes who cry out against such abuses and who have committed their honor, persons, and goods for your benefit. Be courageous and valiantly seize the moment, draw the wood from the fire; that is, take from the useless, ignorant, lascivious, lazy, greedy, stingy monks and priests their daily unendowed alms, and you will see that the loafers and inventors of vice will not be so many. And where the numbers of these people are reduced, so also will vices decrease and daily bread increase. With this I don't mean to dispute the endowments which the consecrated already possess, but taking them additional gifts every day I want stopped. The parish priests and their necessary chaplains and helpers I consider worthy, and all necessary support should be given to them. But all other forms of monkery and priestliness my companion[8] doesn't want praised, and even if you can't root them out completely, nonetheless their numbers will be reduced if you follow my advice outlined above. Commit yourselves to the departed souls and thus improve their situation by faithfully imploring God to preserve you from such harsh judgment and to release them from the torments of their

8. Again, likely a reference to the discussion in *The Fourth Confederate*.

punishment. And take to heart the teachings of my sworn companions, and they will take care of you. If the fat, full, hypocritical, self-serving, blackmailing monks, priests or nuns suggest otherwise, don't pay attention, even if there are many of them and they appear slick and well-healed. Rather, subject such matters to the sound judgment of your reason and to reliable writings. You will find that my companions and I have advised you faithfully. And pray to God for us that He will give us grace to instruct both you and us in what promotes the health of the soul.

I hope and wait.

Warũb man herr Erasmus von Roterodam in Teütsche sprach transferiert.
¶ Warumb doctor Luther vnd herr Vlrich von Hutten teütsch schriben.
¶ Wie nutz vnd notes sy das sollich ding dẽ gemeinen man fur kom̃.

Der. VIII. bundtsgnosz.

Figure 8, *Der VIII. bundtsgnosz.* Bayerische Staatsbibliothek München [Res/4 H.ref. 271 y#Beibd.7]

8

The Eighth Confederate

Why Sir Erasmus of Rotterdam is translated into German. Why Doctor Luther and Sir Ulrich von Hutten write in German.
How useful and necessary it is that such things come before the common man.

We know well that there are many who are angered by, and who regard as useless, God's great gift that so many wholesome things are now being translated into the German language. Therefore, I, the eighth confederate, have been directed by my fourteen companions to show the common man the useful things arising from this. St. Paul writes to the Romans that some learned people conceal the truth in their injustice.[1] That is, they do not want the clear truth to emerge, so that their own evil and wicked lives do not appear damnable before the people, so that one does not learn what God wants from us and does not discover that the lives of the learned are contrary to it. In the Gospel the Lord Jesus says to the wicked learned ones and priests: "You have taken away the key to the heavenly kingdom, that is the knowledge of the Holy Scriptures; and you yourselves have not entered the kingdom nor have you allowed others to enter into it, that is, not only have you been wicked, but you have kept from the simple people a correct understanding of God's commands."[2]

1. Rom 1:18ff.
2. Matt 23:13; Luke 11:52.

Take care, beloved pious Germans, we have an inborn trust and innocence, so we believe that others are as unlikely to want to deceive us as we are to want to deceive them. As a result, we willingly trust those who seem serious and we follow where they lead, especially in matters we see as concerning God and service to God. For no nation in Christendom came later to the Christian faith than the German, and then held to it so fervently. The devil has tried to use to our ruin the very innocence and decency which should contribute to our great well-being. And he has undertaken to introduce among us Italian deceit and inconstancy, also their godlessness and wickedness, and especially the Antichristianism of the Roman curia. For he knew well that we were ripe to be led away from the true path, especially when corruption is presented under a good appearance. And what would appear better than if one brought a sealed letter from the Roman bishop, whom many of high authority and great learning have proclaimed, and themselves regard, as the sole vicar of Christ on earth, to whom all the world is subject, and in whose hands are our salvation and damnation? Some German princes were even led so far astray by this that they accepted the imperial crown from the pope, believing that he had the authority to depose the true Roman emperor and, at his pleasure, to put in his place another, whom he leads around by a fool's halter as he wishes. The pope subjects to his own tyrannical authority as many lands and peoples as he wishes, and the rest he leaves to his chosen emperor. And such a Roman emperor always lies under the feet of the pope like a purchased slave. Therefore, the German princes were led astray by their innocence and have taken on the imperial office, assuming that they are duty-bound to make the whole world subject to the Roman See, and that the pope alone is a god on earth. And although the German lords have come to this dignity through the pope's cunning, nonetheless, they should no longer let themselves be driven from it so long as God grants it to them.

When we Germans saw that our princes and emperor esteemed the pope so highly, we couldn't think other than that we, too, were required to do the same. But our ancestors were also inclined to regard the popes' claims as false and their demands as too unreasonable. Therefore, some German emperors dared to resist vigorously and to throw off the papal yoke. These were such beloved emperors as the Henrys, the Ottos, Frederick Barbarossa, Frederick II and Ludwig the Bavarian.[3] When the papists

3. Some of the names on Eberlin's list of German kings and emperors who stood up to the papacy are obvious: Frederick I, Barbarossa (1152–1190), Frederick II

saw this, they, or the devil through them, dreamed up another deception. There were in Italy two devout men, named Francis and Dominic[4], who took it upon themselves with their companions to preach God's word. And they requested from the pope permission to do this. And they accomplished much good among the people, for they lived truly spiritual lives, which were above suspicion. They accepted only their daily bread for all their work, and they were truly inwardly devout people and God was with them. But afterwards many sought to live by begging, using the names of these two pious men or their devout followers. But the numbers spoiled the game. When a great lazy horde needed to be provided for, the people became fed up with them. They were not like those in the beginning, and yet they wanted to fill their bellies and realize their ambitions under the appearance of poverty and the preaching of their devout forefathers Francis and Dominic. But since they no longer possessed either knowledge or effort or zeal, they didn't know how better to hide their falsehood than through the many privileges they received from the papal curia. And since they wanted to defy the whole world through this, they inflated the power of the pope, giving him ten times more authority than he actually had. They did this not to venerate him, but for their own profit and honor, as one can see from the bulls of their most elevated idol, the pope, claiming that they should be regarded as papal angels and Roman saints.

Then began as well the lucrative trade in indulgences, from which the mendicant friars gladly gave the Romanists three parts so that they could keep the fourth. And although they claim that pious Francis established an indulgence at Assisi, it is well known that he allowed no special prayers to be associated with it, and that he forbade all monetary donations in that place. He was concerned only with the salvation of souls as he understood it. Immediately the pope and his court realized that the mendicant friars were inclined (for completely selfish reasons) to all that would bring them honor and profit; furthermore, that for selfish reasons they were willing to make a god of the pope and a heavenly kingdom of his court, truth out of falsity, something out of nothing. Then they began to strike a bargain with the mendicant orders and commissioned them as their hunting hounds throughout the world with great indulgences and privileges to encourage

(1215–1250), and Ludwig III, the Bavarian (1314–1347). The Henrys are likely Henry III (1039–1056), Henry IV (1056–1106), and Henry V (1106–1125) and the Ottos Otto I (962–73), Otto II (973–83), and Otto III (983–1002).

4. Dominic (c. 1174–1221), *ODCC*, 496–97 and Francis of Assisi (c. 1181/2–1226), ibid, 632–33.

strife and refer all of the resulting discord to Rome so that they themselves receive excessive authority and great amounts of money. Then the authority of the bishops and the parish priests began to diminish, and the universities and all the pulpits and confessionals were forcibly occupied by the mendicant friars. The friars contrived a slick appearance to oppress the whole world, so that no one would stand up to them and their Roman idol, and they established *inquisitores heretice pravitatis*,[5] which you call heretic hunters. These are supposed to suppress, ban, and burn all who truthfully preach evangelical teachings under the guise that they contradict the Christian church, that is, they contradict the tyranny of the mendicant orders and their Roman idol.

Their unchristian authority has so universally destroyed things that we were living in darkness and in the shadow of death.

But such abuses by the mendicant friars succeeded foremost in the German lands, in part because the pope wanted through them to bind the German people to him in excessive obedience since the German emperors mentioned above refused to tolerate papal arrogance any longer. Also because the cunning mendicant friars saw that the innocence of the Germans made them ripe for the picking.[6]

There were prudent people in Germany when originally the first mendicant friars arrived here. They were bare-footed friars[7] and twice they were driven in shame out of Germany and back to Italy. For these devout, wise Germans understood clearly that these people would do nothing good in the time they were among us Germans. But the mendicant friars, the bare-footed friars, kept trying until finally they were able to set down roots in our land. At first they were very simple, as one can still see in the small chapel and small simple cottages in the small cloister of the bare-footed friars in Strasbourg. Just so, in other places they began with poor cottages until, through the appearance of poverty, they came to immense riches. Through them all of Germany has been mortgaged to the pope, all bishoprics, all parishes. Only the bishopric of Salzburg is blessed, which to this day has no mendicant monasteries anywhere in its territory.

The mendicant friars also sought to bring Rome into Germany through their special authority to absolve, to dispense, to constrain, to compel, to

5. Inquisitors of Heretical Depravity.

6. "*das teütsche einfeltigkeit inen ein ebner vogel härd was*"—literally, "that German innocence was for them a virtual flock of birds."

7. The Franciscans, see *The First Confederate*, 25n19.

release, as this would be the best way to get money, until our land was so filled with Roman curials, courtiers, and cardinals, that it was unequaled anywhere else.

Through such things the German people was led unawares from Christian laws to papal laws, from riches to poverty, from truth to falsehood, from loyalty to disloyalty, from uprightness to deceit, from manliness to womanliness; and all of this has come upon us by God's just, hidden judgment. But now God looks on us mercifully in our unjust suffering, and opens our eyes through an inner clear understanding, and helps us externally through the godly, Christian teaching of the highly learned, devout teachers, through which we have been able to come back to Christian truth and to German decency.

Since the pope's messengers, the mendicant friars and courtiers, observe this, they devise all manner of tricks with which they can maintain peace in their prison. And they want to hamper what is pleasing to God and promotes our honor, welfare and good so that their unreasonable, devilish, antichristian conduct might continue; to this they devote all their cleverness and thoughts, work and efforts. They seek to suppress the truth and the preachers of the truth. They slander both the honor and reputation of true teachers, they seek to injure their bodies, they make the people suspicious of their teachings, they claim that such teaching contradicts several hundred years of tradition, that it contradicts the Christian church, that it contradicts the holy teachers, that such preachers are villains, that they're heretics, etc. And with these and similar objections they want to deflect the devout Germans from the godly truth. But the true preachers and teachers have long refrained from paying them back with abusive words, until they saw that it is necessary to show the people the true reasons for the wrongs, contrary to both God and honor, with which they have been burdened until now. And this they write out in the German language so that every devout Christian can read it in his own home and think it over. And it is a sign that such teachers are right that they publish their teachings under their own names in German, so that every sensible person has time to judge them for himself. This is a sign of the truth, because they come forward into the light. But the mendicant friars and courtiers prefer to make their case with words, but not in public writings. They are hedgerow preachers,[8] they run from house to house, lead astray pious but gullible girls and other simple people. But God be praised that they don't accomplish much, because their

8. "*winkel prediger*," literally "corner preachers."

untruth stinks so badly that they are no longer able to smell, just as if they have colds.

These false hypocrites and seducers of devout hearts put a good (but false) face on untruth. Therefore, the true preachers and teachers are duty-bound to reveal as well their personal vices so that God's word is not harmed by their hypocrisy.

Since now the papists claim that their teaching is the holy scriptures, the Christian preachers are called forth to show the people that it has no basis in the scriptures.

The hypocrites say that what the Roman curia decrees is a command of the Christian church. In response the true teachers must show that the Roman curia is not the Christian church, but rather a synagogue of Satan.[9]

The monks say that the pope is an earthly god. In response the true teachers show that this is not true, that he is a bishop like any other bishop, that he has no authority over the temporal Roman Empire, that he should preach and pray—those are his duties—and leave ruling of lands and people to princes and lords.

The hypocrites put on display their holy orders and teachers, through which such teachings are smuggled in. In response the true teachers say that their orders are not holy, but rather more a means to do serious damage to Christendom. And that their teachers have always rebuked each other's falsity, from which comes their errors, and these errors cannot be defended with any scripture.

For this reason all things are translated into German for the benefit and welfare of souls, honor, goods, and lives in Germany.

The monks say such things come down to us from the ancients. So one must shove the truth directly under their noses and show them that such things as letters of indulgence, butter letters of the papal deity,[10] the great begging confirmed by papal foolishness (I mean papal freedom), also all the teachings known as *scholastica theologia*, that all of these things are not old, but rather new things, thought up in the last three hundred years by the mendicant friars and their followers. Further, that such things which did exist were not observed as they now are, and that Christendom existed for a thousand years before they appeared.

But many take the side of the monks against the true teachers, and this is the cause of some of the misunderstanding among the people. They

9. Reve 2:9; 3:9.

10. Letters granting dispensation to eat butter during the Lenten fast, see *FnhdG*, 44.

fancy that what they see before them has always been. This is part of the manifest evil, which has come about from the deceitful monkish teaching, and has made an abomination out of Christian truth. Therefore, all usurers; all priests with many benefices; all bishops with many bishoprics; lazy monks and foolish nuns, who can say nothing other than what the monks want; and all the others who support themselves in these ways cling to the monkish, Antichristian teaching.

Against this the true Christian teachers fight zealously. Erasmus, Luther, Hutten, and many others seek to bring the real truth to the people in German, and to warn everyone against the false prophets in sheep's clothing, in the hope that God will open the eyes of the poor German people so that they recognize and accept the truth and shun the lies which the monks spread both secretly and openly from the pulpit, maliciously without any fear of God, to lead astray the devout simple people.

Some say, Luther and Hutten and others should not ridicule people. But I say, when Christ and Paul saw that the common people were being led astray by the good appearance of the tempters, then they pushed aside that false appearance with all severity.

If the false saints are allowed to scorn devout teachers with no regard for the truth, then such devout teachers are allowed to show the people these knaves in their knavery to promote the truth. Because if the ignorance of the preaching friars,[11] the hypocrisy of the bare-footed Observants,[12] the knavery of the Carmelites, and the Antichristianism of the Carthusians are not brought into the clear light of day, there can be no wonder that the world is still turned upside down.

And it is proof of God's involvement that the papists and courtiers use all their authority with bulls and liberties,[13] that the mendicant friars secretly in the confessional and openly from the pulpit, in houses and on the streets, try with lies and deception to turn the people from the emerging Christian teaching, but all to no avail. Therefore, all the people should strive to translate into German beneficial, Christian, useful things, all that may serve in promoting the Gospel, faithfulness and uprightness. For, if the German nation is revived with its emperor, it can then be of service and

11. The Order of Preachers, the Dominicans.

12. The Franciscan Observants, see *The First Confederate*, 25n19.

13. Eberlin's reasons for using the term *gaben*, gifts or talents, here are not completely clear. Enders (*JEvGS* 3:385) suggests he may be referring to benefices. Götze, (*FnhdG*, 94) suggests *Bestechung*, corruption, as a possible alternative. The context suggests liberties granted by the pope.

assistance to the entire world in obtaining the truth. When the monks and papists refrain from their corrupting schemes, then others, too, will stop writing against them. But if they grow more and more stubborn in their schemes, God will certainly allow, as He did with Pharaoh and his people, that they will be completely obliterated, that the devout Germans will strike them all dead, or send them all home to the pope so he will keep them in his land, as the Germans originally did with the bare-footed friars.

If the mendicant friars did half as much damage to the pope and his court with their Antichristian conduct as they have to the devout Germans and their praiseworthy emperors, he would have rooted them out long ago, as Pope Boniface VIII once commanded that the order of bare-footed friars should be wiped from the face of the earth in one fell swoop, just as earlier the Templars were wiped out.[14] And were this to occur, little misfortune would follow. For the bare-footed order is a source of all begging among monks and nuns, and the origin of such restless running about in the world. The others have learned it from them, and assume it must be right if such hypocrites can use it to their advantage.

Oh, you pious Germans, be daring and seize the initiative, hold to the evangelical teachers and their followers. Be brave, the time is here, God is with you, for God neither can nor will tolerate any longer the great tyranny of the papists under a false Antichristian appearance, the great arrogance and wantonness of the worldly prelates, the great false deception of the mendicant friars through their superstition, or the robbery of simple Christians by monks, priests, and nuns.

Onward with joy.

14. While Boniface VIII (1294–1303) crossed swords with the rigorist Spirituals within the Franciscan Order, there is no evidence he ever sought to eradicate the order as a whole, see Lambert, *Franciscan Poverty*, 177–84. Enders (*JEvGS* 1:217) suggests that Eberlin was writing from memory here which would also explain his mistaken claim that Boniface VIII, not Clement V (1305–1314), suppressed the Knights Templar.

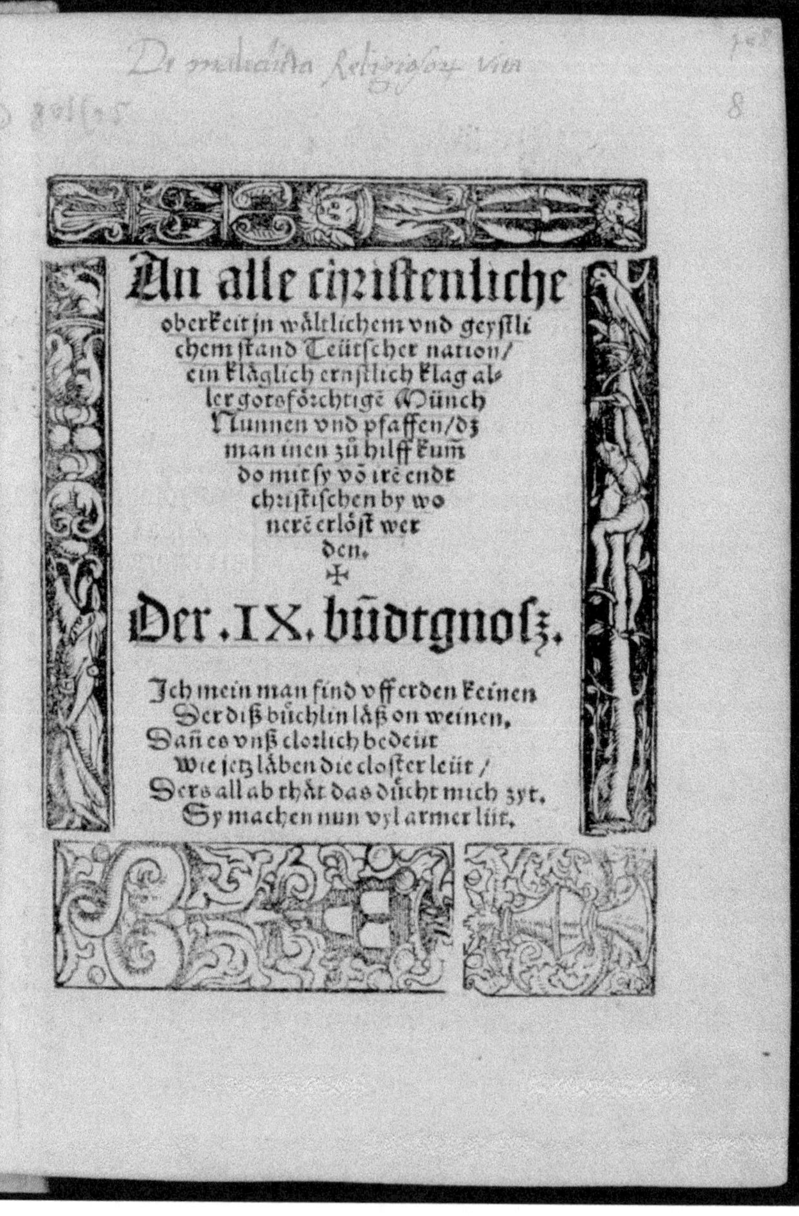

An alle christenliche
oberkeit in wältlichem vnd geystli
chem stand Teütscher nation/
ein kläglich ernstlich klag al
ler gotsförchtigē Münch
Nunnen vnd pfaffen/dz
man inen zů hilff kum
do mit sy vō irē endt
christischen by wo
nerē erlöst wer
den.

Der .IX. bůdtgnosz.

Ich mein man find vff erden keinen
Der diß büchlin läß on weinen,
Dañ es vnß clotlich bedeüt
Wie jetz läben die closter leüt/
Ders all ab thät das dücht mich zyt.
Sy machen nun vyl armer lüt.

Figure 9. *Der IX. bundtgnosz.* Bayerische Staatsbibliothek München [Res/4 H.ref. 271 y#Beibd.8]

9

The Ninth Confederate

To all Christian authorities, both worldly and spiritual, of the German Nation, a wretched, fervent lamentation of all God-fearing monks, nuns, and priests that one should come to their aid and save them from their unchristian neighbors.

There is no one on earth I fear
Who can read this little book without tears,
For it shows us all quite clearly
The lives now lived by the cloistered folk
It seems to me time for a remedy.
They leave so many people broke.

When I, the ninth confederate, read the diligent work of my comrades uncovering for the German people the mischief done to them, I thought it useful and good that I expose as well the great pressing danger and fear experienced by so many people in monasteries. Since they have often implored me to do this, out of brotherly love I have agreed to come to their aid and say the following.

You know well, courageous Germans, how often and frequently you are called upon to aid Christians tormented by the Turks, with the promise of a great indulgence and the favor of God. And this would, indeed, be a Christian act. I don't know what has kept you from it, although I suspect that your great distance from them played a significant part. But I will show you devout, decent Christians much closer at hand who are no less tormented by their seemingly good, Christian superiors than others are by Turks and heathens. Therefore, you should all help them as soon as possible out of brotherly love. Think seriously, oh faithful Germans, how unfaithfully they have treated your children, such that useless, heretical courtiers draw to themselves all benefices—often one of them has 40 or 50—and squeeze them dry so that no one can support himself from them any longer. The Romanists have taken for themselves from our land silver and gold, and everything that is valuable and useful among us. And so we have reached the point that we are unable to give our children a good upbringing unless we commit them to uncertain beggary which is despicable in the eyes of the world. Furthermore, endowed priestly benefices, which could support many people, are either depleted or, through dispensations, gathered into the hands of one person. Also, since benefices must be bought dearly from the pope or the bishops, we force our children to enter into the monasteries, into veritable prisons. In addition, some of us have been misled by the hypocrites into believing that the cloistered life alone is the true Christian life, and that everything outside the monastery walls has been dismissed by Christ with the designation "worldly." In this way, we and our children are led astray, just as, unfortunately, our ancestors have long gone astray. Until, by God's grace, such falsity daily became more obvious and now our children cry pitifully to us for help. Although they also called to us many years ago, we didn't believe them and didn't come to their aid, until they all but perished in body and soul. I fear that for this we will be called to account by God on the judgment day, for they are born German just as we are, Christians just as we are, our own flesh and blood. Other knowledgeable, decent people have passed through many monasteries and they take seriously these complaints, either on the basis of their own judgment or an awareness of the truth growing out of their cries of distress and frightened complaints. And they have learned that the suffering and distress are a thousand times greater than we could ever put down in writing. A small portion of this we want to reveal.

The great complaint of all monks and nuns is that they are all so weighed down with such unchristian, inhuman, oppressive statutes that servitude to the Turks would be less burdensome to their consciences. Their superiors claim that these statutes derive from their authority, that their authority comes from God, and therefore, that whoever is not obedient to them disobeys God. Item, no indulgence, no confession can atone for breaking these statutes; purgatory alone can do that. As a result, the consciences of their charges are always troubled, since there are so many statutes that one can hardly learn them all, much less observe them. If one offends against them, he is troubled in his conscience. And all the poor children are so afflicted by fear and scruples from the moment they enter the monastery that afterwards they will never be free from them. As they get older and wiser, and they realize what madness this is, still they cannot escape in peace. Still they are smothered[1] all their days, and their consciences gnaw at them in vain. Then the superiors say: "You can't dismiss the scruples in good conscience. For, whoever ignores his conscience paves his own way to hell." Were they subject to the Turk, they could rejoice in the hope that when they are mistreated they would soon be redeemed. Also, escape would be permitted to them, should they get the chance. But in the monastery they have to think that they are bound to such things, and they can expect no deliverance for their entire lives. None of them can even think of escaping, no matter how good his reason, because they are told that their vows are binding before God and no dispensation can help them. But see, dear friend, the great false lies and tyranny of the monastic superiors. They themselves want to be free of all their statutes, they want to be lords, and they say that the superiors have authority over the convent. To this end, they grant every liberty to their toadies so long as they remain flatterers and pleasing dissemblers. And so these are subject to less discipline and order than a common, devout lay person outside the monastery. If the superiors are reprimanded for permitting so many sins, their answer is: "We have the power of dispensation." And if one asks them why they don't grant this to the others, they answer: "The others don't conduct themselves in the same way, that is, they aren't pleasing to us." And so, contrary to God and justice, they entangle their subjects in statutes, and with these so compel them that they are willing even to say that God is not God. Everything sinful or shameful that the superiors desire, their charges do willingly. Indeed, they scramble to outdo each other, so eager is each in the hope that he will be delivered, at least in part, from such unreasonable statutes. This pleases the superiors, and they gather together all their favorites, so long as they remain pleasing to them. Moreover, they keep the others in great suffering, and they also use their chosen ones to help torment the others. As a result, there is now less truth, constancy, faithfulness, and uprightness

1. "*Versteckt*," Enders (*JEvGS* 3:383) is not completely clear on the meaning of this term, but he suggests *erstickt*, suffocated, choked, smothered.

among monks than among the bandits in Italy. For only with such wiles can they buy their freedom from their superiors, who are tyrants and can keep their charges in check only with cunning and terror. Whoever helps them in this has clear sailing ahead. But the others who are unable to do this, or who are ashamed of such dishonest conduct, are in greater danger than the devout people in the land of Württemburg under Duke Ulrich, the Devourer of People.[2]

Furthermore, in the monasteries one is not drawn to faithfulness, trust or even honor. Instead, he sees, hears and believes that he does enough simply by complying with his superiors' demands. Therefore, among the cloistered people there is no nobility of the soul, no free, steadfast, vigorous hearts, but all are servile, downtrodden, and half-desperate people. Whoever wants to increase faithfulness, trust, virtue, etc. is more despised than a virgin in a brothel.

Furthermore, all cloistered people complain that the goods which the cloistered currently possess, or which they beg daily, are so misused, without any hint of thanks, that they themselves often say that God cannot tolerate this much longer. The cloistered life is such that the longer one lives among monks and nuns, the less one wants to adopt the monastic life, unless he is a complete fool or utterly wretched; for one experiences there so much risky business, deception and faithlessness, indeed so much knavery, the likes of which one would never find in the world. All monks and nuns say that if people knew how lazy we are and how unwilling to perform our duties in the choir, what useless work it is to sing and read in the church, to observe the chapter prayer, vigils, masses, the office of the dead, that these make so little sense, that they go so unobserved, they wouldn't even give us water to wash our hands.

If the people knew of our ferocious anger, our unrelenting hatred, our obvious envy, our excessive eating and drinking, our obscene, malicious, insolent, fickle, backbiting, mocking, hurtful speech, there would be little wonder that they shunned us. If they knew of our great arrogance, how, in our cowls and appearance, in our superficial divine service, we seek worldly praise, we wouldn't be able to pass off reading three psalms in the church as the canonical hours. We tarry longer at these so that the people will hear them, for the prayer is as long as we want to make it. Also, there are many

2. Duke Ulrich of Württemberg (1487–1550) ascended the ducal throne in 1498 and was declared of age in 1503. In 1519 he was forced to concede his duchy to Emperor Charles V. In 1534, with the help of King Francis I of France, he recovered the duchy. During his exile he developed a reputation as a brigand. See *OER* 4:195; *COE* 3:464–65.

trivial matters we proclaim from the pulpit before the people, and we are more concerned about how they appear to the people than about whether or not we have accomplished them properly. Item, as a proverb among us, and especially among the bare-footed Observants,[3] states: "Something isn't a problem unless the people in the world see it."

All cloistered people complain that the superiors and their supporters are permitted to neglect the common divine office, to hold the community's rules only when they want to, to gorge themselves and tipple, to go out on a stroll, and carry on an affair. They give and take and devour without permission; they mock, provoke and tread under foot others among their brethren as they see fit. Things are such among the monks and nuns in both open and closed monasteries[4] that each does what he wishes; if he is unable to carry on an affair in person, then he does it with words and letters passed through the wall. There are many among them who try to remember something better and would prefer not to act in this way, but the others are so numerous and powerful that a noble soul can't make its mark among them. They call upon obedience, statutes, ancient customs, the examples of saints and all sorts of harsh punishments that are imposed on all who want to act contrary to the wishes of their superiors. And so the superiors and their disciples uphold nothing other than human laws and tyrannical statutes, but Christian, evangelical teaching is ridiculed among them and regarded as a source of all disobedience and knavery. To this life in the monastery has come. None have either the time or the opportunity to devote themselves to a properly repentant life. Only the body appears different, and is more restricted, than that of people in the world, but certainly not the soul. We can't devote ourselves to the contemplative life because our duties in the choir are so great they prevent us from doing anything else. After we bawl in the choir for eight or ten hours day and night, we become so weak in the head that we can't push our reason any further. For many say that everything is in order if they have sung forth in the choir, even though it's impossible to be devout or repentant on account of the amount of singing, on account of the deception, on account of the stupidity, on account of the differences in temperament—what serves one, hinders another.

Even if we wanted to apply ourselves to reading Holy Scripture during the day, there is no one to properly teach us. And if we are taught

3. The Franciscan Observants, see *The First Confederate*, 25n19.

4. Monasteries with less and more strict rules of enclosure. Occupants of closed monasteries required special permission to leave the monastery, as did outsiders to enter it.

something, it is more heathen than Christian. Then, if we want to seek what is wholesome on our own, we are unable to do it and have no useful books on the topic, nor are we allowed to consult learned people outside the monastery. In the monastery we have none, and if one of us knows something, he wants to keep it to himself and won't say anything to the others. If someone wants to dedicate himself to the Holy Gospel and the earliest teachers of the church, they call him a Lutheran, a Hussite, and under such pretense they vex him until the monastery becomes too small for him. In this way, they have forbidden the reading of Luther in many orders and monasteries, under the threat of strictest punishment. Therefore one is scorned for reading him, especially among the bare-footed Observants, who have forbidden this in their general chapter. Even more so among the Preachers[5] and Carmelites, also among the Carthusians and others.

The poor cloistered women are even more hampered in pursuing a penitent spiritual life. Even if they wanted to learn the true teaching, there is no one to teach it to them, and so they are troubled in heart and soul. Thus is the entire cloistered life more a hindrance than an aid to happiness and salvation, more pretense than substance. In all this the good suffer obvious anxiety that after these punishments they must undergo the tribulation of eternal punishment. For they can reckon that the cloistered life of our day is not a Christian activity, but rather preparation for the Antichrist. This has been obvious in many ways for a long time. In particular, this has been known to the mendicant friars, of whom there are certainly 24,000 in Germany, and it's been calculated up to 400,000 in all of Europe. And even if there were some among them who would do, or would like to do, something useful with wholesome teaching in the pulpit or confessional in exchange for their alms, they are so few that among fifty, indeed, among a hundred scarcely one is found inclined to this, as they themselves often lament. And while the simple people believe that the monks would put no one in such a post unless he was even more qualified than a secular priest, in fact, they have only unsuitable candidates, as one can see by the foolishness of the monks.[6] They were not confirmed by the Roman bishop for the purpose of singing and reading in the churches. The orders previously established to sing and read without begging were sufficient for that; and there were plenty of priests already. Rather, the mendicant friars

5. The Order of Preachers or Dominicans.

6. Subsequent comments indicate that Eberlin is referring specifically to the friars here.

were meant to preach and hear confessions where the parish priests needed them. But they wanted to rise above the parish priests and entered into such conflict with them that now this causes great harm to the people.

It was also not necessary that the mendicant friars be established to say special prayers for the people, since according to scripture this falls not to them, but to the parish priests and pastors with the cure of souls. And they should not claim that the common prayers which all Christians pray to God do not please God more and bring Him more honor than those of such lazy, bloated cloistered asses. And as they admit, among their more reasonable members there is always doubt that their begging may not stand up before God. Even if some of them wanted to preach according to their original commission, none can preach the wholesome evangelical teaching to the people without great danger. For, as is now clear, no one opposes the truth more than the mendicant friars. This is a cause of great sorrow for the devout among them, but they must either painfully hold their tongues or suffer great persecution from their stepbrothers, since everything is directed more toward self-interest and winning honor than to caring for souls. They wanted to discover a solid foundation for their begging and found that the pious man Francis,[7] a founder of the bare-footed order, is the beginning of all begging among the orders. Therefore, they investigated further the source of his begging and discovered the following in the printed bare-footed chronicles. Francis was an unlearned, simple man, and although he himself was a devout person, he attempted to do many things that have never been praised by reasonable people. He took it upon himself to write a rule which, his followers claim, he received through divine revelation. But, contradicting that claim is the fact that he lost the first rule and wanted to make another one which is completely different from the first, as can easily be seen when one reads them both, since the first was found again shortly afterward. But the Holy Spirit does not contradict Himself. Furthermore, when he made the second rule, many renowned monks from his order came together and told him they did not want to live according to the second rule. But Francis completed his second rule, which they still have, and to this day there is in no other order more discord than among the bare-footed friars. The reformed oppose the unreformed; among the reformed there is more discord than among heathens and Turks; together, all the bare-footed friars are against the other orders, and against the parish priests, priests, and bishops, as

7. Francis of Assisi (c. 1181/2–1226), *ODCC*, 632–33.

can be proven by the records of litigation resulting from these disputes in the pope's chancery and in the chanceries of all bishops.

At first there was also considerable opposition among the pope's counselors to confirming Francis' rule. The Holy Spirit at first gave sufficient warning to the heads of the Christian church, had one wanted to follow through in frustrating the designs of the mendicant friars. For nearly all of the bishops and parish priests in the whole world, as well as many of the universities, opposed them, until the papal curia realized what benefits these begging folk could bring it. Then it supported the beggars with all its authority in bulls, bans, and liberties. In response, the beggars devoted themselves to raising the pope and his designs so high that he became the equal of God, and through the beggars a broad way was prepared for the Antichrist.

And although pious Francis discussed begging in his rule, he was of the opinion that in the first place his brothers should support themselves by the work of their hands, and for their hard work they should accept nothing other than the basic necessities to nourish their bodies, without money or gold. If, however, they were not properly rewarded for their hard work, then they could turn in good conscience to simple begging. In this way Francis explained the meaning of his rule in his last testament, which the bare-footed friars hold in high regard, even equal to the rule. Further, Francis was always against his brothers building great convents and he had many of them torn down. Also, he insisted that no more than five or six of his brothers live together in a small monastery. He also placed his mantel only on simple, plain, poor people, and not many of them, who simply admonished the people to modesty and godliness. No learned man was ever to take precedence in their rustic lives. He also spoke of the ignorance of his brothers in both his rule and his testament. Even if there have been some learned people among them, they did not receive special treatment. Read the recently published histories of the bare-footed friars and their book of liberties,[8] for God has allowed these to be published so that their game would be recognized. Francis also forbade them to acquire a bull from the pope for any reason whatsoever. Rather, they should always be patient and confidently trust in God, be subject to all, suffer misfortune from all. That was his last testament, and also his rule.

8. Enders (*JEvGS* 1:217) was unable to identify the Franciscan histories and book of liberties to which Eberlin is referring here.

But the gray cowls[9] want to have praise and honor, they want to be full and lazy, and do or suffer nothing for it. They would like nothing better than to bring this about through the thunder of papal bulls, with which they can compel and bully everyone as they please, in violation of their rule and statutes.

For they have always glossed the rule to suit themselves; and then they have had their glosses approved by the pope, as if this somehow made them better. And when a pious, conscientious person has appeared among them, they've persecuted him to the fullest, until they've silenced him through misfortune and calamity. On this read the book by the bare-footed friar Humbertus von Lasslen.[10] Therefore it is certain that Francis was so committed to working with his hands for his food and drink that he insisted if one of his brothers did not know a trade, he should learn one so that with it he could earn his keep and provide a good example to the people. So it is a great evil that so many young, healthy, strong people rely entirely on begging to the misfortune of other upright paupers. For his intention was that his brothers should be industrious people. He was not thinking of learned people. Therefore, he forbade that letters be the first things that someone learned on entering the order; rather, he should first learn a trade if he did not already know one.

So you see that initially the order was not established on the basis of begging, but of manual labor. And if no one wanted to give them the basic necessities for their work, they should not dispute this, but instead patiently seek bread, until they were better rewarded.

But now the monks have gotten so lazy that they won't do their work in the monastery, except grudgingly, and they claim instead that they have to sing in the choir, which isn't prescribed for them.

They say that they preach and therefore they should eat from their begging. In fact, among twenty, hardly one is found to preach, and among thirty preachers hardly half of one is suited to the task, as is so obvious now. And it would have been better if the mendicant friars had never appeared on the earth.

Now, when St. Francis had begun his activities, Dominic[11] also followed along with his schemes, and when several hermits saw the advantages in begging, they, too, wanted to adopt the mendicant life and called

9. The Franciscans, see *The First Confederate*, 25n20.

10. The identity of Humbert of Lasseln is unknown.

11. Dominic (c. 1174–1221), *ODCC*, 496–97.

themselves the Hermits of St. Augustine. Then the Carmelites started begging, until almost the whole world is full of beggars.[12]

Devout, decent people among the mendicant orders need to reflect on the fact that they have to live off alms and do nothing praiseworthy for them, nor may they do any such thing in front of the others. And they fear that they sin by devouring so unjustly what people should earn by the sweat of their brows, and so they fall into the devil's hands. As a result, great knavery continues under the appearance of good in this monkish subterfuge.

The Preachers lament the great, unspeakable ravages that still exist in Christendom because of their order. Therefore, they stick together to suppress and destroy all clever people of the world, as they did with Jan Hus, Jerome of Prague, John of Wesel, Johannes Reuchlin, Martin Luther, Jean Gerson, Erasmus of Rotterdam.[13] Furthermore, if there is among them someone similar to such honorable people, he must suffer the same fate. Indeed, as many chronicles show, they are willing even to undermine the pope and emperor if they want to undertake something displeasing to them. In this way they devour unspeakable profit, which they also pilfer from their poor cloistered sisters.

The bare-footed friars must daily expect great tribulation, which several kind-hearted people among them fear, not without cause. For they do great violence to their rule with excessive begging, with laziness, and with jealousy and hatred and malicious behavior among themselves, so that in 40 years there will be few, if any, useful people among them. An elderly, experienced man from the bare-footed order, who once had some authority among them, told me this. There is more order among all other estates than among them. They rule over their lay brothers or *conversen*, whom they take on in the place of servants, with an iron fist, so that even priests and

12. From its formation in 1209, the Franciscan Order was committed to a life of mendicancy. The Dominicans, formed in 1216, adopted mendicancy in 1221. In 1256 Pope Alexander IV consolidated several small groups of hermits into the Augustinian Hermits and granted them the name and privileges of mendicant friars. The origins of Carmelites are traced to groups of hermits in Palestine in 1156. The order was confirmed by Pope Honorius III in 1224 and made a mendicant order by Innocent IV in 1245. See *ODCC*, 131–32, 289–90, 497–98, 634–36, 1070.

13. Eberlin includes here a list of individuals who ran afoul of the Dominicans in their role as inquisitors: Jan Hus (c. 1372–1415), *ODCC*, 806–7; Jerome of Prague (c. 1379–1416), ibid., 868; John of Wesel (c. 1400–1481), ibid., 898; Johannes Reuchlin (1455–1522), ibid., 1389–90, *COE* 3:145–50; and Jean Gerson (1363–1429), *ODCC*, 669–70. The addition of the names of Erasmus and Luther to this list highlights their place in ongoing attempts by the Dominicans to suppress the truth.

learned people must be subject to them in all things to the derision and general suffering of worldly people, as I have often seen when they visit my house and home. It would be much better that a devil came to visit than these beggars.

The Carmelites claim that their first foundation was not established on the basis of begging, and that their predecessors left this first foundation, which was good, and took up precarious begging. But, since they had no rule, and nothing was required of them other than to do good, no good-hearted person among them noticed the consequences. The Augustinians make similar complaints, but I don't think things are as bad among the Augustinians as among the others. They have almost never distinguished themselves in deceit and discord; furthermore, they also fear evil from perilous begging.

All cloistered women, especially those under the authority of the mendicant friars, complain of great hardship. They are more than evilly served with father confessors and preachers who also have their own allegiances, and what one favors, the others oppose. Furthermore, among them no abbess or prioress can keep peace in her house, because the monks always form factions within the convent, stirring up one group against the abbess, and establishing their own followings. The monks want to deny the poor nuns any chance to see their devout father and mother and siblings, and the nuns say that it seems to them that the monks want to be the only object of their affection. When the provincials, together with other monks, visit a women's convent one or even four times a year, they first have themselves shaved and washed and creases are pressed into their cowls, especially the bare-footed Observants and the Preaching Monks, so that they are pleasing to their "betrothed." But the nuns say that the monks can't find favor with them, and they refuse to look at them. The monks devour roasted or boiled meat and drink the best wine, and the nuns have to cook such meals for them, but are themselves not allowed to eat any meat. They force the nuns to confess nearly every day, so that the monks can practice their hostility or kindness under this guise.

The monks seek in all places how to bring a child into the monastery, but then they leave the poor child to sink or swim without any help, so that they want to scream bloody murder. For this reason, not only do the enclosed cloistered women under their care, but also the Beguines,[14] have

14. Women leading pious communal lives but not members of formal monastic communities, see *ODCC*, 178–79.

significant complaints against them, about which nothing more can be said. I won't report now about the complaints of the Carthusians, the Benedictines, the Bernardines[15] and other similar orders, whose unsuitable lives cry out to the whole world.

For these reasons, dear friends, dear pious Germans, I have been entreated by many decent, pious cloistered folk to show you their distress and torment, and to seek your help for them. The Carthusians, Benedictines, Bernardines, Premonstratensians, Regulars, Williamites[16] have no other purpose on earth than to fleece and skin the poor. But one can't stand up to them on account of their riches. And there are so many mendicant friars that we have to fear there is no way to get rid of them all. Therefore, the pious monks have thought that it would be pleasing to God if they removed their cowls, were ashamed of their laziness, and from now on they supported themselves by doing priestly work—such as preaching, being a parish priest—or by being a parish priest's helper, asking nothing for their services other than the bare essentials. Those unable to do this want to work, to serve, and as they are able to earn their keep in a way pleasing to God. They hope that God will support them, they don't want to seek any special pleasures or riches. For if God sustains them in their sinful "monkish" begging, which offends against God and the statutes of their own rule, He will certainly provide for them if they leave off such things and put their trust in godly provision and in the common command to work for one's keep. It is no sin for them to remove their cowls, or even to take wives, for they were too young when they took their vows of chastity. Indeed, God wants this from them and they do God a service by it.

The nuns desire that their confinement be eased a bit, for many must die or suffer constant illness because they are not permitted trips to the baths and other cures. Although no legitimate original rule states that a women's convent must be sealed up, the devil devised this requirement through the malicious monks; especially that they should eat no meat,

15. The Carthhusians were founded in 1084 by Bruno of Cologne, see *ODCC*, 293–94. The beginnings of the Benedictine Order are usually dated to the founding of the monastery at Monte Cassino by Benedict of Nursia in 529, see ibid., 186–87. In this case the name Bernardines refers to the Cistercian Order (founded 1098) in honor of one of its most renowned members, Bernard of Clairvaux (1090–1153), see ibid., 354–56.

16. The Premonstratensians, the Order of Canons of Prémontré was founded by Norbert of Xanten in 1120. Regulars likely refers to canons regular in general terms. The Williamites are likely a hermit congregation named after a St. William in Tuscany. It may have been one of the congregations incorporated into the Augustinian Hermits in 1256. See *ODCC*, 1321.

which God permitted them; also that they should observe such burdensome choir duty, even more burdensome than the monks'; that it is not contrary to their rule that they are burdened with the monks' statutes; that they can confess to whomever they confide in. Nonetheless, one must be patient when so much shame and damage, contrary to God's will, occurs among them. Even if one fears mischief in following this path, still it is not as ungodly as it was before. Therefore, beloved, pious Germans, reach out your hand to such kind-hearted cloistered folk. If any of them are of a mind to leave their order, don't be angry with them, don't think them any less devout or honorable, for they aren't betraying decency, nor God's law, nor their rule, because no rule has stipulated that there should be such ungodly activities in the monasteries.

You should know that whoever helps such a cloistered person out of this situation will receive a greater indulgence than if he had gone to Rome or to St. James.[17] Whoever helps one of these cloistered folk from this, redeems a soul from a sinful life no less than if he married a common whore for God's sake. Christ will reward you if you help Him win back one of these Christian souls. Oh dear friends, if you knew what sort of Turkish regime there is in the monasteries, what antichristian practices, what a great purgatory for pious persons, you would take pity on them. Their souls torment them more than their bodies do; they are not concerned with temporal things, but they find it unbearable that in their distress they should also find themselves enemies of God. Now they realize that this false cloistered pretense cannot bring them salvation, especially the mendicant friars, since they are young and healthy, and in the eyes of God they don't deserve to eat on the basis of begging, nor is their work in the canonical hours sufficient to justify their begging. Since no one is permitted to preach to you godly, evangelical teachings, but instead one has to preach devilish, antichristian things, he damns your souls.

Therefore, you compassionate Germans, take pity on these people and protect them if they flee to you. Don't think that they must observe their vows. Oh God, these are evil, destructive vows which God has forbidden in Scripture to be observed in this way. They certainly have a good appearance, but great damage comes from them. It is to be feared that God's great anger often comes upon the world on account of the monks' wanton vocation and lives. Should you help one such monk out of this situation for God's sake,

17. Presumably Santiago de Compostela.

you would do more than if you endowed an anniversary mass in perpetuity, a perpetual light, an eternal mass, indeed, even a new monastery.

You pious Christians, do you have a compassionate heart in you, then take pity on the inhuman suffering of the cloistered folk. Do you have a drop of Christian blood in you, then pity them their unchristian practices. Do you have a free German sinew in you, then take pity on their barbarous imprisonment. Are they not your flesh and blood, your countrymen, your fellow Christians? Take pity on them so they aren't corrupted so badly in body and soul.

Oh, you honorable bailiffs, mayors, councils and courts in villages, cities and on the land, visit twice every year the monasteries in your territories, for they incarcerate their prisoners in inhumane conditions. Rescue the prisoners, for no Turk binds more severely than the monks when they have imprisoned their brethren; since the imprisoned are more devout than the free.

I believe that hail and storms and pestilence have descended on many places on account of such prisoners, who cry out to God in their suffering for help and vengeance. Therefore, visit often the prisons in the monasteries. You are held accountable for this before God. You've been told; don't try to make excuses. If they claim that they aren't subject to your authority, that is true only so long as they act justly, but when it comes to unjust actions they are subject to you and to everyone else. God will grant you happiness and good fortune for your service.

Come, come, you pious Germans, put your hand to the plow, be brave, God is with you.

All monks who flee the monastery for the world don't intend to make demands, either on the basis of law or force, on their friends and their monasteries. Rather, their intent is to commit themselves to God and faithfully serve others for their daily bread. For the cloistered life is now nothing but drunkenness, sin, mischief, purgatory, hell.

I didn't want to keep these requests of the cloistered folk from the German nation. Furthermore, I wanted to reveal their purposes to you so that now that you have heard their reasons, no one will be angered by their departure. There are so many decent people in the world. What a pity it would be if no one was pious besides the cloistered folk, what with their cowls, their cords,[18] their veils, their scapulars, their babbling and shriek-

18. The cincture or girdle normally worn with an alb. In the Western church it was usually a simple cord meant to symbolize clerical chastity and spiritual vigilance, see *ODCC*, 679.

ing in the choir, their avoidance of meat and their gossiping, their refusal to wear linen shirts and their jealousy, their frequent fasting and refusal to do good for one another.

Furthermore, since God provides for such a great big world, He will also provide for decent people who leave the monastery for reasons of conscience. Any honorable man should be ashamed if he has a friend in a monastery where he eats in sloth, in God's enmity and to the disgust of the people, what has been produced by the sweat of the poor. It would be more honorable to have a pig keeper as a cousin.

The monks don't need a dispensation from the pope or from their unwilling superiors in the monastery any more than a whore needs a dispensation from her pimp if she wants to become virtuous.

If, however, the monasteries were organized according to true Christian form, they would be happy to return to them. In the meantime, they don't want to be in these synagogues of Satan, these schools of sin, in these hypocritical assemblies, in which no one is able to follow a Christian life without great torment and of which, by God's grace, they certainly have had enough. For each person may avail himself of all seemly freedoms and comforts on earth up to the point where God restricts him with His commandments.

Everything about the cloistered life in our time, all their statutes, rules, vows, their conception of God not drawn from the Gospel, isn't worth one day's fast. For this reason alone they maintain all their hypocrisy and deception, and suppress evangelical teaching. Take your friend home from the monastery. Are you rich? Give him what you give daily to the poor; that doubles your alms.

I can't say any more now—the matter is vast, and my time is up. You hear their pitiful complaint; therefore, give them all possible help.

Be happy, your deliverance is at hand.

New statutē
die Psitacus gebracht hat
vß dem lād Wolfaria wel-
che beträffendt reformie-
rung geystlichen stand.

Wañ man annäm diß re-
formatz/
So gschweigt man man-
che kloster katz/
Die vornen läckt vnd hin-
den kratzt.

Der. X. būdt
gnosz.

BIBLIOTHECA
REGIA
MONACENSIS.

Figure 10. *Der X. bundtgnosz.* Bayerische Staatsbibliothek München
[Res/4 H.ref. 271 y#Beibd.9]

10

The Tenth Confederate

New statutes concerning reform of the spiritual estate which Psittacus[1] brought from the land of Wellfaria.[2]

In adopting these reforms
One silences the cloister cats;
They'll lick you in front,
In the back they'll scratch.

I, THE TENTH CONFEDERATE, want to present for the benefit of all an outline of the fair government of Wellfaria as follows. We the magistrates and councilors[3] of the land of Wellfaria announce to whoever reads, or has read to them, these statutes, by-laws and ordinances that all of these canons were ordained by us, after deliberate reflection, for the benefit our land, cities, villages and hamlets.[4] And we bind you to them under the threat of being labeled a disobedient and godless citizen.

1. The name *Psittacus* is both a play on the name of Eberlin's cousin, Huldrich Sittick, and a pun meaning either "the parrot" or "the ear-blower." See Seibt, *Utopica*, 73 and *JEvGS* 1:221.

2. "*Wolfaria*," the land where one "fares well."

3. "*Ringk manner*," named for the ring or place in rural Swiss communities where the council met, see Laube, *Flugschriften* 1:85n2.

4. "*Fläcken*." There is some ambiguity in Eberlin's use of the term *fläcken*. In some cases it appears to mean "hamlet" or "village" and in some others "region" or "place"

Since both law and reason teach us that one should honor the one true God above all else and place all trust first in Him, we shall have pastors[5] who exhort us to serve God according to His commandments. And therefore, each parish shall have two pastors: a parish priest and a chaplain who will receive the same benefice, but the chaplain shall be under the direction of the parish priest. Every Sunday during mass the parish priest shall teach an evangelical lesson on important parts of our law. During Vespers the chaplain shall give a brief sermon to the children so that they will learn Christian discipline.

On Feast Days

We wish to have only the following feast days: every Sunday, Christmas and the following three feast days, New Years' Day, Epiphany, Maundy Thursday, Good Friday, Easter Eve and Easter Day, Ascension Day, Pentecost, Corpus Christi, Annunciation, the Feast of Our Lady's Ascension, Our Lady's Candlemas, the Feast of Saints Peter and Paul, all of which have in Europe special sermons. The Feast of St. John the Baptist, who fought so dutifully for the truth. All angels feast on Michaelmas. All Saints' Day.[6]

Each church shall have a feast on the day of its patron saint: St. Agnes, St. Cecelia, St. Anastasia, etc.

All other feast days we discard as useless, harmful things, because God is greatly angered by this hypocrisy.

On Fasting Days

Everyone who is able should fast on the three days before Easter.

One should fast on the evenings before all feast days, with the exception of evenings before Sundays.

---

seems the better translation.

5. "*Pfaffen.*" Eberlin uses the term *Pfaffe* to denote both the old-style priests and the new-style pastors. I have translated the term as "priest" or "pastor" depending on the context in which Eberlin is using it. The related term *Pfarrer* I have translated consistently as parish priest.

6. The lesser known feasts retained by Eberlin were celebrated on the following days: The Feast of Our Lady's Ascension (August 19), Our Lady's Candlemas (February 2), The Feast of Saints Peter and Paul (June 29), The Feast of St. John the Baptist (June 24). See Laube *Flugschriften* 1:75.

One should observe the *Quadragesima* before Easter[7] with fasting and singing as one now observes Advent—whoever wants to may fast, but no one should be compelled to this.

No father confessor shall impose fasting as a form of penance. All fasting days should be observed in the following manner: one shall not eat more than twice during the day, that is, in the morning at 10 o'clock and in the evening at 5 o'clock.

All foods are allowed during fasts with the exception of meat, fish and foreign wines.

On pain of strictest punishment no more fasting days should be established, and all other fasting days should be abolished.[8]

How One Should Observe Feast Days

To avoid incurring our displeasure, everyone, and especially adults, shall come to the church on the morning of all feast days to celebrate mass.

In church one should play neither organs nor pipes, nor sing songs with complicated melodies,[9] but only a serious song from the common mass and vespers.

During the mass, the parish priest should preach as was indicated above.

After the benediction everyone should go home and eat; there should be no preaching then because this harms the body and does nothing useful for the soul.

After eating, honest folk may go visit friends or go for a walk.

Young people may bowl, shoot,[10] engage in athletic contests,[11] or perform for the people interesting comedies which we call Easter plays. But in all these things decency must be maintained and offence avoided. The young women may sing rounds with each other, but not with the men, or throw balls or sing *Meisterlieder*[12] respectably.

7. The forty days before Easter, Lent.

8. Cf. Eberlin's discussion of fasting in *The Second Confederate*.

9. *Yn figuris singen*. Eberlin is rejecting more complicated polyphonic liturgical songs and demanding a return to more simple plainsong.

10. Ozment, *Reformation in the Cities*, 98, translates this as throwing darts. Presumably any sort of target practice could be meant.

11. *Barr louffen*, a medieval athletic contest in which two teams race against each other, possibly similar to a relay race. See Laube, *Flugschriften* 1:86n13.

12. Songs composed according to a strict set of rules which flourished since the

No dances should be held on feast days, but we do not prohibit them during the week. We have established so few feast days so that people will observe them properly.

On feast days cards and dice and chess should not be played for any stakes higher than a penny.[13]

At three o'clock in the afternoon everyone shall return to church where there will be a sermon; all the children and young people should be there. And this sermon should occur after the reading and before the hymn, so that one sings a hymn after the sermon.

Every feast day evening one should come to church. There they should not sing, but together pray for the dead as God admonishes, and all should visit the grave sites of their parents, from which comes great benefit. The pastors should impress this on the people.

During mass, after the sermon, instead of an offering everyone should take to the altar whatever he wants to give the poor; or he can bring a note indicating what the poor can expect to receive at his house. During the following week these alms shall be distributed judiciously to the poor.

Under pain of strictest punishment, the canonical hours shall be abolished throughout the land as a poison to true worship.

On Pastors

Each parish shall have two pastors and no more. They should have wives unless they choose to remain celibate. Their wives should have been born in the place where they hold their benefice. And the pastors themselves should be born in the place where they hold their benefices, or not far away from there.

Among twenty parish priests one shall be regarded as a bishop who should manage spiritual affairs with the advice of all the pastors. Every month he should call them all together and impress upon them God's law. Each pastor shall receive annually 200 florins from the common purse of the place and no more.

The bishop shall always receive 15 florins less than the other pastors.

---

middle of the fifteenth century in numerous cities in southern Germany. After the beginning of the Reformation they became an important medium for the spread of reforming ideas, see *ER* 3:41.

13. Cf. Eberlin's discussion of this subject in *The Eleventh Confederate*.

On pain of serious punishment one should not give any pastor anything special for his services, neither as an offering, nor as a penance fee, nor as a donation to benefit the soul.[14]

Each parish priest shall have a deacon who should be a "chantry priest". One shall give him 100 florins annually, and if he is willing and suited, he should be given the benefice when it becomes available.

No pastor should change his benefice unless physical necessity requires him to.

No longer shall there be priestly ordination, but when a pastor or deacon dies or leaves, the parishioners in that place, together with their pastors, shall elect another; then the bailiff and the local court, along with the bishop, shall install him in his office.

Whenever a pastor's wife dies, he may take another.

One shall give no tithes to the pastors.[15]

The pastors should be respectably dressed as is fitting for other honorable men.

They should no longer be tonsured.

They shall have no privileges beyond those of other citizens, but one should show them the same honor as one shows secular officials.

The bailiff and council in a village[16] shall have the same authority over the pastors as over other people.

Any pastor who acts dishonorably in his teaching or in public transgression of God's law should be publicly judged, without any reservations, just like any other public, noxious evil-doer.

If someone no longer wishes to be a pastor, he may give up his office and again be a layman. If he is subsequently re-elected, he may again be a pastor.

Pastors are allowed to pursue all honorable livelihoods or trades.

No pastor shall be a merchant, bailiff, innkeeper or councilor.

They should study and pray, and keep their households in order.

No one under the age of thirty shall become a pastor, under pain of serious penalty.

14. Simon, *Deutsche Flugschriften*, 182n30, suggests that Eberlin is referring here to the endowment of masses for the dead.

15. By way of contrast, *The Seventh Confederate* advises that both the great and small tithe still be given to the clergy.

16. For Eberlin's description of the roles of the bailiff and council in village administration, see *The Eleventh Confederate*.

With their wages pastors may buy land and cultivate it from their homes just like other people.[17]

On Monks

We demand of all our bailiffs in villages and in cities that in accordance with our instructions they compel with force all monks and nuns to put aside the clothing they have worn until now, as such distinctive clothing represents great inequality.

Whoever wants to leave a monastery may do so, unless one chooses to remain in it.

Those in the monasteries should wear ordinary clothing just like other respectable people outside the monastery.

No one should be allowed to pledge oneself to remain in a monastery unless one is thirty years old. And no monastery shall contain more than ten people who want to remain there indefinitely.

All monasteries shall be nothing other than schools for the young, where one teaches boys, women and girls Christian commands and discipline.

In any city or hamlet where there are more than two monasteries for men and two for women, any additional shall be disbanded and converted into hospitals for the poor.

Some of these shall be designated to care for old, poor citizens who have served the city as envoys or public officials for a long time, or for their sick children. Such hospitals shall be appropriately endowed and nicely built. Some shall serve pilgrims, some the city's common poor. All other wealth from the monasteries not needed for schools or hospitals shall be put into the common purse for public buildings and salaries of the city.

On Mendicant Friars

On pain of death, all mendicant orders should be completely disbanded.

Their monasteries shall be converted into communal residences which a city may rent out on annual leases to citizens who do not have their own houses. Many domestic servants may live in a monastery.

17. Baldini, "*Gli Statuti di Wolfaria*," 42, suggests a slightly different translation here: "I preti possono acquistare col proprio salario possedimenti terrieri e, come gli altri uomini, costruirvi l'abitazione con l'aiuto dei propri familiari."

Whoever still wishes to be a monk or nun in spite of the above ordinance, may do so in his or her own house without distinctive clothing or orders and without establishing any common rule.

On Confession

We require that all persons appear once annually before the parish priests or their chaplains; in this way, if they are in need of counsel or special instruction, they may ask the pastor for it; if they are very simple, the pastor may provide this counsel on his own initiative.

We do not wish that anyone feel compelled to tell one's secrets to the pastors unless one wishes to. And this command shall be proclaimed once a year from the open market place.

But whoever wishes may go to the pastors as often as desired for instruction or consultation according to one's own needs.

On Marriage

As soon as a girl is fifteen years old and a boy eighteen, they should be brought together in marriage, with the exception of those who choose to remain celibate. When a marriage breaks up as the result of the death of one of the partners, the survivor should remarry within ten weeks, with the exception of those who choose to remain celibate. When one partner suffers a great obstacle to the performance of his or her conjugal duties, the partners may separate and each may choose a new spouse. I say this on account of great discord. No one shall be ashamed to request a spouse.

Whoever secretly marries without the witness and counsel of honorable people shall be drowned.

There shall be no impediments to marriage on the basis of spiritual association;[18] whatever does not restrict marriage in the law of Moses shall not restrict it among us.

Marriage shall not be regarded as a sacrament among us.

There shall be no prostitutes in brothels.

Confirmation shall not be a separate sacrament among us, neither shall extreme unction nor ordination.

18. I.e., through godparents.

In the churches men and women shall be separated and the children shall be grouped together with members of the same sex.

On the Mass

No masses should be read except on feast days. Then all people shall attend mass and there together pray to God.

On Cemeteries

No cemetery shall be in the vicinity of a monastery, nor shall there be any in villages or in cities; they should be by the parish churches. And by every cemetery there shall be a church or a house where the people can assemble on the evenings of feast days and pray for the dead. Furthermore, there may be many cemeteries, but not more than one parish church.

On Dying

When one is dying, it is not necessary that one be visited by a pastor unless one wishes special counsel or consolation. It is not necessary that one confesses as one now confesses. One may certainly confess unresolved wrongdoing and ask those angered by it for forgiveness.

A pastor or deacon should give the holy sacrament of Christ's body to the sick. As well, friends and neighbors should visit a sick person, pray to God on his behalf, comfort him and read the Gospel law to him.

On Testaments

Each person who has a livelihood shall, as soon as he reaches the age of discernment, establish a testament or inventory of his possessions. One may change such testaments as often as one wishes, but when one dies, the most recent testament will be regarded as binding.

Without the knowledge and agreement of the bailiff nothing should be bequeathed to public institutions, neither to churches nor schools nor hospitals, so that they will not become too rich and no ill may be caused that comes from such bequests, as has so often occurred.

On the Dead

When someone has died, close friends and neighbors should accompany the dead person to the graveyard with their prayers, and on Sunday the names of those who died during the week should be announced and a common prayer held for the departed. No mourning clothes should be worn for more than seven days, under pain of serious penalty. One should do nothing special in remembrance of the dead aside from giving alms and praying. On every feast day one should admonish the people in all sermons to die joyfully, and whoever does not die willingly shall not be buried among other Christians.

On Receiving the Sacraments

Every feast day the pastor shall have consecrated hosts and a chalice, and whoever wishes may receive the sacrament. It is not necessary to make a special confession to the pastor before this. One should not give the sacrament to any sinner who leads a scandalous life. It should be given to all others without their being asked about their confession.

Those who wish to go to the sacrament should do so in the certain hope that God will have mercy on their sins and that they will receive God's help to lead a Christian life. And this preparation will be sufficient. Five sacraments should be observed: baptism, the body and blood of Christ, absolution, prayer, and diligent observation of God's word. The sacrament of the altar shall be given to all mature people,[19] whether young or old, and only to those. The sacrament shall be given to all people in both kinds, and one should put a straw[20] in the chalice, through which one can drink Christ's blood. All shall be free to receive the sacrament of the altar according to their wishes.

Children should be baptized immediately after birth.

19. "*Verstendig*," literally "understanding," i.e., those able to understand its significance.

20. "*Rörlein*," a siphon tube. Use of such a device was widespread since the thirteenth century. See Simon, *Deutsche Flugschriften*, 188n57.

A Common Ordinance Concerning the Number of Old Monks

So that the rabble and vermin of priests, monks and nuns, whose numbers have grown without limit, be suitably decreased, it is our command that, in order to reduce their numbers, for ten years no one be allowed to become a monk or nun; also in the meantime no one should become a priest and all should remain in their callings.[21] After ten years all benefices should be revoked from them with the exception of those detailed in the ordinance above. Old or sick monks and nuns shall be placed in the above-mentioned good hospices until the end of their lives; the same should happen with the priests. With this decree we defrock all priests and make them again laymen with the exception of two in each parish.

Where several noble nuns are in a cloister, they shall be brought together in groups of fifty to a cloister, and there live as free women until they die or marry. One should also give the prebends from wealthy hospices to noble priests.

We order that in each bishopric a *collegium* be established for male persons, well endowed with essentials, for esteemed citizens or peoples' children who are poor or sick; each year one should give them 120 florins for food and essentials. They shall be free, without liturgy or rules. Each should have his own room and a servant, and one of them shall be the housefather.

A similar *collegium* we order to be established for noble maidens or widows, for esteemed female citizens, and each year they should be given 100 florins. Within the walls of the *collegium* each should have her own little house, and one should be housemother with authority over the others. They should be allowed to marry.

On Village Parishes

No village should have a parish priest unless it contains five hundred mature persons. As many villages as are necessary to have five hundred mature persons shall come together to make up a parish. If four or five hamlets belong to a parish, each village should have a chapel, in which on all feast days the people should come together, in cases when legitimate impediments

21. Simon, *Deutsche Flugschriften*, 189n59, suggests Eberlin's meaning here is that all should spend the next ten years keeping a look out for a new vocation.

keep them from attending the parish church, and one should read to them the fifth, sixth and seventh chapters of the Gospel according to Matthew, so that: those who are unable to go to the parish church because of legitimate impediments should come together in this chapel on the mornings of feast days and there pray, and then the chantry priest should stand up and read aloud the above mentioned chapters, for in these chapters are summed all of the evangelical law.[22] Therefore, each village should have a deacon as chantry priest who shall bring the sacrament to the sick who are unable to have a pastor.

Each village shall have its own cemetery.

The schoolmasters shall be admonished to go occasionally on feast days into a poor village and give villagers God's good message.

Note Here

The above-described ordinance concerning the number of years in which we will allow the monks to die out does not refer to the mendicant orders, because these we want to disband immediately.

On Prayer

We forbid, on pain of decapitation, that the people be taught any prayer other than the holy *Pater Noster*.[23]

One should teach no more than the common confession of faith which one is accustomed to pray.

Also, in the churches one should sing neither the Athanasian nor the Nicene Creeds, but only the Apostolic.

All Psalters, Crown Prayers,[24] rosaries, *hortulus anime*, *paradisus anime*[25] and such prayer books, and all similar priestly breviaries should be done away with at once.

22. These chapters of Matthew contain the Sermon on the Mount, which at this point Eberlin saw as the essence of Christ's teaching.

23. Cf. Eberlin's comments on prayer in *The Fourth Confederate*.

24. A devotional exercise associated with the rosary consisting of thirty-three "Our Fathers" and five "Hail Marys." See *JEvGS* 1:215–16. See also, Eberlin's comments in *The Sixth Confederate*, above, 75.

25. Commonly used titles for prayer and devotional books since the end of the fifteenth century, see *JEvGS* 1:220.

On Holy Pictures

No molded, carved, or hewn picture should be in the church. All pictures should be flat and painted. No pictures of saints should be in the churches except those about whom the biblical books tell us.

No precious picture or painting should be in the churches.

On Church Decorations

Churches should be built wide and strong and all precious decorations should be kept out of the churches.

With the exception of the chalice, straw in the chalice and paten there should be no silver or gold in the church.

There should be no precious stones and no elaborate vestments; the two pastors should use only common cloth for vestments, although the colors may be changed.

It is not fitting to make use of expensive things in the church of Christ where one teaches people to disdain such things.

In the churches one should not read, sing or teach anything not described in the biblical books.

We forbid henceforth that any nun or other woman publicly sing or read in church.

On Pilgrimages

No one shall go on a pilgrimage and beg. No one shall go on a pilgrimage which does not include begging unless he first gets permission in writing from his parish priest and his bailiff. If he is rich, he should pay ten florins for this permission. If he is poor, to get this permission he should work alone on the communal fields for ten days, receiving only his food in payment.

On the Roman Seat

Henceforth, no one from our land should go to Rome, neither for business nor for devotional reasons, so that our people do not become Antichristian and more wicked than Sodom and Gomorrah.

No one shall consider or call the Roman bishop our rightful superior.

All the bishops of our land shall come together once a year and then discuss ecclesiastical matters; the bishop in whose diocese the meeting is held should preside over it. These meetings should not always be held in the same place, but should move around.

On Schools

Henceforth, the writings of no scholastic doctor shall be read except as the object of ridicule.

All canon law and decretals shall be publicly burned.

No philosophy shall be read except for what Didymus Faventinus taught in his oration against Thomas Placentinus.[26]

Latin, Greek and Hebrew shall be taught in all schools; every day one should have two lessons on the evangelical law.

In Conclusion

These statutes we want to be taken seriously under the penalties originally ordained, to which all shall comply. Dated in our city of Baldeck on the 35th day of Ubelis in the year in which Easter fell on a Monday.[27]

O Christian man, take this to heart,
No Shrovetide jokes did we impart,
'ere true faith's victory is won,
Many abuses must be gone.
And once the monks are chased away,
Then faith with all its strength will stay.
Time brings roses.

26. *Didymi Faventini adversus Thomam Placentinum pro Martino Luthero theologo oratio*, Phillip Melanchthon's response to the Dominican Thomas Rhadinus who published a theological justification for the papal bull against Luther.

27. There has been some discussion of Eberlin's fictional dating of this and the next Confederate. Lederer, "Welfare Land," 173, suggests that *Baldeck* be translated as Aroundthecorner and *ubelis* as the month of evil, thereby highlighting further Eberlin's satirical intent in the work. Baldini, *Gli "Statuti di Wolfaria,"* 28, has made a similar observation about the name of Wellfaria's capital.

Ein newe ord
nūg weltlichs ſtädts das
Pſitacus anzeigt hat
in Wolfaria beſchri
ben.

Der. XI. būdt
gnoſz.

Figure 11. *Der XI. bundtgnosz.* Bayerische Staatsbibliothek München [Res/4 H.ref. 271 y#Beibd.10]

11

The Eleventh Confederate

A new ordinance concerning the secular estate written in Wellfaria, as described by Psittacus.[1]

I, THE ELEVENTH CONFEDERATE, will present to you what Psittacus says about matters considered by the regents when establishing an ordinance for secular affairs in Wellfaria. However, these statutes have not yet been approved but only proposed, because in that land they may not make rules for all cities and villages unless such an ordinance is first publicly made known in all bailiwicks and the people asked if the rules are pleasing to them. Nonetheless, I will not keep from you their plan.

Beginning

There will be no more honest work or livelihood than field work. All nobles shall support themselves through field work.

Each village will have one nobleman who shall have as many fields as two ploughs can work. This nobleman shall be mayor of the village. As many villages as it takes to have 200 farms will have a knight as its bailiff. Each month this bailiff shall call together the mayors, as well as from each village an alderman from the peasantry, and render judgment with them about pressing complaints of the subjects.

1. On the identity of Psittacus, see *The Tenth Confederate*, 118–19.

Each bailiwick shall make its own laws, which are beneficial to its inhabitants, and such laws shall be ratified by all the people of the bailiwick after they have been personally asked about them.

Each city shall have ten of these bailiwicks under its jurisdiction; however, if they are unable to have that number, they will be designated a walled town and not a city.

Each walled town shall have a magistrate who shall be a baron.

The official presiding over a city shall be a count.

Ten cities shall have a magistrate who shall be a duke or a prince.

No official shall have the authority to act without the aid and advice of representatives established or ordained by the majority of the subjects.

Each walled town, city, and principality shall make useful commands and laws for itself and abide by them.

From among the princes one shall be named king, who also cannot make decrees without the advice and aid of the princes.

No mayor, bailiff, baron, count, prince or king shall derive any special profit from his office, but shall perform all his duties for the comfort and aid of his subjects, and also to further the common good. But they shall be supported from the common purse according to the extent of their work.

None of the above-mentioned officials shall have any special possessions on account of their office except for what is necessary to maintain their own households.

If an official needs help for the common good, all subjects shall put their lives and goods at his service, as he is always the first among them.

As many nobles as peasants shall sit in all councils.

On the Estate of Marriage

We order that all public adulterers be put to death.

None of the above-mentioned offices shall be inherited, but a friend, or the son of a friend, or a father of an office-holder may be elected by all the subjects, as it pleases the people.

On Raising One's Glass[2]

All who raise their glass in public shall be drowned.

2. "*Zü trincken*," toasting or raising one's glass. Eberlin is condemning a practice

On Blasphemers

Whoever swears, other than "in truth" or "by God," shall be publicly beaten with rods.

Slander

Whoever defames another or speaks against his honor, shall be publicly defamed.

On Games

All youths shall be forbidden to play cards or dice games for money or valuables. Only board games shall be allowed for their leisure time.

Adults may play such games at appropriate times, but the stakes shall not be higher than one kreutzer.

No games shall be held except where one can see the players as one passes by.

On Dancing

Each week one day shall be set aside for dancing when whoever wishes may dance, men and women with each other, in a public place for three hours in the afternoon.

No married man shall dance with anyone except his blood relatives or his wife. The same goes for married women.

In gestures and leaps, and songs and piping decency must be maintained without any lewdness, so that leisure will be sought there rather than wantonness.

Such pleasures shall not last more than three hours.

---

common from the fifteenth century to the seventeenth that called for a toast as a form of greeting and which could degenerate into drinking bouts. See Simon, *Deutsche Flugschriften*, 200n8 and Lederer, "Welfare Land," 178.

On Marrying

All people may marry whom they choose without any impediments except where they are prohibited by the law of Moses or on account of friendship or familial relationship.

The pastors shall either have a wife or no woman.

On the Council or Court

In a city the council shall consist of thirty men and the count shall occupy the position of mayor.

In a walled town the council shall consist of fifteen men and the baron shall be the mayor.

Commerce

All Fuggerei[3] shall be done away with.

There shall be no more than three members in any trading company.

No wine shall be imported that is not grown in our land.

No cloth shall be imported that is not made in our land.

No fruit shall be imported that is not grown in our land, unless for pressing health needs.

Food and Drink

All manner of food and drink shall be allowed to all people at all times. Henceforth, no monk or priest shall prohibit this. However, fasting shall be handled as described in the ecclesiastical statutes.[4]

On Communal Property

Game, birds and fish shall be common property for all to catch according to their need and ability.

3. Usury. Eberlin here adopts the common early sixteenth-century identification of the prominent Augsburg banking family, the Fuggers, as the embodiment of usury. See Laube, *Flugschriften*, 2:716.

4. Cf. Eberlin's statements in *The Tenth Confederate*, 118–19 above.

Wood shall be common property for all to cut, so long as it is put to useful purposes.

Bread and Wine

For a half penny one should be able to buy enough bread to provide a strong man with a satisfying light meal.

A measure of wine shall cost one kreutzer.

A measure should be enough to satisfy the thirst of two men drinking in moderation with a light meal.

Beggars

There shall be no beggars in our land. However, at the parish churches every feast day the poor shall be given as much as God commands for each, the remainder shall be made up from the common purse of the city.

The bailiff and court, and all officials should be diligent in their care for the poor.

This shall not be entrusted to the priests, because the priests have been unfaithful to the poor and have falsely sought their own interest. From this has come all the riches the monks and priests have received to this point. These riches were first given to the poor, whose stewards the priests and monks were supposed to be.

All the poor who receive alms shall wear a special sign.

On Trades

Above all, one shall ensure that there are no useless trades in our land.

One shall prevent excessive numbers in the useful trades as well, and make sure that there are not more masters than journeymen.

No livelihood shall be more highly esteemed than field work and blacksmithing.

On War

No war shall be waged without consultation of all princes of our land.

From now on there shall be no artillery.

In combat the nobles shall be in the front lines and the leaders shall be on the field.

In war women, children and the sick shall be spared.

During war one shall not prevent farming.

All farmers and pastors shall be free from military service.

When going to war, each bailiwick shall take a priest with them, and when battle is about to be joined, all priests shall come forward, fall on their knees and pray to God for a favorable peace.

No war shall be undertaken for the extension or expansion of our land.

In war arson is prohibited.

On pain of death houses of God are not to be damaged or robbed.

On Castles

No peasant or non-noble shall occupy a castle, only nobles.

From now on no castle shall be demolished.

No new castles shall be built, however old ones should be renovated.

On Houses and Buildings

In all cities each trade shall have its own quarter.

No excessively sumptuous house shall be built with the exception of public buildings, such as the city hall, market, bathhouse, school, leisure buildings, etc.

Cities shall have wide streets.

On the Bathhouse

All men and boys shall have a designated bathhouse.

All women and girls shall have a designated bathhouse.

Each bathhouse should contain a steam bath and a water bath, so one is able to choose which he wants.

On Beards

On pain of serious punishment, all men should have long beards; no man should have a smooth face like a woman.

It shall be a disgrace to not have a beard.

All men shall have short, unadorned hair.

On Children

All children, both boys and girls, shall attend school from the age of three until they are eight.

Schools shall be maintained from the common purse.

In the schools children shall be taught the Christian law from the Gospel and from the letters of Paul.

In the schools one shall teach the children both Latin and German so they have an equal understanding of these languages. In the upper years they shall learn to read and understand a little Greek and Hebrew.

At the age of eight a child may be put to work in a craft or trade or allowed to continue studying.

On Statutes and Laws of the Land

In each bailiwick no one shall be considered a householder unless he knows the common laws and customs.

We repeal all old imperial and clerical laws.

Each person should know the common law so that each knows what is right and wrong.

There shall no longer be lawyers and advocates; whoever cannot express himself well shall take a fellow citizen with him to court.

On the Ban

No one shall be banned for debt; the pastors should ban only those who openly and repeatedly transgress God's law.

On Indulgences

From now on, anyone who proclaims or reads letters of indulgence shall be publicly punished.

Instead there will be a greater indulgence: doing good for one's neighbor and forgiving one's enemy.

On Currency

In the entire empire there will be one currency, that is one mint and one guaranteed value for the currency.[5]

On Pastors

No pastor shall be a member of a council, neither of princes nor of cities nor of bailiwicks.

On Faithlessness

Whoever fails to fulfill a promise to another, made in earnest without oath or vow, shall be publicly disgraced.

Whoever damages an item lent to him by another, shall pay the owner its previous value.

Whoever will not lend to his neighbor in need, even though he has plenty, shall be publicly punished.

Whoever takes interest on a loan shall be beaten with rods.

Whoever does not repay a loan at the appointed time shall be publicly punished.

On Thieves

A thief shall be sentenced to servitude for one year and should perform menial tasks in the city. He shall wear chains on both feet.

Murderers

A murderer shall be put to death.

Highwaymen shall be made perpetual servants of the community as described for thieves.

5. Eberlin's statement in the latter part of this statute (*das ist ein schlag vnd einer werschafft*) is vague. This reading, suggested by both Simon and Baldini, seems the most logical. See Simon, *Deutsche Flugschriften*, 207n31 and Baldini, *Gli "Statuti di Wolfaria,"* 65.

On Extravagance

Whoever is seen to spend more lavishly than his means allow should be reported under oath to the authorities.

One must respond immediately to excessive extravagance so that it does not create so many poor, unfortunate people.

On Domestic Servants

One shall give no wine to domestic servants under the age of thirty.

No servant should be released from his or her service except for reasons of discord.

No master shall curse or revile a servant, and no servant shall curse or revile a master.

No master shall give a servant his or her wages before they are due.

When they are due, each servant shall be paid in cash.

The master shall maintain and care for ill servants for up to two months at no charge.

On Clothing

All clothing shall be of the same colors except that there should be a distinction between the clothing of men and women.

Clothing shall cover men and women respectably.

Women shall be gracefully yet respectably clothed.

On Amusements

Each month there shall be pleasant, respectable public entertainment, for which the authorities of each region should plan diligently.

No entertainment shall last more than half a day.

No entertainment shall involve excessive feasting.

One shall teach all children to play suitable stringed instruments.

One shall teach all children the arts of measurement, calculation and recognizing the stars.

All children shall be taught to recognize common herbs and common remedies for common illnesses.

Famous doctors shall be employed, using funds from the common purse, who will treat everyone without special fees.

On Corporal Punishment

From now on, no corporal punishment shall be employed that is not prescribed by the law of Moses, because man should not punish more severely than God does.

On Pilgrims

If one is forced to travel and can indicate the reason for that travel in writing from his superiors, everyone shall hold him in high regard. If he has no food, he should be offered hospitality in the communal hospice. It would be good if he were shown kindness out of a special sense of devotion.

On Idleness

On pain of serious penalty no one should be completely idle; everyone shall be assigned to suitable work. Idleness shall be regarded as a public disgrace.

Common Rules

Henceforth, whoever gives money to have a mass read, money for penance, burial money, *item*, whoever praises the canonical hours, whoever gives alms to a mendicant friar, even if he has removed his cowl and goes about as any other man, whoever holds a priest in greater esteem than a bailiff or a councilman shall be publicly punished.

Whoever harms a priest shall be punished as if he harmed a bailiff.

On Jews and Heathens

If unbelievers want to live among us, no one should do them harm, but should treat them in a friendly way like our citizens. However, they shall not be given any civil honors or offices, and they should not dishonor any of our laws or beliefs.

On Heretics

No one should be judged a heretic who holds to the accepted law of the Gospel as determined by the general understanding of our land.

Students, pastors and countrymen, also judges, shall decide together on matters relating to our Gospel teachings and laws.

On Taxes for the Common Purse

Any citizen assessed at less than one hundred florins is not required to pay taxes. But citizens assessed at over one hundred florins will pay one haller[6] each week, and those will be collected every week.

We of Wellfaria have undertaken the above-described ordinance, and it is our intention that we will present it to all the people of every bailiwick to hear if our subjects will accept or criticize it. In that way, after ratification by our land, the laws will have strength to punish the disobedient and reward the obedient. Dated in our capital city of Wolf's Den, in the month Good Time, in the year the mendicants' cowls are put to flight.[7]

M W V H[8]
Lamentation claims me

6. The haller was a coin of very limited worth. The "utopian" features of Wolfaria included incredibly low rates of taxation.

7. On Eberlin's humorous dating of the "Wolfarian Statutes" and its significance for their characterization as a utopia, see *The Tenth Confederate*, above, 129n27; Lederer, "Welfare Land," 175; and Baldini, *Gli "Statuti di Wolfaria,"* 28.

8. Simon, *Deutsche Flugschriften*, 211–12n50, suggests as a possible meaning for this abbreviation "Mit Weile Vetter Huldrich": "With Time Cousin Huldrich."

Ein früntliche antwort aller gotzförchtigen/ erberen/ verstēdigē in Teütschem land vff die jämerliche klag der ordens leüt an sie gethon.

Der. XII. bůdt gnosz.

Figure 12. *Der XII. bundtgnosz.* Bayerische Staatsbibliothek München [Res/4 H.ref. 271 y#Beibd.11]

12

The Twelfth Confederate

A friendly response of all God-fearing, decent, reasonable people in the German land to the pitiful complaint made to them by those in orders.

It is with great pleasure that I deliver this message to the devout folk in the monasteries at the bidding of the German people, and thereby also fulfill my vow as the twelfth confederate. That is the plan.

Devout, spiritual, beloved, faithful friends, kinsmen, kinswomen, brothers-in-law, sisters-in-law, and all fellow Christians who are living in the cloistered estate, we wish you peace and grace from God, and we willingly commit ourselves to continued help and comfort. We have heard with great compassion your appeal so trustingly directed to us, and we have reflected carefully on our answer. By God's grace we have come to understand how the cloistered life, as practiced today, is contrary both to the very essence of Christianity and to the common good. Therefore, it offends us greatly, and we think often of opposing such abuses, but we have concluded that with such deeply rooted abuses, there is no quick solution. And so, whichever of the cloistered folk wish to leave the monastery and put aside the cowl, to support themselves among us in a respectable manner, to them we give full support in their departure. It is not proper that any monk, priest, pope, bishop, nor any of their representatives, should place obstacles in their path.

To all such departed cloistered folk we promise seemly participation in all decent offices and estates, whether spiritual or secular, that may come to them.

We will give five years exemption from all taxes that lie within our authority to any citizen who marries a nun who has left the cloister.

Any woman who marries a monk or priest, from whom she can expect necessary sustenance, if she doesn't already have it, should be held in great honor.

It is our desire that under threat of serious penalty no cloistered person seek a dispensation from the pope, because this is not necessary.

By this decree we forbid all our fellow citizens to give alms to the mendicant friars so long as they continue to wear their cowls.

Henceforth no mendicant friar should preach, except when an entire city or village requests him in particular.

We now outlaw and place under the ban all monks who refuse to accept money,[1] because they do more damage to the common good than anyone can reckon.

We declare that all women's convents shall be open, that is they should have an open "little window,"[2] through which one is able to see and speak, but no man may enter the convent, on pain of serious punishment, except he be a father or a brother.

Cloistered women may leave the convent on respectable or necessary business if accompanied by companions of good repute.

We charge all officials in town and country to appoint their own managers in the monasteries, from whom they will receive an accounting every month.

We forbid that henceforth anyone should enter a monastery except with special permission from a bailiff and court.

The three vows shall no longer be taken in any monastery.

Once each month the bailiffs and courts shall visit their monasteries and investigate the prison under oath.[3]

1. Presumably the mendicant orders whose members took vows of corporate as well as individual poverty.

2. "*Redfenster.*" A small opening in the cloister wall, covered by a grille or grating, through which one could speak with the inhabitants, see *JEvGS* 3:395. Cf. Kerr, *Life in the Medieval Cloister*, 69.

3. Eberlin seems to be suggesting that secular authorities keep a close eye on those incarcerated in monastic prisons for alleged misdeeds in the monastery.

No significant punishment shall be imposed on someone in a monastery without the knowledge and agreement of the secular authorities of the region. If this is discovered to have happened, the monastery and all of its valuables are forfeit to the city, its inhabitants will be allowed to die out, and their possessions will go to the common purse.

Henceforth, no abbot, prior, abbess, mistress, or prioress shall be installed in office except in the presence of the bailiff and court.

All monasteries shall henceforth pay taxes, assessments, and rents like any other citizen; no privileges should exempt them from this. This applies to the mendicant orders as well.

From now on no annual payments or interest on loaned money shall be paid to the monasteries. Instead, the bailiff and court should establish a reasonable schedule according to which the debtor will pay off the principle of the loan, or the city will pay off the principle to the monastery and then receive such payments.

From now on, no interest shall be paid on loaned money.

There shall be no communal graveyards by the churches of the mendicant orders, because it is to be feared that the souls of those who don't want to rest in the parish cemetery must suffer in the next world. However, if the monastery is connected to the parish church, we allow burials there to continue.

Whoever has a child or friend in a monastery, according to the current custom, should know that they have no great honor beyond that of other citizens. If, however, the women's convents become as respectable as free women's convents[4] should be, then we will honor and praise them.

One can certainly calculate what must be collected annually by a monastery so that in addition to communal needs each member receives six ducats for his own requirements, whether for clothing or other necessities.

Cloistered women may work at decent occupations for wages and use the money for their own needs.

Men's monasteries shall become *collegia* just like those free women have,[5] and their goods should be distributed in a similar fashion.

If a monastery is too poor, then it should be helped out with resources from a rich monastery.

4. Presumably the houses of the Beguines or Secular Tertiaries, see below, 146n6.

5. Eberlin seems to be suggesting that the men's monasteries be reformed on the model of Beguine houses, see below, 146n6.

Their foolish poverty shall be done away with in all monasteries; instead, each resident should have his own possessions and use them honorably.

From now on, inhabitants of a monastery shall receive their inheritances; furthermore, when someone dies, his friends outside the monastery should be able to inherit from him.

On threat of strictest punishment, we command all bailiffs and office-holders to remove the black veils worn by some Beguines, also called rule-nuns of the third order of Francis, Dominic, or Augustine.[6] And from now on, the same nuns should come under the supervision of their parish priest, under which so many other decent people of the parish live.

Each village should keep a close eye on them to ensure that they lead upright lives, because when it comes to matters associated with the mendicant friars, one has to fear that they are like a piece of fat among cats.

All such rule-nuns are allowed to marry if they so wish. We declare that their three vows are contrary to justice and right and to their rule. Therefore, they should be abolished and done away with, under the threat of losing all protection by us.

Henceforth, no begging monk shall have or be accorded any more rights than those of a foreigner.

We permit all Clares and Dominican nuns[7] to eat suitable meat on the usual days of the week.

We smash to pieces their inhumane confinement, as we have said above about other monasteries.

We declare that the bare-footed friars and preachers[8] should not serve as their irrevocable visitors and father confessors. Rather, the women

6. Beguines were groups of women, often with close ties to the Franciscans or Dominicans, who did not belong to an official order and did not take formal vows, but who promised to remain celibate and obey a rule. They retained private property and were free to change their status. Sometimes Beguines were also members of the third orders of the mendicant orders. Third orders were composed of laity affiliated with the respective orders. If they took religious vows, they were known as Regular Tertiaries; those not taking vows were known as Secular Tertiaries. See *ODCC*, 178–79, 1610.

7. The second order of the Franciscans, founded by Francis and St. Clare between 1212 and 1214, were also often referred to as Poor Clares. The second order of the Dominicans were cloistered nuns under the jurisdiction of the Master of the Order. See *ODCC*, 497–98, 1308.

8. I.e., the Franciscans (see *The First Confederate*, 25n19) and the Dominicans, the Order of Preachers.

may receive once a year whomever they find acceptable, on the advice of the burgermeister and the neighboring parish priest.

We are sorely vexed on account of the injustices which have occurred to this point in women's convents because of the monks.

On pain of serious punishment, in all women's convents, at the front by the little window there shall be held every day two Bible readings by a respected teacher of Scripture, who will teach the nuns to understand Latin.

No cloistered woman shall recite the canonical hours outside the choir, but every day she should recite for a set time outside the choir the Psalm *Beati immaculate*, so that she recites twenty-three verses of the Psalm for each canonical hour,[9]otherwise she should pray as God prompts her.

Whoever is willing and pleasing to the women may preach to them, be he monk or priest.

We consider it suspect if henceforth anyone confesses to a mendicant friar, unless his abilities and wisdom are known to the whole city, so that our women and children, and also our fellow citizens, are not vexed.

Our advice would be that officials in all villages and cities ensure that the mendicant friars have no authority over nuns, because the nuns learn from them few things that are useful to the soul or decency.

We wish to forbid that any rule should remain except St. Augustine's first rule for men and the free women's status for women.

Furthermore, we do not want to do away with the ways of the hermits as are customary in the land of Württemberg,[10] but they shall have their own possessions and their parish priest shall be their visitor.

We desire that henceforth no monastery shall be exempt from episcopal authority.

We declare null and void all obedience claimed by the pope from free monasteries, and lay it aside.

It is our wish that henceforth no canonical hours will be sung in the monastery churches, especially those of the mendicant orders and the nuns. Instead, whoever wants to hear the canonical hours will find them in the cathedral chapters.

No one should regard the canonical hours as a special form of prayer or as a particularly meritorious form of divine service.

9. Psalm 119, traditionally recited as part of the canonical hours. Because of its length, it was divided up with specific verses assigned to different hours of the monastic day. See *JEvGS* 1:222.

10. It is unclear to what Eberlin is referring here, see *JEvGS* 1:222.

We permit out of kindness that the canonical hours may be sung in the chapters, on account of the common misunderstandings of the people, but we grant this reluctantly.

If the monks or nuns want to observe the canonical hours, they may read them without singing.

The monks, and also the nuns, may sing one mass each day, but no more.

Whichever burghers have their parents buried in a monastery should henceforth observe the anniversaries of their deaths in no other way than by having a common prayer said for their souls from the pulpit and giving common alms to the poor on the anniversary. If the cloistered people wish, they, too, may receive alms like other poor people, and, furthermore, one should not give more than the penny deemed fitting for someone in a monastery.

No one should give gifts or money to the monks as payment for reading masses, because we recognize that such reading of masses is of no use to souls, but only to the greedy monks.

Each city shall be allowed to call out of the monasteries suitable people as preachers, parish priests, and their helpers. And for this they shall receive praise and thanks from us, for it is a great sin and shame that so many able people waste away in the monasteries.

All monks shall be allowed, with the help of city officials, to leave the monastery to go to places where scripture is taught, and there to hear lectures. No authority should hinder this; indeed, all officials of the city should promote this, with force if necessary.

Under threat of loss of reputation and physical punishment we forbid that henceforth anyone enter a mendicant order, just as if it were a brothel. We acknowledge the primary reason for this command is the fact that nothing good can come from the simple folk learning such corrupting things.

All bulls, letters, liberties, authority, etc., dealing with physical, temporal, or spiritual matters, which the mendicant and other monasteries hold from the papal see in Rome, we declare void from this moment, because they cause suspicion and distrust and are unworthy of observance. If the monasteries need something, our bishops in the German land have sufficient authority to provide it.

Henceforth no benefice (especially parochial) shall remain incorporated to the monasteries, on pain of loss of all incurred expenses.

All benefices, pastorates, canonries shall henceforth be free to those who take up residence in them and can be useful.

If, however, a benefice has so much revenue that it is deemed too much for one priest, the bailiff and court shall determine how much is sufficient for the priest and the remainder will be assigned to the common purse for the care of the poor.

If the tithe is too great, it, too, should go to the common purse.

In the case of decent people who receive the tithe in order to carry out responsible tasks, we leave tithe arrangements as they are until a future agreement is reached, because it is more reasonable that they should feed their wives and children from it than that the clergy use it to turn the world upside down. But it would be our wish that lay tithe holders be repaid the principal of their investment from the common purse, and then that the tithe be used to maintain the poor.

We do not begrudge to poor nobles and burghers the tithe for the remainder of their lives, even if they are unable to make a proper case for their claim. But when they die, their heirs will be dealt with according to the judgment and decision of decent, wise people.

It is well known that the majority of those now in monasteries, both men and women, did not know what a wretched and dangerous thing the cloistered life is when they entered the monastery. Furthermore, they often took their vows before the permitted age, especially in the mendicant orders. Therefore, our counsel and advice is that all cloistered people be free to leave the monastery and remove their cowls, so that a terrible punishment from God not come over us. We can better endure that the monks and nuns, too, are subject to normal human weaknesses than that their compelled chastity lead to unnamed sins which call down God's punishment on our entire land. Their departure shall not harm them in body or reputation, much less endanger their souls. Outside the monastery they should be esteemed fellow citizens. We will gladly give them our children in marriage and wedlock. If, however, someone wishes to remain in the monastery in spite of our proposal, we do not wish to remove him with force; he will have to give a reckoning for himself on this matter.

However, in time we want to take it upon ourselves to expel the mendicant friars, especially the Order of Preachers and the bare-footed Observants, so that learned, decent Christian people and our faithful fellow citizens are not so shamefully deceived by them and the people are not taught such unchristian things.

We forbid, on pain of serious penalty, that any monastery be reformed according to the usual means employed until now. If, however, the scandalous lives of the cloistered folk are intolerable to a city or land, they are permitted to expel the cloistered folk and convert the monastery to serve the common good of the territory or city, and for that we will give them thanks and praise.

The monasteries of the Teutonic Knights and the Knights of St. John we assign to poor nobles as almshouses.

This is our well-intentioned, friendly proposal given to you spiritually distressed cloistered folk in answer to your pitiful supplication, in hopes that we will receive on this account reward and grace from God and praise and thanks from you. With this we commend ourselves to your pious prayers.

Dated in a time and place, known to God and us when, we hope, our most gracious lord, Emperor Charles, and all estates of the empire will consider your sincere appeal and our friendly proposal, and that they will be greatly pleased by them.

Put your trust in God alone
And have no fear, it will soon be done.

Ein zuverſichtig ermanung
an die redlichen/erberen ſtarcken vnd chriſtlichen herren
obern vnd vnderthon gemainer Eydgnoſchafft (genant
Schwitzer) das ſy trewlich helffen handthaben Ewange
liſche leer vnd frumme chriſten.

Der. XIII. bundtsgnoſz

BIBLIOTHECA
REGIA

Figure 13. *Der XIII. bundtsgnosz.* Bayerische Staatsbibliothek München [Res/4 H.ref. 271 y#Beibd.12]

13

The Thirteenth Confederate

A hopeful exhortation to the upright, honorable, strong, and Christian lords, officials, and subjects of the Common Confederacy (known as the Swiss) that they faithfully help to preserve evangelical teaching and devout Christians.

We want you to know, Oh strong Christian Confederates,[1] Oh defenders and guardians of all those despairing and oppressed, that we fifteen have together sworn an oath to expose to the common German nation the general, conspicuous mischief which has lain on us all for so long. I am the thirteenth of that number and it falls to me to make an appeal to your honor in the hope that you will receive my request in the way it was intended. Each and every one of you knows that loyalty and good faith in noble endeavors don't die with the body. Rather, we should suffer all worldly injuries rather than break a promise. We have a clear example of such constancy today in all those called the Swiss (*Schwitzer*) because they sweat (*schwitzen*) blood rather than deny loyalty and their oath to their captain, even in the face of mortal danger. But what can be more noble than the oath all Christians have sworn in baptism to our godly captain, Christ, which afterwards we have so often reaffirmed in the reception of the sacrament, for each and every partaking of the sacrament is a renewal

1. Eberlin here refers to the Swiss, members of the Helvetic Confederation, as Confederates. To distinguish the Swiss from the fifteen confederates I have capitalized the initial C of Confederate when referring to them.

of our sworn oath? What we have sworn in baptism has been witnessed by God and his angels, indeed, by all of Christendom as represented in the people called to each baptism. What is more noble and pressing than that which we have sworn, that is faithful obedience to our God, to protect and keep his evangelical law, and to be declared enemies of the devil and all his wiles? You know that we were created, redeemed, and every minute without interruption are ruled by God. All our thoughts stand open before his eyes. Without him, we are unable to raise even a stalk of straw from the ground. You know as well that God seeks nothing more earnestly than our well-being. On the other hand, you also know that the devil seeks with all his wiles to undermine our well-being, through pleasure and pain, through fortune and misfortune. How necessary it is, then, that we hold as dearly to God as we do to our fortune, health, and blessedness, and turn away from the devil, not just for one day but for our whole lives. For the moment that we yield to the devil through any sort of sin, we make God and all creatures our enemies. God wishes good for us, the devil evil. God loves us, the devil hates us. God seeks the salvation of our souls, the devil seeks the ruin of our body and soul. To remind us of this, God has given us the sacrament of baptism, through which he visibly binds all who want to be Christians to carefully take to heart what salvation and perdition are. Therefore, since we have all been baptized and sworn an honorable oath to God and Christendom, it follows that we should let go of life and limb, honor and possessions before we become unfaithful and forswear ourselves.

For it is praiseworthy among you men that you keep your promises and oaths, even if that means a loss of temporal life or all earthly possessions. How much more praiseworthy is it before God and all the angels and all devout Christians that one holds in high regard fulfilling that oath given to God, even if that means losing all that a person has and is; because that loss means also a greater victory. As Christ also says, whoever loses his life for my sake will find eternal life.

Is it not regarded as so dishonorable among you if someone takes flight in the face of danger to his life that you yourselves would not let such a deserter live, that among you he would lose his house and home and everything he has? How much more dishonorable is it before God and the saints for a Christian to desert the sworn oath about which I have spoken above? How greatly will God be angered by such a Christian and because of him by an entire land that doesn't punish his misdeeds?

You should also know that Christ, our captain, has given us a law, contained in the Holy Gospel and in the biblical books of the New Testament. This law is filled with all worthy, wholesome, useful, and noble commands. We have sworn not to falsify, not to deny, but to hold firmly and steadily to this law, even if sometimes in our lives we sin against it out of human weakness. However, we will not suffer that this law be subjected to false interpretation, or gloss, addition or subtraction, or to any other abuse. Moreover, we want to atone for our sins, unfortunately all too often committed against the law, under the shield and protection of a correct understanding of the same law. And even though we act unjustly through our inability to hold the law, we still want to open up for others the way to godliness. This and other similar matters you can certainly judge, either all together or individually, according to the level of your understanding. It is not necessary to talk a lot about this. And the more and better you understand it, I hope, so much more will the offenses against this just responsibility distress and grieve you. I am not speaking here about all our sinful lives when we act against God and his law through blasphemy, lewdness, pride, jealousy, hatred, etc. Rather, I lament the false, deceitful interpretation of our law and that such corruption has gone so far that pain and torment await all those who proclaim a proper understanding of the Christian law to others.

In the universities a heathen interpretation of the Christian law is taught which also contradicts the common sense understanding held by many. From the pulpit is taught not only this heathen interpretation, but also Antichristian statutes under the guise of Christian instruction. They weigh down the light law of Christ contrary to his command; they confound our consciences with hellish scruples; with so many papal commands and human statutes; with so many censures of excommunication, irregularity, and interdict; with so many regulations about fasting, feasting, food, and drink, from all of which Christ set us completely free. They burden us with so many fantasies and superstitious rules about confessing, although the Christian church demands of us nothing other than a faithful, confident acknowledgment of our sins before a priest without any specially scrupulous accounting; with many and varied forms of penance which God has not commanded, even though not sinning further has always been regarded as the best penance; with so much deception about indulgences, indulgence letters, with the reservation and then dispensation in so many types and cases of the conscience; with the theft of our benefices and parochial livings, through which every day ignoble, soul-less, faithless, bloated, lazy people, known as courtiers, derive advantage. We Germans are daily burdened with such things, molested in our consciences and goods.

You may notice how little is said from the pulpit about the Holy Gospel, about the teachings of the apostle Paul, of Peter, and of John. The greater part of preaching is about the teachings of Aristotle, Thomas, Scotus;[2] about imperial or canon law; about fables; about worldly matters. But sermons should be nothing other than fervent, clear exhortations to do what the evangelical law reveals and teaches. As a result, Christian people are now completely fed up with hearing the fables of preachers and their souls thirst for the living word of God.

You also notice now how all effort is directed entirely toward self-interest and reputation so that all sermons are poisoned and there is little or no attention to our salvation. As a result of the false demands of our preachers we are now more unfaithful, more deceitful, more treacherous, more envious, more angry, more arrogant, indeed, more soul-less than heathens and Turks. For our priests and monks take money and gloss over for each person his evil designs, so that we almost entirely forget God's. Many very learned, devout, honest people have seriously considered this and have taken it upon themselves to interpret and teach the Christian law in Christian terms. They don't wish to harm anyone's possessions, for they do this with no thought of self-interest. They don't wish to harm anyone's honor so long as God's honor is promoted. They compel no one to do the right thing. They believe that the Christian law should be preached in a pure, suitable and Christian manner in the churches. Therefore, even if one does not already live according to the law, one will allow it to be taught in conformity with the Christian faith; should I not wish to live a Christian life, nonetheless, I allow another to teach in a Christian manner. They intend further that one present to the Christian people the words of Christ and the apostles briefly, clearly, and faithfully, unmixed with heathen teachings, with human laws, with false explanations, through which clearly self-interest and reputation are sought rather than God's glory and the salvation of souls. When other, false, self-serving tellers of fables, dream preachers, and tempters note the diligence of devout Christian doctors now coming forward, such as Erasmus of Rotterdam, Martin Luther, Karlstadt,[3] Melanchthon, etc., then they come along and want to try by every means

2. Thomas Aquinas (c. 1225–1274), *ODCC*, 1614–17; John Duns Scotus (c. 1265–1308), ibid., 513–14.

3. Andreas Bodenstein von Karlstadt (1480–1541). See *OER* 1:178–80; *COE* 2:253–56.

to obstruct the truth, with invented lies, as if one intended to act against papal obedience, against the faith, against the common good of the empire. In this way they make the true teaching suspicious before the simple Christians, whom they have led around on a fool's halter for so many years, corrupting their souls and goods. For all opponents of these devout teachers are concerned with nothing other than self-interest and reputation, as is obvious to all wise people who can truly judge things rationally. Therefore, they try to rile up papal holiness and imperial majesty against the truth and Christian teachers, and so neither the pope nor the emperor have been correctly informed about this affair. But the money gluttons, the slanderers of people, the seducers of souls take it upon themselves, under the appearance of goodness, unjustly to rouse the pope and emperor against God and his law, to the great detriment of human salvation. For it is worth noting that were the pope and emperor properly informed about matters, they would shield and protect all the devout doctors mentioned above. But since the heads of the church are led astray by envious, injurious people with God's leave, we should faithfully implore God that he would enlighten them so that they recognize the faithfulness and truth of the sincere teachers, how they seek the honor, welfare, and benefit of the empire, and, on the other hand, they see the deceit and unfaithfulness of the envious who seek not the common interest, but their own advantage, to the great detriment of the church and the empire. We are also charged with exhorting, admonishing and warning all our fellow Christians, in word and deed, to take to heart the full understanding of what needs to be done in such cases. For indeed the lives, reputations and goods of true teachers and their supporters and followers are not secure from the knaves. For this reason we fifteen have sworn together to present to you noble Confederates what concerns the salvation and damnation of the soul. For you are good-hearted people and devoted to realizing the acknowledged truth. We have no doubt that when you know what is pleasing to God, you will risk life and limb to guard and protect it. It also grieves us very much that all devout Germans, especially those of the noble Confederacy, are led astray by the tempters, that you noble Swiss, along with all of us Germans, hold false teachings for Christian, monkish self-interest for the good of your souls. Although, by God's grace, you devout Confederates have always been less inclined than other Germans to be led around by the nose, through bans, sycophancy and other things. For you and your ancestors, as wise people, have certainly been able to observe where preaching has aimed for many years. Now that God has looked on the German nation with the fullness of grace and sent us people who again direct us to Christian teaching and the common good of the entire land, we should be thankful and ready to serve. Therefore, our friendly, Christian request of you triumphant, robust, upright Confederates is that you would faithfully guard and protect our Christian law. You have always had the word, you help the downcast and the oppressed receive justice without fear, you support now Christian justice and are prepared to ensure that the evangelical law is preached in the churches and that heathen, human, misleading interpretations are silenced. Should honorable, devout Christian teachers or people flee to you as protectors and defenders of the truth, stand by them faithfully. Don't let papal bulls, bans, commandments, and the like frighten you, since the false seducers produce such decrees without the knowledge of the pope and other princes. And while truthful people are unable to get an audience with the lords, these devilish men manage this with money and gifts, through which they incline the closest servants of the lords to them; as a result there is no access for the truth. We are certain that if you were to read just once the clear gospel teaching, along with the godly explanation the Apostle Paul provides in his epistles, you would understand how miserably we have been led astray for so many years by the monks and priests in the pulpit and the confessional. Although there still are, and have always been, many devout, honorable priests who never were pleased by such things, nonetheless, the false appearance and numbers of the others have prevailed.

You are called Swiss, your greatest honor should be that you sweat even blood in defense of the holy evangelical law and hold firmly to its teachings.[4] You should be sweaty defenders, protectors, and deliverers of unjustly oppressed devout Christians. You are called Confederates, therefore, hold to the oath you pledged to God in baptism and so often reaffirmed in receiving other sacraments. Also, help us so that we can fulfill the oath we took to God according to the evangelical law, so that we will not be driven from Christian teaching, so that we will not be so unjustly deprived of the goods, honor, and life by false Christians and teachers, which contradicts both God and justice. That you receive a pension to support temporal lords and lands does not concern us; you can pledge yourselves to whomever you want. But in what relates to the salvation of souls and the Christian law, we wish that you would commit yourselves to God alone and

4. Eberlin here returns to his inventive etymology of the name Swiss introduced at the beginning of this work.

fight and contend for this. Follow the example of the troops of St. Moritz's company who were ready to commit life and limb to temporal lords in temporal matters. But when it came to the Holy Gospel, to Christian law, they could not be swayed, even by the threat of death.[5] We have no doubt that if the devout Confederacy holds faithfully to Christian law and to devout Christians, unchristian power, deception, and unfaithfulness will make no progress. God has given you a strong body, a courageous nature, a name feared in all the world, a secure land, a decent judgment and disposition, godly sustenance from earth and cattle, a productive people. You should be thankful for these gifts and increase and honor your good name through these Christian acts of protecting and defending God's gospel. And we believe that God has set you aside from eternity as a special people, that you would serve others by one day protecting His law. Arise then, you noble warriors, and awaken your hearts and minds and your Christian kin, stand faithfully by your God and His law. Then He will nourish, multiply, and honor you and your children and your servants both now and hereafter. He will be graceful to you and us. Amen

Let us stand by Him with a stout heart
Who shed his blood on the cross for our part.

5. Eberlin is referring here to the legend of St. Mauritius and the Theban legion which refused to persecute fellow Christians and suffered martyrdom as a result, see *JEvGS* 1:222.

Figure 14. *Der XIIII. bundtgnosz.* Bayerische Staatsbibliothek München [Res/4 H.ref. 271 y#Beibd.13]

14

The Fourteenth Confederate

Sir Erasmus of Rotterdam reveals in the book *Encomion Morias* the shameful service we now render to the saints.

It is no wonder that I, the fourteenth confederate, find it difficult to fulfill my duty in writing this, since so many of my wise colleagues have already applied themselves diligently to the task. Nonetheless, that I may do my part, I will present what Erasmus of Rotterdam has written in the book *Praise of Folly* concerning the foolish service rendered to the saints. Not that the most famous teacher Erasmus is against honoring God and the saints, which, in fact, he keenly commends. But the abuses associated with this displease him greatly; these are his words, accept them all in their shocking truth.

Great is the number of those who light little candles for the mother of God, even in the middle of the day when no light is needed. But few are those who take pains to imitate her chaste life, her humility, her love of heavenly things, even though this is true service and most pleasing to the saints.[1]

People who take pleasure from telling or hearing about incredible, fictitious, miraculous signs of the saints are completely foolish. They can't get their fill of fables they dream up about the appearance of ghosts, souls, devils from hell and thousands of similar miracles. These they find all the more believable the more extravagant their claims. Such fabulous miracles are not only entertaining to hear, they also bring profit to the priests and preachers.[2]

1. Cf. Erasmus' statements in *Praise of Folly* in *Collected Works of Erasmus* 27:120.
2. Ibid., 113.

Listrius[3]

With these words Erasmus condemns not true miracles but invented, and especially those dreamed up to further self-interest, by which more money can be squeezed out of widows, the elderly and the gullible. For whoever believes fully the Holy Gospel, does not put much stake in invented miracles such as these, and as we can see, whoever believes fully in such fables has little regard for the Gospel truth. Erasmus is also reviled for speaking here against the wretched people known as the Pardoners,[4] who exploit the holy relics of the saints and without shame preach about the biggest fabricated miracles, which afterward they mock over wine.

Erasmus[5]

There are some who foolishly convince themselves that if one looks on a contrived, great painting or wooden image of St. Christopher just once a day, on that day no harm will come to him.[6] Or, whoever says a few little prayers to a picture of St. Barbara every day will come home from war safe and sound.[7] Or, whoever honors St. Erasmus on certain days with special little prayers and candles will soon get rich.[8] Also that someone conceived

3. Gerardus Listrius was a physician who wrote a commentary on *Praise of Folly*, published with most editions of the work beginning in 1515, from material largely supplied by Erasmus, see ibid., 78; *JEvGS* 1:222; and *CE*, 2:335–36.

4. "*Questionirer*." Enders defines this term as an "*Ablaßkrämer*," a seller of indulgences (*JEvGS* 1:222), or an "*Almosensammler*," a collector of alms (3:394). Götze, (*FnhdG*, 172), identifies a "questor" as an "*Ablaßkrämer*." In this context, it seems that the more comprehensive English term Pardoner is the better fit. Bowden, *A Commentary*, 276, describes a Pardoner, also referred to as a *quaestor*, as someone involved in three practices: selling indulgences, selling relics, and preaching.

5. The next three paragraphs are a loose translation of Erasmus' parody of the cult of saints from *Praise of Folly*, see *Collected Works of Erasmus* 27:114–16.

6. St. Christopher is the patron saint of wayfarers. According to legend, he was a giant who carried travelers across a river, and on one occasion carried the Christ child. It was a common medieval custom to place a large painting of the saint opposite the south door of a church in the belief that the sight of it would safeguard passers-by from accident that day. See *ODCC*, 338 and Jacobus de Voragine, *The Golden Legend*, 377–82.

7. St. Barbara was invoked for protection against thunderstorms and fire and was the patron saint of artillerymen and firefighters, see *ODCC*, 156.

8. St. Erasmus, aka St. Elmo or St. Ermo, was one of the martyrs of the Diocletian persecutions and is the patron saint of seafarers.

of St. George on the basis of the pagan Hercules.[9] Item, it is a heathen Hippolytus, whose horse they adorn with luxurious ornaments and whom they honor in the churches, bringing special offerings to him.[10] And it is a regal oath if sworn by St George's helmet. But what should I say about those who buoy themselves up with invented indulgences, and measure out their time in purgatory with hour-glasses, and count off the year, month, day, hour, the *Caren* and *Quadragena*,[11] as if they had everything laid out in a table and have no doubt they have calculated everything correctly. Some take great pleasure in magical prayers, thought up by knaves for either entertainment or profit, which some people use for riches, some for honor, some for pleasure, some for daily bread, some for health, and some for strength in old age. Some hope that through such prayers they will receive a seat of honor next to Christ in heaven, although they are in no rush to take that seat. Rather, first when they grow tired of earthly pleasures do they want to embrace heavenly joys. With an indulgence a merchant or a soldier or a judge seeks, by throwing a penny into the offering box, to atone immediately for the entire mass of his life's sins: so many false oaths, so much lewdness, debauchery, bickering and quarreling, murder, deceit, perjury, treachery, just as though he made a bargain with God through the indulgence and entirely atoned for his guilt so that he could begin anew his former ways.[12] But what is more foolish, indeed what is more blessed, than those who assure themselves of the greatest blessedness if every day they recite eight verses from the Psalter, and these verses, so they say, were revealed to St. Bernard by a devil.[13] Such foolish things are believed not only by simple Christians, but by people in religious orders as well.

9. St. George was likely martyred before the time of Constantine. The legend of slaying the dragon was first credited to him in the twelfth century and became popular in the thirteenth after it appeared in *The Golden Legend*. See *ODCC*, 664–65 and Jacobus de Voragine, *The Golden Legend*, 232–38. Eberlin here is repeating Erasmus' claim that the legend of the dragon is likely derived from the story of Hercules and the Hydra, see *Collected Works of Erasmus*, 28:477n307.

10. In Classical mythology, Hippolytus was dragged to death by his horses at the instigation of his father Theseus after his stepmother, Phaedra, claimed he had seduced her. A third-century saint is said to have been martyred after being dragged by horses. See *ODCC*, 519; Jacobus de Voragine, *The Golden Legend*, 446–49; and Erasmus, *Collected Works of Erasmus*, 28:477.

11. Both terms refer to a forty-day fast, see *JEvGS* 1:223 and *FnhdG*, 131 and 171.

12. ". . . *das er uff ain news mag anfahen den vorigen raien* . . ." Literally, "that he can begin again the same dance."

13. According to legend, the devil revealed to St. Bernard (1090–1153) that he would

Is it not also folly that each land has its own special saint and that to each saint they assign a particular task and a particular honor: one is supposed to help with toothaches, another with labor pains, another when someone has lost something, some in cases of shipwreck, some are supposed to protect cattle or sheep and others similar things, so that I can't explain them all. But what does one ask the saints for besides foolish things? Look at all the gifts hung on the vaults and walls of the churches. Neither the image nor the offering indicates in any way that someone has escaped folly, or that he became wiser by a hair than he was before. But they do show that one has escaped the dangers of the deep, that some have been stabbed, but not mortally. Some have escaped from battle, but left others to do the fighting. Some have been hung on the gallows, but with the help of a saint the rope broke and the thief ran away so that he could rob another day. Some have broken out of the tower. Some have recovered from a fever against the wishes of their doctors. Some have drunk poison and not been harmed, much to the dismay of their wives. Some have upset their cart, but the horse came home unhurt. Some have fallen, but not been injured. One was caught with another man's wife and escaped the husband. But none thank the saints that he has left behind his folly, for no one asks them for wisdom. Therefore, it is a sweet thing for folly that we would rather do without all other things before folly. And there is no limit to the number of foolish miracles, but the priests let them be because they serve their interests. However, should a wise man stand up and tell the truth, he would say that if you want to die well, you should live well. You atone for sin when you join to your penny true remorse for past sins, also tears, as well as vigils, prayers, fasting and when you improve your entire life. For it pleases a saint when you imitate his life and not just when you buy indulgences or offer a candle or a picture to the saint. Should one preach this and similar things, which are the truth, there would be a great murmuring against him because he wanted to draw the people away from folly to the truth.

Also belonging to the foolish people mentioned above are those who, while still living, arrange what sort of show should be put on with the burial of their corpse: how many candles, how many people wearing black mourning clothes, how many singers, how many keeners and mourners; as if the souls in the next world experience such follies arranged for them,

be saved if he recited seven special verses from the Psalms every day, but refused to reveal which seven verses. The saint responded that their identity was of no concern since he recited the entire Psalter every day, see Erasmus, *Collected Works of Erasmus*, 28:477n311.

or as if the spirits must be ashamed when such things are not arranged for them on earth.

Listrius

If a prince dies, a horse bedecked with black ornaments is led into the church and its reins are tied to its foot so it appears that the horse is hanging its head in mourning and grief. What folly.

A Supplement

We should accept these words of Erasmus and Listrius not that they lead us away from true honor for God and the saints, but rather that we see with what foolish matters we are occupied even in service to God and the saints. The world is so blind that it will not investigate and decide whether something is dangerous or useful, good or evil, no matter how unseemly it is. The greedy priests and monks see this and then use human folly to their own advantage. Is it not an obvious, clear deception that the people believe the pains of purgatory are removed through indulgences with such certainty that one can reckon the days and years in indulgence bulls, seal them with a bishop's seal, and then read them publicly in the church before learned and unlearned people? And yet, a wise man would think that God would not let such false monks and priests know his secret judgments. What great blindness it is that superstitious miracles are ascribed to the pictures of saints. This often causes more laughter than reflection, and serves more the mockery of the saints than their praise.

The Preachers[14] say that God revealed to their Thomas[15] that his explanation of scripture was accursed and that an unlearned pope gave witness to its truthfulness.[16] So it is well known that for 200 years his teaching has been rejected, even by his similarly misled schoolmates. And it is clear that Thomas' teaching is a corruption of Christendom, which has more to do with the Antichrist and with Aristotle than with Christ and the apostles, and that no one can regard him as a saint without doubts.

14. The Dominicans, the Order of Preachers.

15. Thomas Aquinas (c. 1225–1274), *ODCC*, 1614–17.

16. The source of this legend about St. Thomas is unknown.

The bare-footed friars[17] make just as much of their Francis[18] as of Christ, so that even holy Francis himself is greatly offended. I would hold Francis for no saint had he not rejected completely and entirely the vocation and lives of the begging monks, as they now practice them, especially the hypocritical, deceptive life that the bare-footed Observants[19] now lead, which they themselves say God and Francis will no longer tolerate. See what they say about their Francis. Whoever furthers the spread of the bare-footed order will die a blessed death. Whoever opposes the barefooted order will not die a good death; is it not folly that all the holy martyrs died wretchedly? Every year Francis takes out of purgatory all those there from his three orders. When Francis died, he completely emptied purgatory. His order will remain until the last day. And yet, all wise people know that the bare-footed order strives against reason and scripture. And since Francis regarded as his brothers all devout, perfect Christians, some of whom there will always be until the last day, such a prophecy may be more a fable invented by the deceitful monks than by the holy father. And furthermore, if indeed Francis held such an opinion, nonetheless, it is doubtful that he would have numbered himself among the perfect Christians given his reputation for humility. Item, whoever has a good will cannot last in his order; his order will spit him out, just as the sea does the dead. As if there were not a 100,000 malevolent, lewd, obscene, insolent, backbiting, vengeful, and in every way roguish people in his order. And among them honorable, devout, learned and clever people can't remain in peace and quiet.

Item, if there were no people to replenish the bare-footed order, would God they had left it to those first born to it. And they say so much about their Francis that they are silent in their praise of Christ and His holy, evangelical teaching. They have more to say about their popish, foolish rules than about St. Paul's epistles. They think of neither God nor His mother, except in so far as it serves the glory of their Francis. Indeed, through Francis they want to be esteemed and valued, and under the guise of the saint's honor they seek their own honor and advantage. They themselves say, "We have no greater honor than when we present ourselves as poor in attire and devout in countenance. Also, we are given much more. And anything valuable one has, he should not let the people see." They have a saint named

17. The Franciscans, see *The First Confederate*, 25n19.

18. Francis of Assisi (c. 1181/2–1226), *ODCC*, 632–33.

19. On the Franciscan Observants, see *The First Confederate*, 25n19.

Ludowicus who was one day a bare-footed friar and the next a bishop.[20] Then his regimen became easier, and this was fitting, because he may have perished in the mendicant life. They claim of him that he was able to arrange that a barren woman was with child (which is to be understood thus: when a young, strong bare-footed friar said previously on three successive days several little prayers alone for the woman, which no one sees or hears, etc.) and if a woman would want to abort at the birth, the beloved saint could help her with that too (in so far as she would not give the child to a bare-footed friar, even if he is a deserving father).

They have a saint named Anthony.[21] Whoever calls on him finds lost spoons, knives and keys, also lost needles and pins. With such folly they go out among the simple people, so that they can support themselves to the great detriment to true Christianity and the common good.

The Preaching monks invented the seven golden (*guldin*) masses, which are called golden because you must pay a florin (*guldin*) to have each of them said.[22] The same applies with the Rosencrantz and Our Lady's Mantel[23] and in addition many brotherhoods, to be enrolled in which one has to give a Kreuzer, and then whenever the names are read each year, one has to pay another penny. They consider their Dominic a saint, and I consider him holy in that he cursed all Preaching monks (for it is believable that in the spirit he recognized all the evil they have perpetuated until now, as with the conception of Mary and with the brothers in Berne, etc).[24] For they have been cursed down to this day, since at his end

20. St. Ludwig (1274–1297) was the son of Charles II of Anjou. As the result of a vow taken during a serious illness, he was ordained and entered the Franciscan order, but the same year he was made Bishop of Toulouse by the pope. See *JEvGS* 1:224.

21. St. Anthony of Padua (1188/1198–1231), a Franciscan and the first lector of theology in the Franciscan Order. He was invoked primarily for the return of lost property, likely on the basis of the story that a novice once ran away with his Psalter, but then returned it after being frightened by an apparition. See *JEvGS* 1:224; *ODCC*, 81.

22. Cf. Eberlin's comments in *The Sixth Confederate*, 75–76n19.

23. A series of devotional practices dedicated to the Virgin Mary described in *A Mirror of the Christian life* by the Franciscan Dederich of Münster. See *JEvGS* 1:224.

24. Ebebrlin is referring to the Jetzer Affair. In 1506 a tailor named Jetzer arrived in Berne and stayed at the local Dominican priory. While there he claimed to have had visions of the Virgin Mary, who informed him that she had spent three hours in a state of original sin. This revelation was welcomed by the Dominicans, who saw in it confirmation of their campaign against the Franciscan teaching on the immaculate conception. Jetzer's notoriety spread quickly and people flocked to the city to see the man who had spoken with the virgin. After the charade was exposed, some of the Dominicans were implicated in the hoax and four friars were condemned to death. They were burned at the

he cursed all who brought or accepted real estate into his order, which is stated in his legend.[25]

Read the recently printed books that have come out on the bare-footed statutes, rule, histories, and also on the fables of the Preachers, many of which they themselves invented, you will find shameful, deceitful things, and if there is someone among them who is displeased by such things so contrary to the Christian faith, he must either flee or suffer a lingering martyrdom.

The Carmelites' marriage to and relationship with Mary serves as a shield for them; even though they follow her in neither modesty nor humility, nor contempt for the world, nonetheless, they claim that they and Mary are first cousins.

The swindlers of entire lands known as the Stationers,[26] have authority from the bishops to undertake all manner of knavery.

The Valentinians claim St. Valentine, whose feast is in February, but that is disproven if one searches the histories, for their Valentine was a bishop, as they claim, but not that one, and it is a great pity that one gives them half a farthing in Rufach.[27]

Saint Bernard's message leads the people to believe that the Bernardines come from Saint Bernard, the great teacher, who was called the Mellifluous,[28] but that's not true.

The Holy Ghosters and Anthonites[29] take up collections at the hospitals for the poor, with whom, however, they share hardly a straw on which to sleep in their great hunger.

---

stake in May 1509. Jetzer, who claimed that the Dominican leadership had orchestrated the whole thing, was banished (Gordon, *Swiss Reformation*, 32–33).

25. On his deathbed Dominic cursed all those who would bring secure incomes or landed goods into his order. In 1425, Pope Martin V removed this restriction on the order's activities, see *JEvGS* 1:225.

26. Mendicant friars like the Pardoners who sell indulgences, but also travel with holy relics, see *JEvGS* 1:225.

27. Benedictine monks of the cloister of St. Valentine at Rufach in Alsace. See *JEvGS* 1:225.

28. Bernard's contemporaries called him mellifluous (honey-tongued or sweet-tongued), see *JEvGS* 1:225. In the Middle Ages the Cistercians were sometimes referred to as the Bernardines in recognition of the Bernard's significance to the early history of the order.

29. The Hospital Brothers of St. Anthony founded by Gaston de Dauphiné in 1095. See *ODCC*, 80.

The world is full of such deceit, and there won't be an end to it until the peasants finally hang and drown the good and the bad together; thus is deceit justly rewarded. I believe that all those in our day who support the begging orders and Pardoners commit a greater sin than if they stole or promoted whoredom. For such crimes would be evident so that both sides would take seriously the corrupting mischief that comes from them.

M W V

I warn you in good faith

Allē und ietlichē
christgelöubigē menschen ein
heilsame warnūg das sy
sich hüten vor nüwen
schedlichen leren.

Der.XV.bundt
gnosz.

Figure 15. *Der XV. bundtgnosz.* Bayerische Staatsbibliothek München [Res/4 H.ref. 271 y#Beibd.14]

15

The Fifteenth Confederate

To each and every believer in Christ, a wholesome warning to guard against new, dangerous teachings.

Since all of my fourteen colleagues have already written, it is fitting for me, the last and fifteenth, to conclude with this advice. Know, beloved, devout Christians that, both together and individually, we are obligated to remain firm in the Christian teaching, which Christ proclaimed to us by himself and through his apostles and evangelists. So many thousands of martyrs have suffered for it, so many holy doctors have faithfully studied it, and for so many hundreds of years it has stood on firm foundations. Therefore, it would be a disgrace for us to abandon for the sake of new inventions such an ancient, firm truth, which the patriarchs and prophets spoke of many hundreds of years before Christ's birth. But in the last few years there have arisen unlearned teachers who don't know God's law, false prophets whom God didn't send, and illegitimate lawgivers who intend nothing good, all of whom have attracted to themselves almost the entire world through their glistening appearance and poisonous sweetness. Through them so many renowned people have been led astray that we must fear that the elect have nearly fallen into the abyss of God's anger. For what is God's anger other than a blinding of reason into a perverted understanding of Holy Scripture and God's commandments, from which follows godless desires and everything evil.

Therefore, to escape such evil it is necessary above all else that each person adopt the most effective means to avoid harm.

The first means to do this is that each person should himself read, or have read to him, the four gospels and Paul's epistles, as one finds them in the second part of the Bible. And no one should deny that he has the necessary understanding, for the spirit of Christ, through which such things are written, will, without doubt, stand by, either through inner inspiration or outer teaching, all those who read these writings in good faith. Further, when God is sought in them, it is not possible to read through these scriptures without special illumination from God. When these writings have been read carefully, even a simple lay person will understand for the most part what in the newly arisen teaching is for, and what is against, our law. Without a doubt, it was through the devil's rabble and obstacles that the Holy Bible was appropriated to the priests, monks, and professors and denied to the simple Christians as something dangerous. But in understanding the Holy Bible, pious prayer is more helpful than keen reading, humble faith more than elevated disputation, a kind heart more than lengthy babbling. And for no other reason than a gracious God wants his teaching to be common for everyone, to whom he did not deny his suffering and death and wholesome, salutary sacrament.

There are also lay people, rich and poor, men and women, with sharp minds; they, too, are loved by God; God has not abandoned them, indeed, much less than he has the greedy monks and priests and vain professors.

It is written that no one is taught in the Holy Scriptures, except by God. He who is not taught by God will remain untaught, and God reveals to the simple what he hides from the highly esteemed and wise.[1] Therefore, whoever loves his soul should not scorn my advice. He should read the scriptural passages recommended above or have them read to him, because Holy Scripture is the sword of the spirit with which we all must protect ourselves against error. And these are dangerous times when the devil is active. Therefore, whoever doesn't have the sword of the Bible, let him sell his coat and buy a Bible with the money he gets; the time is here.[2] No one can claim poverty as his excuse. Can you buy bread to feed your body? Then you are no Christian if you don't have more regard for the bread of the soul, which is God's word. Are you unable to read by yourself? Then hire a poor student who can read to you as much as you need in a day for a piece

1. See Matt 11:25ff; Luke 10:21–22.

2. See Luke 22:36.

of bread. Do you not have a book? Are you too poor? Then beg for a book; it is more fitting to beg for the Gospel than for a piece of bread. Ask others for God's sake to read to you from the Gospel.

Don't say, "I hear it from the priests in the pulpit," because you hear from the pulpit or in the mass only the smallest part and, indeed, the least understandable part of the Gospel. And that same small part is properly explained for the salvation of souls by only a few. It is much more helpful and useful that you read thoughtfully by yourself so that you can reflect on and re-read passages where you have difficulties. Otherwise, the words of the priest fly by without understanding. Furthermore, you will get much greater benefit from what the priest says if you read it beforehand.

I tell you truly that in our time there is an overriding need to take great care with God's word, for in it lies our salvation. And had our ancestors taken such advice, without doubt our times would not be so dangerous. But what harmed our ancestors should be a warning to us, because blessed is he who learns from the suffering of others. However, I will explain to you what the new, misleading teachings are.

Whoever says that something in the law of Christ is a counsel and not a command errs. Only keeping celibate is a counsel.

Whoever says that indulgences are good errs.

Whoever says that a person can prepare himself for God's grace by his own ability errs.

Whoever says that a person, if he is already saved, can do a good work, no part of which is sin, errs. For the prophet says all our righteousness is like an unclean cloth before God.[3] And Christ says that we can make no good preparation for grace on our own, without me you can do nothing.[4] And according to Paul on our own we cannot even think of something good.[5]

Whoever says that we can do enough for the forgiveness of our sins errs. For Christ alone has done enough for that and if we have faith in Him, we will partake of His satisfaction. As the prophet says, He has taken away our sin.[6]

Whoever says man has a free will, he can do good or evil if he chooses, errs. For God says, Oh Israel, your depravity comes from you, but your

3. Isa 64:6.

4. John 15:5.

5. 2 Cor 3:5.

6. Zech 3:4.

salvation comes from me alone.[7] He desires to and can sin on his own, but by himself he can do nothing good. As is written, Lord you have worked all our good works in us.[8]

Whoever says that human nature is fine and noble errs, for we are corrupted right to the marrow. As God says, from childhood on human thought and reason tend toward evil.[9] The grace of God alone can bring us back to the right path. Since we are corrupted, how can our thoughts and works be good before God; a bad tree cannot bring forth good fruit.[10]

Human preparation does not help bring true repentance and suffering for sin. As the prophet says, Lord restore us, and so we will be restored.[11] And whoever says otherwise errs.

Whoever says that anointing, confirmation, ordination of the clergy, and marriage are godly sacraments errs; these are self-serving teachings.

Whoever says that a man, foreseen in the end for eternal damnation, is a true member of the Christian church here on earth lies, because no one is a member for whom Christ is not an eternal, saving head.

Whoever says that according to God's law the priests should not be subject to the laity in temporal matters in terms of both judgment and punishment errs, for St. Peter says otherwise.[12]

Whoever says that the religious estate bound by three vows is a more sure path to salvation than the married estate errs.

Whoever says that the handling and transformation of the holy *corpus Christi* wrought by the priest in the mass is an offering for the living and the dead errs. Therefore, the greater part of the goods and money used to endow masses and pious anniversaries, thirtieths and sevenths, etc.[13] is wagered and lost.

Whoever claims anything other than that true faith, given to mankind by God, alone is the beginning of salvation errs.

Whoever says that God rewards good works first and foremost errs, because God rewards the good wills in the good works, and the will is good that has godly faith. God rewards His gifts in us and not our works.

7. Hos 13:9.

8. Matt 7:20; Eph 2:10.

9. Gen 8:21.

10. Matt 7:18.

11. Jer 31:18.

12. 1 Pet 2:13.

13. See Eberlin's comments in *The Seventh Confederate.*

It is a truth that works which appear good, such as fasting, keeping vigils, praying, etc. can certainly occur without true faith, but true faith can never be without good works, because true faith given by God is not idle, it always works good.

Whoever says that voluntary begging, as we have among the mendicant orders, is meritorious for salvation errs, because begging is only allowed for the poor and ill. Others should work for their upkeep. God has commanded this.

Whoever says that in the case of reserved matters or sins one must seek out for confession a specific higher authority than the common parish priest errs.

Whoever says that brotherly love or bodily need are not sufficient reasons to break all papal, episcopal, and monastic rules or commands without any other dispensation errs and contradicts the teachings of St. Paul and St. Peter.

Whoever says that a person is obliged to confess sins other than those he can recall in good faith without exceptional burdens, and which in his own understanding he recognizes as mortal sins, errs. And the priests should not be harsh in the confessional, nor should they ask many questions if they don't want to go astray. Rather, they should absolve what the sinner confesses for the sake of God and the sinner's faith.

Whoever says there is no purgatory errs.

Whoever says that after confession a penance should be imposed errs.

Whoever says that one is bound on pain of mortal sin by commands of the church or rules of an order, even if one breaks them in secret without offense to others, errs. It follows from this that a priest, monk, or nun may neglect to recite the canonical hours, if they are prescribed individually, outside the churches or choir, and the neglect remains secret and doesn't offend others. Indeed, since one chooses to do this, no one is obliged to it on pain of mortal sin. And if afterwards you have scruples of the conscience on this account, this is from your lack of faith, not from your neglect. From this follows that secretly breaking a fast without offending others, even if one is not ill, is not a mortal sin.

It is also important to know that all preaching mixed with the teachings of Aristotle, Scotus, Thomas, Hales, Ockham, Gabriel Biel, Albertus,[14]

14. John Duns Scotus (c. 1265–1308), see *ODCC*, 513–14; Thomas Aquinas (c. 1225–1274), ibid., 1614–17; Alexander of Hales (c. 1185–1245), ibid., 39; William of Ockham (c. 1285–1347), ibid., 1745–46; Gabriel Biel (c. 1420–1495), ibid., 207–8; Albert the Great (c. 1193–1280), ibid., 34–35.

etc., also with a concoction of ecclesiastical law and such human ordinances, is suspect and should not be heard by the people. Instead, one should hold the priests to presenting pure evangelical teaching.

Whoever says it is better to give a penny offering to the priest at the altar than to a pauper errs, even if the priest is destitute.

Whoever says it is better to give alms to the begging monks than to another unknown beggar errs. But, know that if you want to be sure, give alms first of all to your poor fellow citizens. Then, if you have something left over, give to foreign beggars as well.

How strictly one is bound to the confession and to papal obedience, one can learn from other wholesome books now on the market.

Look, friend, such things were taught in Christendom for twelve hundred years and were well established, but in the last four hundred years new baseless teachings have taken root, primarily through the activities of the universities and begging monks. These teachings have caused great damage to true Christianity and the common good, so that both our morals and our goods have suffered and we have become more evil than heathens and poorer than beggars. But by leading us astray our deceivers (who are the monks, priests, and professors) have become rich and powerful, so that now in their leisure they possess almost half the world and can pursue all manner of depravity without punishment. Besides, we have to support them with our hard work and poverty and receive nothing in return except an evil example, contempt for ourselves and our children, and poisonous, unchristian teachings. No one should say that such teachings seem good on account of their longevity, because you know that the previous 1,000 years were longer than the last 300. Furthermore, when some devout teachers wrote something contradicting them during this time, their books were suppressed and their teachings declared heretical so that such Antichristian inventions and teachings were promoted. And in 300 years no teacher is held in greater honor than he who has fought the hardest against the evangelical foundation under the appearance of doing good. It's no wonder that many people cling to and have clung to such teachings, because monks and priests have racked their brains day and night as to how they might deceive us. Meanwhile, we have been anxious and fearful about providing daily bread for ourselves, our children and servants, and we could hardly expect that our ministers and devourers of saints would have prepared for us such a massacre of souls under good appearances. But God be praised that the true light is returning. God has not forgotten us in our need,[15] even if the devil and Antichrist, and all the evil monks, priests, and professors contend against it. We should beseech God for grace that we might receive this light.

I wanted to give you this admonition and ask each of you in particular that you let it serve you well.

Don't let the time drag on, I will come soon, God willing.

15. The text states "unser noch." The context suggests that "*noch*" should be "*Not*."

Select Bibliography

Primary Sources

A. Modern Editions of the *Fifteen Confederates*

Baldini, A. Enzo, ed. and trans. *Gli "Statuti di Wolfaria" di Johann Eberlin (1521)*. Turin: Academia delle Scienze, 1986. (tenth and eleventh *Confederates*)

Berger, Arnold E., ed. *Die Sturmtruppen der Reformation: Ausgewählte Flugschriften der Jahre 1520–1525*. Leipzig: Philipp Reclam jun., 1931. (first, eighth, tenth, and eleventh *Confederates*)

Enders, Ludwig, ed. *Johann Eberlin von Günzburg. Ausgewählte Schriften*, vol. 1. Flugschriften aus der Reformationszeit, vol. 11. Halle: Niemeyer, 1896.

Laube, Adolf, et al., eds. *Flugschriften der frühen Reformationsbewegung (1518–1524)*. 2 vols. Berlin: Akademie, 1983. (first, tenth, and eleventh *Confederates*)

Simon, Karl, ed. *Deutsche Flugschriften zur Reformation (1520–1525)*. Reprint, Stuttgart: Philipp Reclam jun., 1980. (tenth, eleventh, and fifteenth *Confederates*)

B. Other Primary Sources

Baldini, Artemio Enzo. *L'Educazione di un Principe Luterano. Il Furschlag di Johann Eberlin von Günzburg, tra Erasmo, Lutero e la Sconfitta dei Contadini*. Milan: Angeli, 2010.

Brieger, Th. *Quellen und Forschungen zur Geschichte der Reformation*. Vol. 1, *Aleander und Luther. Die vervollständigen Aleander Depeschen*. Gotha: Perthes, 1884.

Erasmus, Desiderius. *The Collected Works of Erasmus*, vol. 27. *Literary and Educational Writings*, vol. 5. Edited by A. H. T. Levi. Translated and annotated by Betty Radice. Toronto: University of Toronto Press, 1986.

———. *The Collected Works of Erasmus*, vol. 28. *Literary and Educational Writings*, vol. 6. Edited by A. H. T. Levi. Translated and annotated by Betty I. Knott. Toronto: University of Toronto Press, 1986.

Förstmann, Karl Edward, ed. *Album Academia Vitebergensis*. Old series, vol. 1, *1502–1560*. Leipzig, 1841. Reprint, Aalen: Scientia, 1976.

Horace. *Satires, Epistles, and Ars Poetica*. Translated by H. Rushton Fairclough. Cambridge: Harvard University Press, 1929.

Jacobus de Voragine. *The Golden Legend of Jacobus de Voragine*. Translated by Granger Ryan and Helmut Ripperger. New York: Arno, 1969.

Masser, Achim, editor. *Johann Eberlin von Günzburg. Ein zamengelesen bouchlin von der Teutschen Nation gelegenheit, sitten, vnd gebrauche, durch Cornelium Tacitum vnd etliche anderer verzeichent*. Innsbruck: Institüt für Germanistik, 1996.

Mayer, Hermann, editor. *Die Matrikel der Universität Freiburg i. Br.* Vol. 1, *1460–1656*. Freiburg: Herders, 1907.

Murner, Thomas. *Thomas Murners Deutsche Schriften mit Holzschnitten der Erstdrucke*. Edited by Franz Schultz. Vol. 9, *Von dem großen Lutherischen Narren*, edited by Paul Merker. Strasbourg: Trübner, 1918.

Pelikan, Jaroslav, ed. *The Preaching of Chrysostum: Homilies on the Sermon on the Mount*. Philadelphia: Fortress, 1967.

Schaff, Philip, and Henry Wace, ed. *A Select Library of Nicene and Post-Nicene Fathers of the Christian Church*. 2nd series, vol. 6, *St Jerome: Letters and Select Works*. New York: Christian Literature Co., 1893.

Wackernagel, Hans Georg, ed. *Die Matrikel der Universität Basel*. Vol. 1, *1460–1529*. Basel: Verlag der Universitätsbibliothek, 1951.

Secondary Sources

Ahrens, Hans-Herbert. "Die religiösen, nationalen und sozialen Gedanken Johann Eberlin von Günzburgs mit besonderer Berucksichtigung seiner anonymen Flugschriften." DPhil diss., Universität Hamburg, 1939.

Andrews, Frances. *The Other Friars: The Carmelite, Augustinian, Sack, and Pied Friars in the Middle Ages*. Woodbridge, UK: Boydell, 2006.

Baldini, Artemio Enzo. "Istanze utopiche e dibatto poltico agli inizi della Riforma luterana. Dall 'Wolfaria' di Johann Eberlin all 'Newen Wandlung eynes Christliche Lebens.'" In *Alberto Tenenti. Scritti in memoria*, edited by P. Scaramella, 302–15. Naples: Bibliopolis, 2005.

———. "Nobile e contandini negli scritti di Johann Eberlin: un riforatore tra Erasmo e Lutero." *Il Pensiero politico* 28 (1995) 439–53.

———. "Riforma Luterana e Utopia: Gli 'Statuti del Paese di Wolfaria' di Johann Eberlin." *Il Pensiero politico* 19 (1986) 3–31.

Baur, August. "Rezension der Herausgabe von Eberlins Schriften durch Ludwig Enders." *Göttingische Gelehrte Anzeigen* 159 (1897) 1–7.

Bell, Susan Groag. "Johann Eberlin von Günzburg's *Wolfaria*: The First Protestant Utopia." *Church History* 36 (1967) 122–39.

Bowden, Muriel. *A Commentary on the General Prologue to the Canterbury Tales*. New York: Macmillan, 1949.

Brecht, Martin. "Johann Eberlin von Günzburg in Wittenberg." *Wertheimer Jahrbuch 1983* (1985) 47–54.

Brinker-von der Heyde, Claudia. "Neue Weltordnung in Zeichen des Antichrist: Radikale Reformer entwerfen die ideale Gesellschaft." In *Reisen, Entdecken, Utopie: Untersuchungen zum Alteritätsdiskurs im Kontext von Kolonialismus und Kulturkritik*, edited by Anil Bhatti and Horst Turk, 29–40. New York: Lang, 1998.

Buck, Lawrence P. "The Reformation, Purgatory, and Perpetual Rents in the Revolt of 1525 at Frankfurt am Main" In *Pietas et Societas: New Trends in Reformation Social History. Essays in Memory of Harold J. Grimm*, edited by Kyle C. Sessions and Phillip N. Bebb, 23–33. Kirksville, MO: Sixteenth Century Journal Publishers, 1985.

Bujňáková, M. "Johann Eberlin von Günzburg—'Wolfaria'—Eine Gesellschaftsutopie aus dem 16. Jahrhundert." *Philologica Pragensia* 32 (1989) 184–94.

Cole, Richard G. "Eberlin von Günzburg and the German Reformation." PhD diss., Ohio State University, 1963.

———. "Law and Order in the Sixteenth Centutry: Eberlin von Günzburg and the Problem of Political Authority." *Lutheran Quarterly* 23 (1971) 251–56.

———. "The Pamphlet and Social Forces in the Reformation." *Lutheran Quarterly* 18 (1965) 195–205.

Deuerlein, Ernst. "Nachtrag zu Johann Eberlin von Günzburg." In *Lebensbilder aus der bayerischen Schwaben*, edited by Götz Freiherrn von Pölnitz, 6:495. Munich: Heuber, 1958.

Dipple, Geoffrey. *Antifraternalism and Anticlericalism in the German Reformation: Johann Eberlin von Günzburg and the Campaign against the Friars*. Aldershot, UK: Scolar, 1996.

Doku, Sharon Oboshie. "Johann Eberlin von Günzburg's Lutheran Utopia *Wolfaria* (1521): Laws for a New German State." BA honors thesis, Harvard University, 2005.

Edwards, Mark U. *Printing, Propaganda, and Martin Luther*. 1994. Reprint, Minneapolis: Fortress, 2004.

Edwards, O. C. *A History of Preaching*. Nashville: Abingdon, 2004.

Eliav-Feldon, Miriam. *Realistic Utopias: The Ideal Imaginary Societies of the Renaissance*. Oxford: Oxford University Press, 1982.

Geiger, Gottfried. "Die reformatorischen Initia Johann Eberlins von Günzburg nach seinem Flugschriften." In *Festgabe für Ernst Walter Zeeden zum 60. Geburtstag am 14. Mai 1976*, edited by Horst Rabe, Hans-Georg Molitor, and Hans-Christoph Rublach, 170–201. Münster: Aschendorff, 1976.

Gorciex, Bernard. "L'Utopie en Allemagne au XVIe at au début du XVIIe siècle." *Études Germanique* 30 (1975) 14–29.

Gordon, Bruce. *The Swiss Reformation*. Manchester, UK: Manchester University Press, 2001.

Götze, Alfred. "Ein Sendbrief Eberlins von Günzburg." *Zeitschrift für deutsche Philologie* 6 (1904) 145–54.

Heger, Günther. *Johann Eberlin von Günzburg und seine Vorstellungen über eine Reform in Reich und Kirche*. Berlin: Duncker & Humblot, 1985.

Hitchcock, Willliam R. *The Background of the Knights' Revolt, 1522–1523*. Berkeley: University of California Press, 1958.

Kerr, Julie. *Life in the Medieval Cloister*. London: Continuum, 2009.

Koslofsky, Craig. *The Reformation of the Dead: Death and Ritual in Early Modern Germany, 1450–1700*. New York: St. Martin's, 2000.

Lambert, M. D. *Franciscan Poverty: The Doctrine of the Absolute Poverty of Christ and the Apostles in the Franciscan Order, 1210–1323*. St. Bonaventure, NY: Franciscan Studies Institute, 1986.

Lederer, David. "Welfare Land: Johann Eberlin von Günzburg and the Reformation of Folly." In *Ideas and Cultural Margins in Early Modern Germany: Essays in Honor of H. C. Erik Midelfort*, edited by Marjorie Elizabeth Plummer and Robin Barnes, 167–81. Farnham, UK: Ashgate, 2009.

Leitzmann, A. "Zu Johann Eberlin von Günzburg." *Beiträge zur Geschichte der deutschen Sprache und Literatur* 43 (1918) 275–78.

Lucke, Wilhelm. "Die Entstehung der '15 Bundesgenossen' des Johann Eberlins von Günzburg." DPhil diss., Universität Halle, 1902.

Neidiger, Bernhard. *Mendikanten zwischen Ordensideal und städtischer Realität: Untersuchungen zum wirtschaflichen Verhalten der Bettelorden in Basel.* Berlin: Duncker & Humblot, 1981.

Noack, Lothar. "Johann Eberlin von Günzburg (um 1460–1533) und seine Flugschriften in der deutschsprachigen Flugschriftenliteratur der Jahre 1520–1524." DPhil diss., Universität Leipzig, 1983.

Oberman, Heiko. *The Roots of Antisemitism in the Age of Renaissance and Reformation.* Translated by James Porter. Philadelphia: Fortress, 1984.

Opitz, D. D. "The Social Vision of Johann Eberlin von Günzburg: From Utopian Humanist to Evangelical Reformer." PhD diss., Boston University, 1995.

Ozment, Steven. *The Reformation in the Cities: The Appeal of Protestantism to Sixteenth-Century Germany and Switzerland.* New Haven: Yale University Press, 1975.

———. "The Social History of the Reformation: What Can We Learn from Pamphlets?" In *Flugschriften als Massenmedium der Reformationszeit. Beiträge zum Tübinger Symposion 1980*, edited by Hans-Joachim Köhler, 171–203. Stuttgart: Klett, 1981.

Packull, Werner O. "The Image of the 'Common Man' in the Early Pamphlets of the Reformation." *Historical Reflections* 12 (1985) 253–77.

Peters, Christian. *Johann Eberlin von Günzburg ca. 1465–1533: Franziskanischer Reformer, Humanist, konservativer Reformator.* Quellen und Forschungen zur Reformationsgeschichte 60. Gütersloh: Gütersloher, 1994.

Plard, Henri. "L'Utopie Communiste Agraire d'Eberlin de Günzburg: Le Pays de Wolfaria." In *L'Humanisme allemand (1480–1540): XVIIIè Colloque International de Tours*, edited by Joël Lefebvre and Jean-Claude Margolin, 387–403. Paris: Vrin, 1979.

Radlkofer, Max. *Johann Eberlin von Günzburg und sein Vetter Hans Jakob Wehe von Leipheim.* Nördlingen: Beck, 1887.

Riggenbach, Bernhard. *Johann Eberlin von Günzburg und seine Reformprogramm: Ein Beitrag zur Geschichte des sechzehnten Jahrhunderts.* 1874. Reprint, Nieuwkoop: De Graaf, 1967.

Rivoletti, C. "Strategie della finzione nelle utopie del Cinquecento europa. Sulla ricezione dell Utopia di Thomas More nei testi di Eberlin von Günzburg, Antonio Brucioli, Anton Francesco Doni, Kaspar Stiblin e Tommaso Campanella." *Morus: Utopia e Renascimento* 3 (2006) 69–93.

Schmidt, Johann Heinrich. "'Die 15 Bundesgenossen' des Johann Eberlin von Günzburg." DPhil diss., Universität Leipzig, 1900.

Seibt, Ferdinand. *Utopica: Modelle totaler Sozialplannung.* Düsseldorf: Schwann, 1972.

Sessions, Kyle C. "Christian Humanism and the Freedom of a Christian: Johann Eberlin von Günzburg to the Peasants." In *The Social History of the Reformation*, edited by Lawrence P. Buck and Jonathan W. Zophy, 137–55. Columbus: Ohio State University Press, 1972.

Stöckl, Kurt. "Untersuchungen zu Johann Eberlin von Günzburg." DPhil diss., Universität Munich, 1952.

Strobel, Georg Theodor. "Nachricht von Johann Eberlin von Günzburgs Leben und Schriften." *Literarischen Museum* 1 (1778) 363–85.

Szittya, Penn. *The Antifraternal Tradition in Medieval Literature*. Princeton: Princeton University Press, 1986.

———. "The Antifraternal Tradition in Middle English Literature." *Speculum* 52 (1977) 287–313.

Vogler, Günther. "Reformprogramm oder utopischer Entwurf? Gedanken zu Johann Eberlin von Günzburgs 'Wolfaria.'" *Jahrbuch für Geschichte des Feudalismus* 3 (1979) 219–32.

———. "Von Eberlin zu Stiblinus. Utopisches Denken zwischen 1521 und 1555." In *Reform Reformation Revolution*, edited by Siegfried Hoyer, 143–50. Leipzig: Karl-Marx-Universität, 1980.

Vogler, Günther, Max Steinmetz, and Adolf Laube. *Illustrierte Geschichte der deutschen frühburgerlichen Revolution*. Berlin: Dietz, 1974.

Weidhase, Helmut. "Kunst und Sprache im Spiegel der reformatorischen und humanistischen Schriften Johann Eberlins von Günzburg." DPhil diss., Universität Tübingen, 1967.

Werner, Julius. *Johann Eberlin von Günzburg: Ein reformatorisches Charakterbild aus Luthers Zeit*. 2nd ed. Heidelberg: Winters, 1905.

Wulkau, Curt. "Das kirchliche Ideal des Johann Eberlin von Günzburg." DPhil diss., Universität Halle-Wittenberg, 1922.

Name and Subject Index

Absolution, 125, 175
Adultery, 32, 132
Advent, 119
Agatha, St., 45
Agnes, St., 118
Albert the Great, 175
Aleander, Girolamo, 1, 6–7, 9
Alexander of Hales, 175
Alexander IV, 110n12
All Saints' Day, 118
Alms, 31, 67, 74–76, 88, 110, 115, 120, 125, 135, 140, 144, 148, 150, 162n4, 176
Alsace, 4, 23, 49
Anastasia, St., 118
Andlau, 44n3, 49
Annaberg, 15
Annates, 31
Anne, St., 77
Annunciation, 118
Anthony, St., 167
Antichrist, 24, 28, 30, 92, 95, 97–98, 106, 108, 113, 128, 155, 165, 176–77
Antwerp, 13
Apostolic Creed, 127
Aquinas, Thomas. *See* Thomas Aquinas
Aristotle, 28, 65, 74, 156, 165, 175
Ascension Day, 118
Ash Wednesday, 40n7
Athanasian Creed, 127
Augsburg, 11–12, 15
Augustine, St., 47, 65, 70, 77, 83n2, 147
Augustinian Hermits, 109–11, 112n16

Baden, 9–10
Baptism, 37, 61, 66, 125, 153–54, 158
Barbara, St., 162
Bare-footed friars. *See* Franciscans
Barr, 4, 49n11
Barrabas, 24
Basel, 3, 4n12, 5, 9, 11, 14
Bavaria, 31
Bede, 65
Beguines, 111, 145n4, 145n5, 146
Benedict of Nursia, 112n15
Benedictines, 112
Benefice, 27, 30n25, 31–32, 57n5, 62, 87–88, 97, 102, 118, 120–21, 126, 148–49, 155
Bernard, St. 112n15, 163, 168
Bernardines, 112, 168
Berne, 167
Bible, 14, 47, 57, 59, 66, 74–75, 78, 128, 147, 172
Biel, Gabriel, 41, 175
Blasphemy, 32
Bonaventure, 74
Boniface VIII, 98
Brassicanus, Johann, 23
Brothers of Saint Anthony, 54, 168
Burials, 81–83, 85, 125, 140, 145, 148, 164. *See also* Funerals

Canonical hours, 7, 50, 53–59, 85, 87, 104, 113, 120, 140, 147–48, 175
Canon law, 1, 9–10, 29, 74, 129, 134, 156, 176

Carmelites, 77–78, 97, 106, 110–11, 168
Carthusians, 97, 106, 112
Cathedral chapters, 54–59, 106, 147–48
Cecelia, St., 118
Celibacy, 12, 112, 114n18, 120, 123, 146n6, 149, 173
Cemeteries, 124, 145
Chalice, 125, 128
Chaplains, 81, 88, 118, 123
Charles II, 167n20
Charles V, 8–9, 21–30, 32–33, 104n2, 150
Charles the Fat, 49n11
Christendom, 10–11, 21–22, 36, 41, 85, 92, 95, 110, 165, 176
Christmas, 118
Christopher, St., 162
Chrysostum, John, 38, 47, 65, 77
Cicero, 71
Cistercians, 112n15, 168n28
Clare, St., 146n7
Clement V, 98n14
Cochlaeus, Johannes, 1, 24
Cologne, Bruno of, 112n15
Compline. *See* Canonical hours
Confession, 9, 25–26, 30–31, 35, 36n1, 38, 40, 48, 56–57, 64, 73, 78, 85, 94, 97, 102, 106–7, 111, 123–25, 146–47, 155, 158, 175–76
Constance, Council of, 25n19
Constantine, 163n9
Convents, 13, 43–51, 54, 86, 103, 108, 111–12, 144–45, 147
Corpus Christi, 118, 174
Courtiers, Roman, 21, 26–29, 31–32, 38, 95, 97, 102, 156
Crown Prayers, 75, 127
Crusades, 54n2

Dauphiné, Gaston de, 168n29
Demosthenes, 71, 73
Dertusiensis, 25–26
Devil, 6, 24–26, 32, 43, 45, 47–48, 92–93, 95, 110–12, 115, 154, 161, 163n13, 172, 177
Dominic, St., 93, 109, 167, 168n25
Dominicans, 16, 77, 110n12, 110n13, 111, 146, 149, 165, 167–68
Drunkenness, 32, 38, 114

Eberlin von Günzburg, Johann,
Against the False Religious known as the Bare-Footed Friars and Franciscans, 16
Against the Imprudent, Unreasonable Departure of Many Cloistered, 13
Against the Profaners of God's Creatures, 15
The Bell Tower, 16
The Consolation of the Seven Devout Priests, 14
Epistle to the Parson of Highsense (Hohensynn), concerning Dr. Martin Luther's Teaching, 5
A Friendly, Encouraging Exhortation to the Christians at Augsburg, 13
How a Servant of God's Word Should Conduct Himself, 17
How Very Dangerous, that a Priest does not Have a Wife, 12
I Wonder that there is no Money in the Land, 17
A Little Book Which Answers Three Questions, 14
A New, and the Last, Statement of the Fifteen Confederates, 14
On the Abuse of Christian Liberty, 13
A Second True Admonition to the Council of Ulm, 15
A Sermon in Erfurt on Prayer, 17
Seven Devout but Disconsolate Priests Complain to One Another about Their Plight, 14
A Short Written Report on Faith to the Citizens of Ulm, 15
A Splendid Mirror of the Christian Life, 16
A Warning to the Christians of the Margraviate of Burgau, 18
Eck, Johannes, 1
Eckhart, Johann, 11
Edwards, Mark U., 1

Enthusiasts, 13, 17
Epicureanism, 41
Epiphany, 118
Erasmus of Rotterdam, 8–10, 19, 22, 31, 69, 71n7, 72n8, 73–74, 91, 97, 110, 156, 161–62, 165
Praise of Folly, 10, 69, 161
Erfurt, 17
Eucharist. *See* Mass and Sacrament of the Altar
Exaltation of the Cross, 40n7
Excommunication, 30–31, 65, 94, 108, 137, 144, 155, 157–58

False prophets, 97, 171
Fasting, 40, 43, 47, 51, 70, 75, 118, 124, 134, 155, 163n11, 164, 175. *See also* Lenten fast and Lords' Fasts
Feast days, 40n7, 83, 118–20, 125, 127, 135, 139, 155
Francis, St., 77, 93, 107–9, 146n7, 166
Rule of, 25n19, 107–10, 168
Francis I, 104n2
Franciscan nuns, 4, 146
Franciscans, 1, 4, 6, 8–9, 15–16, 19, 25–27, 33, 77, 94, 97–98, 105–11, 146, 149, 166–68
Franciscan Observants, 4, 6, 8–9, 25–27, 33, 97, 105–6, 111, 149, 166
Frederick I, Barbarossa, 92
Frederick II, 31, 92
Freiburg im Breisgau, 3, 5n19
Friars. *See* Mendicant orders, Augustinians, Carmelites, Dominicans, and Franciscans
Fritzhans, Johann, 15
Funerals, 81, 84, 104. *See also* Burials

Geiger, Gottfried, 7–8, 10, 11
Gengenbach, Pamphilius, 11
George, St., 163
Gerbelius, Nikolaus, 23
German lands, 1–4, 8–10, 14, 16, 18, 21–22, 24, 26–31, 33, 36, 38–39, 61, 82, 87–88, 92, 94–95, 97–98, 101–2, 106, 112–14, 143, 148, 153, 156–58
German language, 8, 10, 13, 19, 91, 95–97, 137
German Peasants War, 3, 17–18
Gerson, Jean le Charlier de, 41, 110
Glapion, Johannes, 9, 25–26, 30–31
Good Friday, 118
Gospel, 5–6, 10, 12, 16–18, 22, 24, 28, 30–31, 41, 47–48, 51n14, 59, 62–63, 65–67, 72, 75–78, 83, 85, 91, 93, 96–97, 105–7, 113, 124–25, 127, 137, 141, 147–48, 155–56, 158–59, 162, 165–66, 171–73
Grace, 28–29, 46, 67, 89, 102, 115, 143, 150, 157–58, 173–74, 177
Greek, 31n30, 129, 137
Grey Friars. *See* Franciscans
Günzburg, 3, 16

Hagenau, 23
Hebrew, 31n30, 129, 137
Heger, Günther, 8
Heinrichmann, Jakob, 23
Henry III, 92
Henry IV, 92
Henry V, 92
Hercules, 162
Heresy, 24, 94–95, 141, 176
Hermits of the Blessed Virgin of Mount Carmel. *See* Carmelites
Hilspach, Michael, 23
Hippolytus, 163
Holy Communion. *See* Mass and Sacrament of the Altar
Holy Cross Day. *See* Exaltation of the Cross
Holy Ghosters, 168
Holy Trinity, 70–71
Honorius III, 110n12
Horace, 70
Horb, 23
Hortulus anime, 127
Hospitalers. *See* Knights of the Order of the Hospital of St. John of Jerusalem
Hospitals, 27, 54, 122, 124, 168
Hugh of St. Caro, 74
Hugh of St. Victor, 74
Humanism, 4–5, 8–9, 18–19

Hus, Jan, 110
Hussites, 106
Hutten, Ulrich von, 8–9, 10n36, 17, 19, 21, 24, 26–27, 29, 31, 91, 97
The Robbers, 17

Immaculate Conception, 167n24
Indulgences, 28, 31, 66, 75, 93, 96, 101–2, 113, 137, 155, 162n4, 163–65, 168n26, 173
Ingolstadt, 3
Innocent IV, 110n12
Inquisitors, 94, 110n13
Italy, 28, 33, 94, 104

James, St., 75, 77, 113
James of Voragine, 77n24, 163n10
Jeremiah, 75
Jerome, St., 47, 51, 65, 70, 77
Jerome of Prague, 110
Jetzer Affair, 167n24
Jews, 40
John, St., 75, 77, 156
John the Baptist, 77
John of Wesel, 110
Judea, 22
Judgment Day, 46, 54, 102, 166
Julius Caesar, 73

Kaisersberg, Johann von, 23
Karlstadt, Andreas Bodenstein von, 9, 12, 15, 31, 156
Kleinkötz, 3
Knights of the Holy Cross or Holy Spirit, 54
Knights of the Order of the Hospital of St. John of Jerusalem, 54, 150
Kraft, Ulrich, 23
Krautwasser, Ägidius, 23

Laity, 1, 7, 10, 24, 29, 36, 39, 55, 58, 73–76, 77n22, 78, 86, 103, 110, 121, 126, 146n6, 149, 172, 174
Lasslen, Humbertus von, 109
Latin, 31n30, 47–48, 73, 129, 137, 147
Lauingen, 9–11
Laziness, 29, 38, 53, 55, 59, 65–67, 74, 81, 84–85, 87–88, 93, 97, 104, 107, 109–10, 112, 140, 156
Leipheim, 16
Leipzig, 12, 15
Leipzig Disputation, 1
Lenten fast, 7, 35–41, 96n10, 119, 163
Leuterschausen, 18
Listrius, Gerardus, 162, 165
Lord's Supper. *See* Mass and Sacrament of the Altar
Lords' Fasts, 40n7
Lucke, Wilhelm, 7, 11
Lucy, St., 40n7
Ludwig, St., 167
Ludwig III, the Bavarian, 92
Ludwig, Duke of Bavaria, 31n28
Luke, St., 75
Luther, Martin, 1, 2, 5–9, 11–13, 15–19, 21, 24, 26–29, 31, 74, 91, 97, 106, 110, 156
Address to the Christian Nobility, 8
On Confession, 11
Lutheran, 106

Mark, St., 75
Marriage, 39n5, 44, 46, 49–50, 120, 123, 126, 132–34, 144, 146, 149, 174
Martin V, 168n25
Martyrs and Martyrdom, 45, 159n5, 162n8, 163n9, 166, 168, 171
Mary, 77, 78n25, 167–68
Mass, 28, 32, 43, 58, 59n7, 74–75, 81–88, 104, 114, 118–20, 121n14, 124–25, 140, 148, 173–74. *See* also Sacrament of the Altar
Anniversary, 75, 81n1, 83–86, 88, 114, 174
Golden, 75, 167
Perpetual, 84–85
Seventh, 81, 85, 174
Thirtieth, 75, 81, 85–86, 174
Matins. *See* Canonical hours
Matthew, St., 75
Maundy Thursday, 118
Mauritius, St., 159n5
Maximilian, 25n18, 26

Medici, Guilio de, 6
Meersburg, Bishop of, 12
Melanchthon, Phillip, 2n4, 23n11, 129n26, 156
Memmingen, 24
Mendicant orders, 5, 9–10, 16, 21, 26–31, 63–65, 69, 70–74, 76–78, 87, 93–98, 106–13, 122, 127, 140, 144–49, 166–67, 169, 175–76. *See also* Augustinians, Carmelites, Dominicans, and Franciscans
Merchants, 73
Michaelmas, 118
Miracles, 161–62, 164–65
Monasteries, 5n18, 7, 11, 13, 27, 30, 32, 46, 51n14, 54–58, 62, 64–65, 73–74, 76, 87, 94, 101–9, 113–15, 122, 124, 143–46, 148–50
Monastic rules, 10, 51, 54, 59, 105, 107–13, 115, 123, 126, 146–47, 168, 175
Monica, St., 83
Monks, 9–11, 13, 24, 27–28, 30, 32, 36, 39–40, 48, 51, 53–59, 62–66, 70, 73, 76, 78, 84–86, 88–89, 95–98, 101–2, 104–7, 109–15, 122–23, 126–27, 129, 134–35, 143–44, 147–48, 156–58, 165, 172, 175–77
Monte Cassino, 112n15
More, Thomas, 10
  Utopia, 10
Moritz, St., 159
Moses, 36, 123, 134, 140
Murner, Thomas, 2
  The Great Lutheran Fool, 2

Nadler, Jörg, 11
Nesen, Wilhelm, 24
New Year's Day, 118
Nicene Creed, 127
Nicholas of Lyra, 74
Nobility, 15, 28, 30, 32–33, 54, 56, 75, 131–32, 135–36, 149–50, 153, 158, 165
Nones. *See* Canonical hours
Norbert of Xanten, 112n16
Nuns, 4, 7, 9–11, 13, 24, 32, 39, 43–51, 53, 58, 84, 89, 97–98, 101–2, 104–6, 110–12, 122–23, 126, 128, 144, 146–49, 175
Nuremburg, 12, 16, 24
Nuremburg *Reichstag*, 14n55, 16n65

Oaths, 28, 61, 138–39, 144, 153–54, 158, 163
Oecolampadius, Johann, 23
Order of Canons of Prémontré. *See* Premonstratensians
Origen, 47, 65
Otto I, 92
Otto II, 92
Otto III, 92
Our Lady's Candlemas, 118
Our Lady's Mantel, 167
Our Lady's Psalter, 75

Palestine, 110n12
Pallium, 31
Papacy, 8, 14n55, 27–31, 33, 35, 38–39, 41, 57, 61, 65, 92–98, 102, 106, 108–10, 115, 128, 143–44, 147–48, 155, 157–58, 166, 175–76
Papal bulls, 33, 64–65, 67, 93, 97, 108–9, 129n26, 148, 158, 165
Paradisus anime, 127
Pardoners, 162, 168n26, 169
Paul, St., 36, 40, 48, 63, 75, 77, 91, 97, 137, 156, 158, 166, 172–73, 175
Paula, St., 51n14
Peasants, 30, 54, 75, 78, 86, 169
Pellikan, Konrad, 5, 12
Penance, 37, 119, 121, 140, 155, 175
Pentecost, 40n7, 118
Peraudi, Cardinal Raymond, 4
Peter, St., 75, 77, 156, 174–75
Peters, Christian, 4, 10, 12, 15, 19
Petris, Adam, 5
Pforzheim, 23
Pharisees, 85
Philo of Alexandria, 48
Pilgrimage, 128
Pope. *See* papacy
Poor, 27–29, 32, 39, 49, 53–54, 74, 76, 78, 83–84, 86–88, 109, 112, 115, 120, 122, 128, 135, 139, 148–49, 168, 172, 175–76

Poor Clares. *See* Franciscan nuns
Poverty, 17, 44, 64, 67, 93–95, 146, 172
Prayer, 25, 33, 40, 47–48, 51n14, 53, 55, 58–59, 70–71, 75–76, 83–84, 87–88, 104, 107, 120–21, 124–25, 127, 147, 150, 162–64, 167, 172, 175
Preachers, Order of. *See* Dominicans
Preaching office, 8, 24, 28–29, 31, 35, 38, 61–67, 70, 72, 75–78, 85, 94, 97, 105–6, 148, 155–56, 158, 173
Premonstratensians, 112
Presentia, 85–86
Priests, 9–10, 14, 24, 27–29, 31–33, 36, 38–40, 53, 55–56, 58–59, 62, 64–65, 75–76, 81, 84–89, 91, 94, 97–98, 101–2, 107–8, 110, 112, 118–21, 123, 126–27, 134–35, 140, 143–44, 146-49, 155–56, 158, 161, 164–65, 172–77
Prime. *See* Canonical hours
Printing press, 2, 22–23
Probst, Jacob, 13
Psalters, 127, 163, 167n21
Psittacus, 10, 17, 117, 131
Pulpit. *See* Preaching office
Purgatory, 45, 67, 103, 113–14, 163, 165–66, 175

Reformation theology, 11–12, 15, 18–19
Regular Tertiaries, 146n6
Remlingen, 18
Reuchlin, Johann, 22, 110
Rheinfelden, 9n35
Rhenanus, Beatus, 5
Riggenbach, Bernhard, 15
Rome, 1, 6, 27–29, 32, 33, 38, 113, 128, 148
Rosary, 75, 127
Rosencrantz, 167
Rothenburg ob der Tauber, 17
Rottenburg am Neckar, 16
Rufach, 168
Sacraments, 66, 85, 123–25, 127, 158, 172, 174
Sacrament of the Altar, 37, 125, 153. *See also* Mass
Saints, 10, 47, 57, 66, 75, 77, 85, 93, 97, 105, 128, 161–68, 176
Salvation, 30, 46, 66–67, 75, 82, 92–93, 106, 113, 154, 156–58, 173, 174–75
Salzburg, 94
Santiago de Compostela, 113n17
Sapidus, Johann, 23
Scherdüng, Johann Kröner von, 4
Schlettstadt, 23
Schmidlin, Johann, 23
Schmidt, Johann Heinrich, 7
Scholastic theology, 11, 72, 96, 129
Schools, 23–24, 29, 31, 48–49, 54, 56, 74, 122, 124, 127, 129, 136–37
Schwärmer. *See* Enthusiasts
Scotus, John Duns, 41, 71, 74, 156, 175
Scripture. *See* Gospel
Secular authority, 8–10, 14n55, 28, 29n24, 32, 61, 64–67, 74, 92, 95, 114, 121, 131–32, 134, 137–38, 140–41, 144–45, 147–48, 153
Secular Tertiaries, 145n4, 146n6
Sermon on the Mount, 127n22
Sermons, 6–7, 10, 16–17, 64, 66, 69–74, 82–83, 118, 120, 125, 156
Sext. *See* Canonical hours
Seyler, Hans, 15
Shrovetide, 82, 129
Sickingen, Franz von, 31
Sigk, Matthias, 3, 9
Simler, Georg, 23
Sin, 28, 44, 46, 51, 54–56, 59, 62, 66–67, 71, 87, 103, 110, 112–15, 125, 148–49, 154–55, 163–64, 167n24, 169, 173–75
Sittick, Huldrich, 117n1
Speyer, 11
Stationers, 168
Steiner, Heinrich, 15
Strasbourg, 94
Stuttgart, 23
Swabia, 23
Switzerland, 9, 11–12, 16, 117n3, 153, 157–59

Tacitus, 18n72
Taxes, 27–28, 40n7, 86, 141, 144–45

Temple servants, 54, 57–58, 84–88
Templars, 98
Terce. *See* Canonical hours
Teutonic Knights, 54, 150
Thomas Aquinas, 40, 74, 156, 165, 175
Toulouse, Bishop of, 167n20
Tübingen, 4–5, 23
University of, 5
Turk, 28, 66, 85, 101–3, 107, 113–14, 156
Tuscany, 112n16

Ulm, 6, 9, 15–16, 23
Ulrich, Duke of Württemburg, 104
Usury, 28, 32, 64, 134, 138, 145
Uttenheim, Crato von, 23

Valentine, St., 168
Valentinians, 168
Vernacular. *See* German language
Vespers, 53n1, 118–19. *See* also Canonical hours
Vigils, 43, 51, 58, 84–85, 104, 164, 175
Vows, 32, 49–50, 61, 103, 112–13, 115, 122, 138, 144, 146, 167n20, 174

Warfare, 32, 55, 67, 135–36, 162, 164
Wartburg, 15
Wehe, Johann Jakob, 3, 16–17
Wellfaria, 10, 19, 117–141
Wertheim, 18
Wertheim, Duke George of, 18
Wertheim, Duke Michael of, 18
Wilhelm, Duke of Bavaria, 31n28
William of Ockham, 41, 175
William of St. Amour, 25n19
William, St., 112n16
Williamites, 112
Wimpfeling, Jakob, 23
Wittenberg, 6, 9, 11–19, 31n27
Wolfaria. *See* Wellfaria
Women, 4, 7, 24, 32, 43–44, 49–51, 54, 73, 85, 106, 111–12, 119–20, 122–24, 126, 128, 133–34, 136–37, 139, 143–47, 149, 167, 172
Worms, Diet of, 1, 8
Württemburg, 104, 147

Zurich, 9, 11
Zwickau, 11
Zwingli, Huldrych, 9

Scripture Index

Old Testament

Genesis
8:21 174n9

Psalms
119 147n9

Isaiah
75
64:6 173n3

Jeremiah
31:18 174n11

Hosea
13:9 174n7

Zechariah
3:4 173n6

New Testament

Matthew
6 38
7:18 174n10
7:20 174n8
9 86
11:25ff 172n1
23:5 25n19
23:13 91n2

Luke
10:21–22 172n1
11:52 91n2
22:36 172n2

John
15:5 173n4

Romans
1:18ff 91n1

2 Corinthians
3:5 173n5

Ephesians
2:10 174n8

1 Peter
2:13 174n12

www.ingramcontent.com/pod-product-compliance
Lightning Source LLC
LaVergne TN
LVHW010937100826
845153LV00001B/68

* 9 7 8 1 4 9 8 2 2 6 7 1 4 *